Other Books by Francine Prince

The Dieter's Gourmet Cookbook
Diet for Life

Francine Prince's
New Gourmet Recipes for Dieters

No sugar, no salt, low-fat, low-cholesterol!
More than 200 new gourmet recipes
from around the world—
that anyone can create!

A FIRESIDE BOOK
Published by Simon & Schuster, Inc.
New York

Not related to Dieter's Gourmet Foods and Dieter's Gourmet, Inc., publishers of DIETER'S GOURMET COOKBOOKS VOLUMES I and II.

FIRESIDE and colophon are registered trademarks
of Simon & Schuster, Inc.
Designed by
Manufactured in the United States of America
Printed by
Bound by
10 9 8 7 6 5 4 3 2

Library of Congress Cataloging in Publication Data

ISBN: 0-671-62750-3

Acknowledgments

To my very special friend, Vera Kay, for her many suggestions concerning Old World recipes. And to my dear husband, who tasted all of my recipes— not just once but many times—while they were still in the development stage.

Caution

The nutritional information in this book is based on the experiences of my husband and myself, and on our studies of the pertinent literature. It is not intended, nor should it be regarded, as medical advice. When contemplating a change of diet, it is advisable to seek the guidance of your physician.

Contents

What Do You Want When You Diet?

If you're a food lover—and who isn't?—you want more in diet food than just low calories. You want:

☑ Ample portions
☑ Breads, rolls, and cakes
☑ Sweetness
☑ Creaminess
☑ Exciting flavors
☑ Pasta
☑ Potatoes
☑ Feasts for the eye
☑ Snacks
☑ Stimulating textures
☑ Rich-tasting sauces
and
☑ The kind of desserts you dream about

When you switch to a diet, you want no near-starvation miseries, no sense of deprivation, no transition woes. You want your meals to be something special, something wonderful, something to look forward to, not away from. You want your food to be so delicious that the thought of binge-ing or straying will never enter your mind.

In short, you want to diet like a gourmet.

But you also want your food to be healthful. And, in light of what science knows now about nutrition, that means you want food

☑ Low in calories
☑ Low in fat
☑ Low in saturated fat
☑ Low in cholesterol
☑ High in fiber
with
☑ No additives
☑ No caffeine

and especially with
☑ No sugar, and
☑ No salt

To meet your health specifications, you have to do without butter, eggs, cream, whole milk, chocolate, mayonnaise, most meats (including sausages and other delicatessen and bacon), rich sauces, pickles, ketchup and other condiments, all processed foods, pancakes, pies, luscious desserts—and everything else that makes eating one of life's greatest joys.

And you want *gourmet* food?

Impossible!

And it was—until I introduced my haute cuisine of health in my 1980 bestseller, *The Dieter's Gourmet Cookbook: Delicious Low-Fat, Low-Cholesterol Cooking and Baking Recipes Using No Sugar or Salt!*, and expanded the cuisine a year later in my even more successful *Diet for Life.* (*Diet for Life* is a complete program for slimming down, and staying slim and healthy for the rest of your life. It also contains more than 100 haute cuisine of health recipes.)

Accolades poured in from all over the nation.

Universal Press columnist Bob Walton called my recipes "better than a gourmet tour of New York's Upper East Side."

Bob Kleinman, the director of the South Ohio Health Center, whose health/food column appears in scores of papers nationwide, raved: "Oh, it is *good!* If I could stand out on our Arcade Square [in Dayton, Ohio] with a drum, and sell copies of your books, I would. The food is that great, and I am that sold!"

"The biggest bonus for those on a diet . . . as well as those who live with a dieter," the editors of *Ladies' Circle* emphasized, "is that all of Francine's recipes are appetizing, scrumptious, mouth watering delights. We're sure that this is a diet you'll really love—and you'll enjoy the sense of healthful well-being that comes from sound nutrition."

The voice of grass-roots America was especially loud in the chorus of praise.

From the *Fayettville* (North Carolina) *Observer:* "A collection of mouth-watering recipes that seem too good to be true."

The *Ypsilanti* (Michigan) *Observer:* "Definitely gourmet. This collection of healthful recipes is an inspirational guide to all dieters."

The *Albuquerque* (New Mexico) *Tribune:* "A godsend."

The *Haverhill* (Massachusetts) *Gazette:* "An exercise in elegant eating that is not a diet in the ordinary sense at all. The homemaker can expand the joys of cooking and eating—in a healthy fashion."

The *Alexandria* (Virginia) *Gazette:* "A diet that works . . . with elegant and tasty dishes."

And from *Today's Post* (King of Prussia, Pennsylvania): "The food is delicious, and no one would suspect it as being totally good for you, let alone life-saving. The dishes taste like the forbidden food of the gods."

Yes, you *can* have *healthful* gourmet food. And *that's* everything you want when you diet.

Or so I thought.

But you wanted more.

THE NEW HAUTE CUISINE OF HEALTH RECIPES WERE MADE TO YOUR ORDER

From an avalanche of mail, from my chats with people like you everywhere in the nation—small towns, suburbs, rural areas, big cities—and from questions addressed to me on radio and TV shows, and on the lecture platform, I learned:

You want quick/easy haute cuisine of health recipes. And I've created

them for you, often taking advantage of those amazing cooking machines—the food processor, the open indoor rotisserie/broiler, the wok, and the clay pot. You'll find the time- and effort-saving recipes you asked for under Quick/Easy Gourmet Cooking, starting on page 125.

And—

You want haute cuisine of health recipes inspired by your favorite dishes from

Regional U.S.A.	Italy
The Middle East	China
Great Britain	Greece
North Africa	Japan
France	Eastern Europe
Norway	Mexico
Scotland	Austria
Spain	India

You'll find what you asked for under Sumptuous Specialties beginning on page 19, and in the Quick/Easy section as well. All these dishes are prepared for American tastes, but as you read the recipes you'll easily identify the country—perhaps even the region—of their origin.

So, with this book, you *do* have everything you ever asked for in diet food.

And something more—something you never dared hope for.

The haute cuisine of health—slimming and healthful as it is—is not diet food. It's a way of eating—a superbly delectable cuisine—based on healthful ingredients. You can invite your boss home to dinner, your mother-in-law over to lunch, even have a large party using my recipes—and your guests will never know they're eating "diet" food. And the food—delicate and elegant—has that stick-to-the-ribs quality heretofore found only on a professional sports team's training table.

If you enjoy the habit of eating, if eating is an occasion for you, if eating is one of the most pleasant satisfactions of your days—then my recipes are for you. Even when you're not on a diet.

How to Use Nutritional Statistics to Slim Down, and Stay Slim and Healthy for the Rest of Your Life

After each recipe the following line appears, which you'll find in no other book.

CAL   F   P:S   SOD   CAR   CHO   PRO

Numerals below the heading give you *complete* nutritional information on each serving (or measure) of the recipe.

Here's what each heading means, and what the numerals under it mean to you:

CAL

CAL stands for food energy in *calories.* If you're an average American, on a total consumption of 1,250 calories a day you can lose about 3 pounds of fat a week. The heavier you are, the more weight you'll lose. Make up daily haute cuisine of health menus—breakfast, lunch, afternoon snack, hors d'oeuvres, dinner—totaling about 1,250 calories, and you're on your way to weight loss deliciously. If you would like to have wine with your dinner from time to time, there's no reason why you shouldn't. A 3½-ounce glass of wine contributes only 87 calories; and red wine is no more caloric than white.

When you get down to your desired weight, multiply it by 15—and that's the number of calories you need daily to keep your new low weight

rock-steady. Make up new daily haute cuisine of health recipes to provide about that number of calories. Do keep your weight down, because overweight can shorten your life and help bring on numerous diseases, including heart attack and diabetes.

F

F stands for *fat* in grams. My dietary program, which conforms more closely to federal nutritional guidelines than any other, calls for a daily intake of 20 percent fat in terms of total calories. That translates to about 28 grams of fat a day on a 1,250-calorie-a-day diet. Don't exceed that number when you're putting your menus together.

When you're down to your desired weight, calculate the amount of fat permissible per day by multiplying your daily caloric allowance (see the *CAL* section) by 20 percent and dividing by 9.

Fats are needed for the proper functioning of every cell in the body, and for the metabolism of vitamins A, D, E, and K. Excess fats have been associated with heart attack, high blood pressure, obesity, and diabetes, among other diseases. So think twice before going on a fad high-fat diet.

P:S

P:S stands for the *ratio of polyunsaturated fat (P) to saturated fat (S).* The higher the *P* value, the more healthful the ratio. The ratio recommended by federal nutritional guidelines is 1:1 minimum. In most of my dishes the ratio is 4:1 or better. That means those dishes contribute at least four times more polyunsaturated ("good") fat than saturated ("bad") fat. On a daily menu, the P:S ratio for one dish may sink below 1:1—say, 0.6:1—provided all other dishes that day have P:S ratios above 1:1. Polyunsaturated fats combat degenerative diseases, including atherosclerosis, a precursor to heart attack.

SOD

SOD stands for *sodium* in terms of milligrams. Sodium is the major constituent of salt. The body needs only about 200 to 400 milligrams of sodium a day. For every 1,000 milligrams of sodium consumed over 400 milligrams, the body retains 2 pounds of excess water. Most Americans consume about 4,300 milligrams of sodium (about 1½ teaspoons of salt) each day, and lug around about 8 pounds of unnecessary and unattractive water weight.

When you switch to a low-sodium diet, you can drop about 8 pounds of water in 2 weeks—without sacrificing a single calorie. On an haute cuisine of health reducing or weight-maintenance daily menu, it is virtually impossible to exceed 500 milligrams of sodium daily. Judge for yourself when you total up the numerals under *SOD* on your daily haute cuisine of health menu.

It's a good idea to keep your salt intake *low,* since excess salt is associated with high blood pressure, bloat, and many nutrition-related diseases.

CAR

Car stands for *carbohydrates* in grams. Your permissible daily allowance on a 1,250-calorie-a-day reducing diet is 187.5 grams (which represents 60 percent of your total caloric intake). To calculate permissible carbohydrate intake on a weight-maintenance diet, multiply your daily caloric intake (see the *CAL* section) by .2, and divide by 4.

The carbohydrates in my haute cuisine of health are mainly complex—they come from vegetables and grains, for the most part—and are good for you. Sugar (sucrose), a simple carbohydrate, plays havoc with blood-sugar levels when taken in excess quantities, and is associated with degenerative diseases,

including heart attack. It is, therefore, to be shunned. But don't use nonnutritive sweetners either; they're suspected carcinogens. I sweeten my dishes with sweet herbs and spices, fruits and fruit juices, and honey (which is *not* sugar).

CHO

CHO stands for *cholesterol* in milligrams. Too little cholesterol could adversely affect the efficient performance of your body. This waxy alcohol (it is *not* a fat) helps form the electrical insulation of your nervous system, is a building block for several hormones, helps govern the health of cell membranes that control the flow of nutrients into the cell, and aids in the digestive process by contributing to the manufacture of bile.

But too much cholesterol may deposit on the artery walls, eventually clogging the coronary arteries, a condition that could lead to heart attack. The safety zone for cholesterol consumption—not too little, not too much—is 160 to 185 milligrams a day. You'll have no difficulty planning daily haute cuisine of health recipes within that zone.

PRO

PRO stands for *protein* in grams. On my balanced dietary program (20 percent fat, 60 percent carbohydrates, and 20 percent protein in terms of total calories), you consume about 62.5 grams of protein a day on a 1,250-calorie reducing diet. To calculate your permissible protein allowance on a weight-maintenance diet, multiply your daily caloric intake (see the *CAL* section) by 20 percent, and divide by 4.

The right amount of proteins, including those from animal sources, produces sufficient quantities of the essential amino acids necessary to good health. But excessive protein can raise the uric acid levels in the blood, possibly leading to gout, an excruciating disease. It can also disturb the body's metabolic balance, which can contribute to the onset of nutrition-related diseases. A balanced diet is more healthful than a fad high-protein diet.

My haute cuisine of health is a lifetime feast for rock-steady weight after reducing, and continuous health and vitality. It was one of the great delights of my life to create these new recipes for you. I hope you will be just as happy preparing them for yourself and your loved ones—dieters and nondieters alike. Good eating and good health!

Part I
Sumptuous Specialties

Meat

Double Delight

Veal cut from the leg is the lowest in fat of all veal cuts (35 percent in terms of total calories). Here thin-pounded veal scaloppine slices, cut from the leg, are married to equally slender slices of chicken breast. The meats are enveloped in a unique breading of my flavorful bread crumbs and toasted wheat germ, with just the suggestion of cheese and spices. Sautéed to perfection on a bed of shallots and garlic, these "fillets" are indeed a double delight.

4 slices veal (¾ pound) cut from the leg, pounded thin
¾ pound chicken breast, boned and skinned, pounded and cut into 4 pieces (see note)
2 tablespoons fresh lime juice
⅓ cup Bread Crumbs (page 85)
2 tablespoons toasted wheat germ (no sugar added)
½ teaspoon ground ginger
1 teaspoon grated no-fat Sap Sago cheese
8 dashes ground red (cayenne) pepper *

* I use cayenne pepper because some authorities believe it has a healthful effect on the circulatory system, whereas both white and black peppers have, in some cases, been associated with high blood pressure.

½ teaspoon dried tarragon leaves, crushed
2 tablespoons evaporated skim milk (¼ percent milk fat)
1 tablespoon each Italian olive oil and sweet (unsalted) 100 percent corn oil margarine **
2 large shallots, minced
1 large clove garlic, minced
   Minced fresh parsley
   Lemon wedges

1. Wipe veal and chicken with paper toweling. Lay slices in dish. Sprinkle with lime juice, turning to coat. Cover and let stand at room temperature for 1 hour.

2. Combine bread crumbs and next 5 ingredients in bowl. Stir to blend. Set aside.

3. Drain and dry veal and chicken. Lay one slice of chicken over one slice of veal. Repeat with balance of veal and chicken. Secure with toothpicks.

4. Pour evaporated milk into small bowl. Sprinkle half of crumb mixture into large flat plate. Dip each veal-chicken combination into milk, then lay on crumbs. Sprinkle with balance of crumbs, pressing into meat. Cover tightly with plastic wrap and refrigerate for 30 minutes.

** I use corn oil because of all the healthful oils, it's far and away the best tasting. I use Italian olive oil because no one should be deprived of its special exquisite flavor. Olive oil has an acceptable but low P:S of 1.4:1, but when the oil is blended with corn oil (P:S of 2.7:1), the total blend has a P:S of 2:1 to 4:1-well above the standard for healthful nutrition set by federal guidelines

5. Heat half of combined oil and margarine in nonstick skillet until hot. Spread shallots and garlic over skillet. Add veal-chicken combinations and sauté over medium-high heat for 4 minutes on one side.

6. Add balance of oil-margarine mixture to skillet. Turn veal-chicken combinations and sauté for 4 minutes on second side. Turn and sauté again for 4 minutes; turning and sautéeing one more time. (Total cooking time is about 16 minutes, depending on thickness of meat. I prefer this dish cooked to a golden brown on the outside, and slightly pink and juicy on the inside.)

7. Transfer to warmed individual serving plates. Sprinkle with parsley and garnish with lemon wedges.

Yield: Serves 4

Note: Chicken should be pounded first, then cut to same size as veal.

CAL	F	P:S	SOD	CAR	CHO	PRO
310.5	14	1:1	107	5.5	95	38

Sautéed Chili Steak

Chili con carne seasoning (available in most supermarkets) is a blend of the dried pods of the chili (capsicum) plant and cumin, garlic, coriander, and oregano. Please don't confuse it with chili con carne *powder,* which contributes two forbidden ingredients, salt and black pepper. The *seasoning,* far milder than the chilis of Mexico, is delightful in marinades; and that's the way I use it here. For a touch of South-of-the Border taste, try this fork-tender steak.

4 *lean beef fillets (eye round), ½-inch thick (1½ pounds)*
8 *dashes ground red (cayenne) pepper*

¾ *teaspoon combined dried rosemary and thyme leaves, crushed*
2 *tablespoons corn oil*
2 *large cloves garlic, minced*
2 *shallots, minced*
1 *tablespoon peeled and minced fresh ginger*
½ *small sweet pepper, cut into ¼-inch slivers*
¼ *pound fresh mushrooms, washed, dried, trimmed, and sliced*
⅓ *cup Rich Chicken Stock (page 94)*
1 *teaspoon tomato paste (no salt added)*
¾ *teaspoon chili con carne seasoning (no salt or pepper added)*
2 *tablespoons medium-dry sherry*

1. Wipe meat with paper toweling. Rub on both sides with ground red pepper and crushed herbs.

2. Heat 1 tablespoon of the oil in iron skillet until hot but not smoking. Sauté steak for 1 minute on each side. Meat should be lightly browned. Transfer to dish.

3. Heat balance of oil in skillet. Add garlic, shallots, ginger, sweet red pepper, and mushrooms. Sauté until lightly browned, stirring constantly. Return steak to skillet. Sauté with vegetable mixture for 1 minute, turning twice.

4. Combine stock, tomato paste, and chili con carne seasoning. Add to skillet. Bring to simmering point. Reduce heat. Cover tightly and simmer for 35 to 40 minutes, spooning with sauce often and turning meat twice.

5. Transfer to warmed individual serving plates; cover to keep warm. Turn up heat under skillet. Add sherry. Stir and cook sauce for 1 minute. Pour over meat and serve.

Yield: Serves 4

CAL	F	P:S	SOD	CAR	CHO	PRO
216.5	11	2.8:1	72	6	57.5	4

Pork Fillets in Red Wine

Pork tastes simply marvelous. (It's my husband's favorite meat, a preference he shares with 600 million Chinese.) Don't be deterred from feasting on it because of its notorious reputation for fattiness. The fillets I use come from loin chops. When well trimmed, they seldom ooze a drop of fat in cooking. Of all the pork cuts, they're the tenderest, tastiest, and have the most pleasing texture. A meat that can be cooked almost any way you choose, pork is here given the French haute cuisine treatment, with results that can only be described as *formidable!*

4 *lean pork fillets (1¼ pounds), well trimmed*
¼ *cup apple juice (no sugar added)*
4 *dashes ground cloves*
¼ *cup Matzoh Crumbs (page 85)*
2 *tablespoons toasted wheat germ (no sugar added)*
2 *tablespoons corn oil*
2 *large cloves garlic, minced*
2 *large shallots, minced*
3 *large fresh mushrooms, washed, dried, trimmed, and sliced*
1 *tablespoon minced sweet green pepper*
⅓ *cup red wine*
¼ *cup Rich Chicken Stock (page 94)*
1 *tablespoon minced fresh parsley*
½ *teaspoon chili con carne seasoning (no salt or pepper added)*
1 *teaspoon dried thyme leaves, crushed*
4 *dashes ground red (cayenne) pepper*
1 *teaspoon freshly grated orange rind, preferably from navel orange*

1. Wipe fillets with paper toweling.
2. Comine apple juice and cloves in small bowl. Beat with fork to blend.

3. Combine crumbs with wheat germ and spread on plate. Dip each fillet into apple juice, then into crumb mixture, coating evenly on both sides. Refrigerate for 30 minutes.
4. Heat 2¼ teaspoons oil in nonstick skillet until hot. Sauté fillets until golden brown on one side. Add 2¼ teaspoons oil to skillet. Sauté on second side until golden brown. Transfer to plate.
5. Heat balance of oil in skillet and sauté garlic, shallots, mushrooms, and green pepper, turning constantly, until lightly browned.
6. Add wine and cook 1 minute. Add stock, half of parsley, and remaining seasonings. Bring to simmering point and cook 1 minute.
7. Return browned fillets to skillet. Baste with sauce. Cover and simmer gently for 25 minutes, spooning with sauce and turning meat twice.
8. Transfer to warmed individual serving plates. Sprinkle with balance of parsley and serve.

Yield: Serves 4

CAL	F	P:S	SOD	CAR	CHO	PRO
314	17	1.8:1	61.5	17	58.5	23

Baked Fresh Ham Slice

The leanest cut of pork comes from fresh ham. Cook it with the respect and tender care it deserves and its natural toughness will melt away. Here it is cosseted in a sweet-and-spicy marinade before baking, then soothed by apple slices and pineapple chunks in the oven. It emerges eager to please; and bathed in a heartwarming sauce, it becomes a fork-tender delight.

1 slice center-cut ham (1¼ pounds), well trimmed
1 tablespoon apple cider vinegar
1 tablespoon corn oil
2 shallots, minced
2 cloves garlic, minced
2 teaspoons peeled and grated carrot
¼ cup unsweetened pineapple juice
¼ cup apple juice (no sugar added)
2 tablespoons raisins
1 teaspoon ground ginger
3 dashes ground cloves
½ teaspoon chili con carne seasoning (no salt or pepper added)
1 large crisp, sweet apple, such as Washington State, cored, peeled, and thickly sliced
⅓ cup pineapple chunks packed in unsweetened pineapple juice, drained
2 teaspoons arrowroot flour dissolved in 2 teaspoons water
1 navel orange, peeled and thinly sliced

1. Wipe meat with paper toweling. Cut into 4 equal pieces. Place in small casserole.
2. In blender, combine all but last 4 ingredients. Blend on high speed for 1 minute. Pour over meat, turning to coat. Cover and let marinate at room temperature for 1 hour.

3. Bake, covered, in preheated 350°F oven for 50 minutes.
4. Add apple. Re-cover and bake for 10 minutes.
5. Add pineapple. Re-cover and bake for 5 minutes. Transfer meat and fruit to warmed serving platter. Cover to keep warm.
6. Slowly dribble arrowroot mixture into gravy, using only enough to thicken lightly. Pour over meat.
7. Garnish with orange slices and serve.

Yield: Serves 4

CAL	F	P:S	SOD	CAR	CHO	PRO
268.5	13	1.3:1	60	20.5	63	22

Fresh Ham with Cranberries

Fresh cranberries are available in fall and winter; once the leaves begin to fall, hurry to your local supermarket and stock up. These tart red berries, long prized in the cookery of the Scandinavian countries (where a local variety spicier than ours, lingonberries, is grown), are now coming into their own in my haute cuisine of health. For a surprising All-American gourmet delight, new style, savor these cranberries with melt-in-your-mouth fresh ham.

2 slices fresh ham (1½ pounds), each ½-inch thick
¾ teaspoon dried sage leaves, crushed
½ teaspoon ground ginger
2 tablespoons corn oil
2 large cloves garlic, minced
1 small onion, minced
1 tablespoon minced sweet green pepper

¼ cup each apple juice (no sugar
    added) and Rich Chicken Stock
    (page 94)
¾ cup fresh cranberries
6 dashes ground red (cayenne)
    pepper
4 whole cloves
2 medium yams, peeled and sliced
    ⅜-inch thick
1 large sweet, crisp apple, such as
    Washington State, peeled, cored,
    and sliced ⅜-inch thick
2 teaspoons arrowroot flour
    dissolved in 1 tablespoon water

1. Wipe meat with paper toweling.
Rub with sage and ginger.
2. Heat 1 tablespoon oil in iron skillet until hot. Brown meat lightly on
both sides. Transfer to plate.
3. Heat balance of oil in skillet.
(Take care that the skillet does not
overheat.) Sauté garlic, onion, and
green pepper, stirring constantly, until
lightly browned.
4. Add apple juice and stock.
Stir, and scrape skillet to loosen any
browned particles. Add cranberries,
ground red pepper, and cloves. Bring to
simmering point. Reduce heat. Cover
and simmer for 15 minutes, turning
meat once.
5. Add yams, immersing in liquid.
Cover and simmer for 25 minutes.
6. Turn meat. Add apples. Re-cover
and simmer for 10 minutes. Turn off
heat. Let stand for 5 minutes.
7. Arrange meat in center of
warmed serving platter, surrounded
with yams and apples. Turn heat up
under skillet. Slowly dribble arrowroot
mixture into sauce, using only enough
to thicken lightly. Spoon over meat,
yams, and apples and serve immediately.

Yield: Serves 4

CAL	F	P:S	SOD	CAR	CHO	PRO
395.5	16	2.1:1	78.5	29	76	3

Meatballs with Apples

It's a wonder to me why other
haute cuisines relegate the apple, for
the most part, to the dessert end of the
menu. Apples, everybody's favorite,
can mingle into an amazing variety of
main courses. I've taken advantage of
their sweetness and tartness and plain
downright appleness to transform the
mundane into the marvelous. These
meatballs are an example.

½ pound each lean ground beef and
    veal
3 tablespoons Bread Crumbs (page
    85)
8 dashes ground red (cayenne)
    pepper
2 teaspoons minced fresh parsley
5 tablespoons unsweetened
    pineapple juice
4½ teaspoons corn oil
2 large cloves garlic, minced
¼-inch slice fresh ginger, peeled and
    minced
1 tablespoon minced celery
2 tablespoons minced sweet red
    pepper
¾ teaspoon dried rosemary leaves,
    crushed
1 tablespoon tarragon vinegar (page
    99)
⅓ cup Rich Chicken Stock (page 94)
2 whole cloves
1 large tart green apple, peeled,
    cored, and thickly sliced

1. Place meat in a bowl. Add
crumbs, 4 dashes ground red pepper,
and parsley. Blend well. Add 3 tablespoons pineapple juice and mash with
fork until blended.
2. Heat 2¼ teaspoons oil in nonstick skillet until hot. Sauté garlic, ginger, celery, and sweet red pepper until
very lightly browned.

3. Sprinkle with rosemary. Stir. Add vinegar and cook for 30 seconds.

4. Pour skillet mixture into meat mixture and blend. (Your fingers will do the job best.) Shape into 16 balls (see note 1).

5. Wipe out skillet. Heat balance of oil in skillet. Sauté meatballs until lightly browned on all sides, pouring off any exuded fat.

6. Add stock, balance of pineapple juice, balance of ground red pepper, the cloves, and apple slices. Bring to simmering point. Cover and simmer gently for 20 minutes, turning meatballs and apples and spooning with sauce twice.

7. Transfer meatballs and apple slices to warm serving bowl. Cover to keep warm. Turn heat up to slow boil. Reduce sauce by half (it will thicken naturally). Pour over meat and apple slices. Serve piping hot.

Yield: Serves 4

Notes:

1. Meat may be prepared through step 4 several hours ahead. Cover and refrigerate until ready to cook.

2. This dish freezes well. Freeze in plastic pouch. When ready to use, drop pouch in boiling water for 15 to 20 minutes.

CAL	F	P:S	SOD	CAR	CHO	PRO
256.5	13	1.2:1	67.5	7.5	73	24.5

Tarragon Veal Chops

I sing my praises of tarragon elsewhere in this book (page 42). The most romantic of herbs, it has an exciting, warming taste all its own, with a faint accent of anise. It lends distinction to many classic sauces, including Béarnaise, and to this new sauce for veal chops.

2¼ teaspoons each corn oil and Italian olive oil, combined
4 loin or rib veal chops (1½ pounds), well trimmed
½ teaspoon dried thyme leaves, crushed
6 dashes ground red (cayenne) pepper
3 large cloves garlic, minced
2 large shallots, minced
2 tablespoons minced sweet green pepper
1 small onion, minced
3 large fresh mushrooms, washed, dried, trimmed, and thickly sliced
¼ cup dry vermouth
⅓ cup Rich Chicken Stock (page 94)
1 tablespoon minced fresh tarragon leaves (see note)
1 teaspoon freshly grated orange rind, preferably from navel orange

1. Wipe chops with paper toweling. Rub with thyme and ground red pepper.

2. Heat combined oils in skillet until hot. Add chops and brown lightly on one side. Turn. Add garlic, shallots, green pepper, onion, and mushrooms. Sauté with meat until lightly browned (about 3 minutes), stirring and moving ingredients around skillet every minute or so.

3. Add vermouth. Cook and stir for 1 minute. Add stock, tarragon, and orange rind.

4. Turn chops and spoon with sauce. Cover tightly. Turn heat down to simmering and simmer for 30 minutes, turning chops every 10 minutes. (Cooking time will vary slightly depending on thickness of chops.) Remove from heat and let stand, covered, for 5 minutes.

5. Transfer chops to warmed individual serving plates. Spoon with sauce and serve.

Yield: Serves 4

Variation: Lean loin or rib pork chops may be substituted for veal. Extend cooking time to 45 minutes or longer, until meat is fork-tender.

Serving suggestions: Serve over just-cooked rice, cracked wheat, or kasha.

Note: This dish tastes best with fresh tarragon. If it is not available, substitute fresh dill.

CAL	F	P:S	SOD	CAR	CHO	PRO
312.5	18.5	0.8:1	79.5	5.5	106	28

Chili Veal Chops with Turnips

Turnips—almost utterly neglected by the maestros of haute cuisine—have a powerful flavor, in delightful contrast to the more commonly used blander vegetables. In this unusual veal dish, turnips combine with chili to create a masterpiece of robust fare. For the adventurous gastronome, here's a strong new taste sensation.

1½ cups peeled and cubed yellow
      turnip (1-inch cubes)
4 loin veal chops (1½ pounds), well
      trimmed
1 tablespoon fresh lemon juice
1 teaspoon each dried rosemary
      and thyme leaves, crushed
2 teaspoons unbleached flour
4½ teaspoons combined corn oil and
      Italian olive oil
3 large cloves garlic, minced
2 large shallots, minced
1 tablespoon minced sweet green
      pepper
2 tablespoons minced fresh anise

½ cup dry red wine
½ cup Rich Chicken Stock (page 94)
1 tablespoon peeled and grated
      carrot
1 teaspoon chili con carne
      seasoning (no salt or pepper
      added)
1 tablespoon minced fresh parsley
1 teaspoon tomato paste (no salt
      added)

1. Boil turnip in water to cover for 15 minutes. Drain. Cover and set aside.

2. Wipe chops with paper toweling. Sprinkle on both sides with lemon juice. Let stand at room temperature for 30 minutes.

3. Pat chops lightly with paper toweling. Sprinkle with herbs, press into meat. Dust with flour, rubbing with fingers to spread.

4. Heat 2¼ teaspoons combined oils in iron skillet until hot but not smoking. Add chops and sauté on each side for 4 minutes. Transfer to plate.

5. Add balance of oil to skillet. Sauté garlic, shallots, green pepper, and anise for 1 minute.

6. Add wine. Stir, and scrape with spoon to loosen browned particles.

7. Add stock, carrot, chili con carne seasoning, parsley, and tomato paste. Bring to simmering point. Return chops to skillet, turning to coat. Add cooked turnip; spoon with sauce.

8. Cover tightly with aluminum foil and bake in preheated 350°F oven for 20 minutes. Remove from oven, uncover, and turn. Re-cover, return to oven, and bake for 20 minutes.

9. Transfer chops to warmed individual serving plates. Cover to keep warm. Place skillet over medium-high heat for 1 to 2 minutes, reducing sauce until lightly thickened. Spoon over chops.

Yield: Serves 4

CAL	F	P:S	SOD	CAR	CHO	PRO
329	16	1.4:1	83	10.5	88	23.5

Baked Medallions of Veal with Piquant Sauce

"Piquant" has two levels of meaning. On one level, it means agreeably stimulating to the palate, with overtones of pleasant tartness and pungency. On another level, it means having a lively, arch charm, and the power to provoke enjoyable excitement. Both levels of meaning mingle in this piquant sauce for meltingly tender baked veal.

For the veal:
4 medallions of veal (1¼ pounds), cut from the leg, ½-inch thick
⅓ cup partially thawed frozen orange juice concentrate (no sugar added)
1 tablespoon fresh lime juice
¼ teaspoon ground ginger
2 dashes ground nutmeg
6 dashes ground red (cayenne) pepper
¼ cup each Bread Crumbs (page 85) and toasted wheat germ (no sugar added)
¼ teaspoon corn oil, for baking pan
1 navel orange, thinly sliced

For the sauce:
⅓ cup partially thawed frozen orange juice concentrate (no sugar added)
¼ cup unsweetened pineapple juice
1 teaspoon each fresh lime juice and apple cider vinegar
1 large shallot, minced
2 teaspoons juniper berries, crushed
¼ teaspoon ground ginger
2 dashes ground red (cayenne) pepper
1½ teaspoons medium-dry sherry

1. Prepare the veal first. Wipe meat with paper toweling.

2. In bowl, combine concentrate, lime juice, and spices. Spread bread crumb mixture on plate.

3. Dip each medallion into juice mixture, letting excess drain; then dip into crumbs, coating evenly. Place on plate. Refrigerate at least 30 minutes before cooking.

4. Place meat in lightly oiled baking pan. Bake, uncovered, in preheated 375°F oven for 40 to 45 minutes, turning carefully with spatula once midway.

5. Start to prepare sauce about 10 minutes before meat is done. In saucepan, combine all ingredients except sherry. Heat to simmering point. Reduce heat and simmer, uncovered, for 10 minutes. Strain into bowl. Wash saucepan. Pour sauce back into saucepan. Bring to simmering point. Add sherry. Simmer for 1 minute.

6. Transfer meat to warmed serving platter. Spoon with sauce; garnish with orange slices.

Yield: Serves 4

Serving Suggestion: Steamed green beans or broccoli makes an excellent accompaniment to this flavorsome dish.

	CAL	F	P:S	SOD	CAR	CHO	PRO
Veal:	350.5	17	1:1	83	22	106	37
Sauce:	45	–	–	3.5	29	–	1

Sautéed Lamburgers with Onions

The word "onion" derives from the Latin word *unus*, meaning "one," and in a variety of my haute cuisine of health dishes the onion is indeed "Number 1." Pungent and aromatic, it adds a gourmet taste to even the simplest of meat dishes, as you can prove to yourself by biting into one of these luscious lamburgers.

1 *pound ground lean lamb, cut from
   leg*
2 *tablespoons rye Bread Crumbs
   (page 85)*
2 *tablespoons minced fresh Chinese
   parsley leaves*
¼ *teaspoon ground ginger*
6 *dashes ground red (cayenne)
   pepper*
1 *teaspoon peeled and grated carrot*
1 *whole scallion, minced*
1 *teaspoon tomato paste (no salt
   added)*
3 *tablespoons low-fat plain yogurt*
2 *large cloves garlic, minced*
1 *tablespoon plus 1½ teaspoons
   corn oil*
2 *large onions, thinly sliced,
   separated into rings*
¼ *pound fresh mushrooms, washed,
   dried, trimmed, and sliced*
2 *tablespoons sherry*

1. In bowl, combine first 9 ingredients plus 1 clove minced garlic. (Your fingers can do the blending best.) Shape into 8 burgers, each ½-inch thick. Set aside.
2. Heat 1 tablespoon oil in nonstick skillet until hot. Add balance of garlic, the onions, and mushrooms. Sauté for 5 minutes over medium heat, without browning. Transfer to plate.
3. Heat balance of oil in skillet.

Add burgers. Sauté on one side for 3 minutes. Pour off any exuded fat. Return onion-mushroom mixture to skillet. Sauté burgers with onions and mushrooms until done. (Do not overcook; total cooking time for medium-rare patties is 7 minutes.) Transfer to warmed individual serving plates.
4. Turn heat up under skillet. Add sherry, stirring rapidly. Spoon equal amounts of vegetables and sauce over each lamburger and serve.

Yield: Serves 4

CAL	F	P:S	SOD	CAR	CHO	PRO
232	–	–	87.5	10.5	69	3.5

Lamb-Stuffed Zucchini Boats

Zucchini is a summer squash, which is known abroad by the deceptive name "marrow." Paradoxically, winter squash tends toward sweetness, but the squash of the sunniest season possesses a tart austerity. That makes it an admirable complement for this richly herb-, spice-, and cheese flavored lamb stuffing.

2 firm zucchini (about 8 to 9 ounces
  each), well scrubbed
½ cup each Rich Chicken Stock
  (page 94) and water
¼ cup cracked-wheat cereal
½ pound ground lean lamb
1 tablespoon corn oil
2 large cloves garlic, minced
2 shallots, minced
1 tablespoon minced fresh basil or 1
  teaspoon dried sweet basil leaves,
  crushed
8 dashes ground red (cayenne)
  pepper
½ teaspoon curry powder (no salt or
  pepper added)
2 tablespoons dry vermouth
1 tablespoon tomato paste (no salt
  added)
2 tablespoons Matzoh Crumbs (page
  85)
1 tablespoon minced fresh parsley
1 teaspoon grated no-fat Sap Sago
  cheese (optional)

1. Cut zucchini in half lengthwise. Insert serrated knife through pulp to a depth of ¼ inch from skin. Cut around entire half vegetable in scooping motion. Repeat for other half. Remove pulp with melon scooper, taking care not to break shell. Cut pulp into ¼-inch cubes. Set aside. Place shells in baking dish.

2. In enameled or heavy-bottomed saucepan, combine stock, water, and cracked wheat. Bring to boil. Reduce heat. Cover and simmer very gently for 20 minutes, stirring twice. All water will be absorbed. Stir, cover, and let stand for 10 minutes. Turn into bowl.

3. Heat nonstick skillet over medium-high heat. Add meat, breaking up pieces with spoon. Sauté for 3 minutes. With slotted spatula, transfer to plate. Pour off exuded fat and water. Wash and dry skillet.

4. Heat oil in skillet until hot. Sauté garlic and shallots for 1 minute.

5. Add zucchini pulp and sauté for 2 minutes, stirring constantly.

6. Return meat to skillet. Sprinkle with basil and spices. Stir and sauté for 2 minutes.

7. Add vermouth. Sauté for 1 minute. Stir in tomato paste.

8. Pour into bowl with cooked cracked wheat. Add matzoh crumbs and parsley. Blend well.

9. Pile into zucchini shells, smoothing tops with knife. Sprinkle with Sap Sago cheese.

10. Bake, uncovered, in preheated 425°F oven for 20 minutes. Cover with aluminum foil and bake for an additional 10 minutes.

Yield: Serves 4

Serving suggestion: Serve Smooth Tomato Curry Purée (page 97) in a sauceboat along with zucchini.

Note: This dish may be prepared in the morning, refrigerated, and popped into the oven for a luxurious dinner treat. Remove from refrigerator 1 hour before baking.

CAL	F	P:S	SOD	CAR	CHO	PRO
183	2.7:1	–	48	16.5	33	16.5

With Sap Sago: No appreciable difference

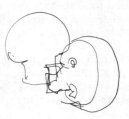

Mild Chili

You don't have to come from South of the Border to know that *chili con carne* means "chili with meat." This stew of red beans and ground beef, heated to tongue-biting delight by the ground dried pods of the capsicum plant, chili, is a favorite everywhere in the U.S.A. This version, which makes unthought-of use of chicken stock and red wine, is as mild a chili con carne as you can find. And it's like no other chili you've ever tasted.

1 cup dried red beans, washed and
   drained
4¼ cups water
1 tablespoon each corn oil and
   Italian olive oil, combined
6 ounces each ground lean veal and
   beef
3 large cloves garlic, minced
2 large shallots, minced
2 tablespoons minced sweet green
   pepper
4 large fresh mushrooms, washed,
   dried, trimmed, and coarsely
   chopped
½ teaspoon dried thyme leaves,
   crushed
½ teaspoon each ground ginger and
   crushed cuminseed
2 teaspoons chili con carne
   seasoning (no salt or pepper
   added)
⅛ teaspoon ground red (cayenne)
   pepper
½ cup red wine
1½ cups Rich Chicken Stock (page 94)
1 bay leaf
2 tablespoons tomato paste (no salt
   added)
7½ teaspoons yellow cornmeal
2½ teaspoons arrowroot flour
   dissolved in 1 tablespoon cold
   water
   Minced fresh parsley

1. Place beans and water in water-less cooker or stainless-steel pot. Cover

and bring to boil. Turn off heat and let stand for 2 hours.

2. Bring beans and water to boil again. Reduce heat to simmering and simmer until tender (40 to 45 minutes). Drain, reserving liquid.

3. Heat combined oils in nonstick skillet until hot. Sauté meats, garlic, shallots, green pepper, and mushrooms until lightly browned. As meat browns, break up chunks with spoon.

4. Sprinkle with thyme and spices; stir to blend. Add wine and cook for 1 minute.

5. Pour contents of skillet into wa-terless cooker. Add stock, bay leaf, and tomato paste. Bring to simmering point. Cover and simmer for 1 hour.

6. Add beans and cook for 15 min-utes. Remove bay leaf.

7. Blend cornmeal with dissolved arrowroot flour. Slowly add to chili. Cook until thickened.

8. Pour into tureen. Sprinkle with parsley and serve.

Yield: Serves 6

Variation: Mash beans with fork before continuing with step 6.

Serving suggestion: Serve with chopped onion and grated no-fat Sap Sago cheese on the side.

CAL	F	P:S	SOD	CAR	CHO	PRO
223	9.5	1.4:1	60.5	16.5	43.5	18

Fish

Crisp Whiting

Sometimes called kingfish or silver hake, these delectable denizens of the deep are often so small that a whole fish makes a satisfactory main course for one. The white flesh is fine-textured and flaky, and it delights the palate with its gentleness. Inexpensive, and quick to make in this mouthwatering sautéed version, it can easily become a staple on your menus. It is on mine.

4 whitings (¾ pound each), cleaned, heads removed
4 sprigs fresh parsley
¼ cup evaporated skim milk (¼ percent milkfat)
3 tablespoons yellow cornmeal
⅓ cup unbleached flour
4 dashes each ground red (cayenne) pepper and ground ginger
¼ teaspoon each dried marjoram and tarragon leaves, crushed
2 tablespoons corn oil
Lemon wedges and fresh parsley sprigs

1. Wash fish inside and out under cold running water. Dry thoroughly with paper toweling. Tuck a fresh parsley sprig into each cavity. Secure with skewers. Make 3 to 4 gashes on each side of each fish.
2. Pour milk into bowl. In another bowl, combine cornmeal, flour, spices, and herbs. Spread mixture on flat plate.
3. Dip each fish into milk, then roll in dry mixture, coating well.
4. Heat 1 tablespoon oil in skillet until moderately hot. Add fish. Sauté for 8 to 9 minutes on one side until browned. Add balance of oil to skillet. Turn fish, and sauté for 8 to 9 minutes on second side. Do not overcook.
5. Serve on warmed individual dishes, garnished with lemon wedges and parsley.

Yield: Serves 4

CAL	F	P:S	SOD	CAR	CHO	PRO
263	46	3.3:1	131.5	15	84	31

Poached Striped Bass Steaks

Of the two types of bass, freshwater and saltwater, I prefer the type that comes from the briny deep. The flesh seems to have been made to order for gourmets: succulent, firm yet tender, and subtly flavored. Poaching preserves the flavor and velvety smoothness of the fish; and my court bouillon adds just the right seasoning accent to make this a dish hard to surpass.

2 striped bass steaks cut from large fish (1½ pounds), each steak cut in half along length of bone
4 to 5 cups water
1 cup dry vermouth or white wine
4 large shallots, coarsely chopped
1 small onion, coarsely chopped
2 large cloves garlic, coarsely chopped
6 dashes ground red (cayenne) pepper
½ teaspoon dried rosemary leaves, crushed
2 whole cloves
1 carrot, peeled and sliced
Bouquet garni (4 sprigs fresh parsley, 1 bay leaf, and ½ teaspoon crushed fennel seeds tied together in washed double cotton cheesecloth)
Lemon wedges

1. Pat fish dry with paper toweling. If you use a poacher, lay fish on rack in one layer. If you don't use a poacher, prepare fish for poaching as follows: Place fish on double layer of washed cotton cheesecloth; fold cloth around fish and tie ends with white thread; set fish aside on plate.

2. Combine balance of ingredients except lemon wedges in poacher or stainless-steel pot large enough to hold fish in one layer.

3. Bring liquid to boil. Reduce heat. Cover and simmer for 15 minutes. The court bouillon you have prepared is now ready for poaching fish.

4. Lower fish into court bouillon. Bring to simmering point. Cover and simmer for 12 to 15 minutes, depending on thickness of fish. Uncover and let cool in court bouillon for 10 minutes. Gently remove from pot and drain. Reserve court bouillon (see note).

5. Serve fish on warmed individual plates. Garnish with lemon wedges.

Yield: Serves 4

Serving Suggestions:
1 Serve hot with Sublime Couscous (page 65) or Gingered Potatoes (page 59).
2. Serve chilled with Cucumber Sauce (page 144) or My Mayonnaise-Type Dressing (page 140).

Note: Court bouillon may be frozen and used once more.

CAL	F	P:S	SOD	CAR	CHO	PRO
223	4.5	1.5:1	124	12	94.5	32.5

Baked Striped Bass

Overcooking any fish, and this jewel of a fish in particular, means instant disbarment from the order of gourmets. When a fork slides easily into the thickest part of the fish, you know it's done. This test applies to any whole fish. Elsewhere in this section (page 30), I rapturously describe the gastronomic joys of striped bass.

1 striped bass (3 pounds), cleaned, head left on
2 tablespoons fresh lemon juice
2 sprigs each fresh parsley and dill
1 tablespoon corn oil plus 1 teaspoon for broiling pan
2 large fresh mushrooms, washed, dried, trimmed, and sliced
1 teaspoon peeled and minced fresh ginger
½ rib celery, coarsely chopped
1 small onion, coarsely chopped
2 large cloves garlic, coarsely chopped
¼ cup dry vermouth
1 cup canned tomatoes (no salt added), chopped
1 teaspoon dried tarragon leaves, crushed
1 teaspoon each minced fresh parsley and dill
6 dashes ground red (cayenne) pepper
¼ cup evaporated skim milk (¼ percent milkfat)

1. Rinse fish inside and out under cold running water and dry with paper toweling. Lay on plate. Make 3 gashes across fish on each side. Sprinkle with lemon juice; rub into skin and cavity. Fill cavity with parsley and dill sprigs. Secure with skewers. Let stand at room temperature for 30 minutes.

2. Heat 1 tablespoon oil in nonstick skillet until hot. Add mushrooms, ginger, celery, onion, and garlic. Sauté over medium-high heat for 2 minutes. Mixture should be wilted but not browned.

3. Add vermouth. Cook 1 minute.

4. Add tomatoes, herbs, and ground red pepper. Heat to simmering point, stirring well to blend. Cover and simmer for 3 minutes.

5. Pour mixture into blender. Blend on high speed for 1 minute. Pour into saucepan.

6. Line broiling pan with aluminum foil. Rub with 1 teaspoon oil. Coat fish on both sides with half of puréed sauce. Place in broiling pan. Reserve balance of sauce in saucepan.

7. Cover fish tightly with another sheet of aluminum foil. Bake in preheated 400°F oven for 15 minutes. Remove foil and baste with cooking juices. Re-cover and bake for 15 minutes, or until fish flakes easily when tested with fork.

8. Pour off cooking juices into sauce in saucepan. Keep fish warm. Slowly add evaporated milk to saucepan. Heat to simmering point. *Do not boil.* Remove from heat and cover.

9. Skin fish. Serve portions, spooned with warm sauce, on warmed individual serving plates.

Yield: Serves 4

Variations:

1. Add ½ teaspoon no-fat grated Sap Sago cheese to saucepan while reheating sauce (step 8).

2. Serve with small red potatoes that have been parboiled for 10 minutes, then skinned and added to roasting pan during last 10 minutes of cooking. Two to 3 potatoes per serving make a satisfying carbohydrate companion to the fish.

CAL	F	P:S	SOD	CAR	CHO	PRO
232.5	8.5	3:1	110	7.5	81.5	32.5

Variation 1: No appreciable difference

Variation 2:

263.5	9	2.9:1	111	14.5	81.5	33.5

Fillet of Sole in Red Wine

The true sole is found only in European waters. What passes for sole in our fish markets are any number of closely related flatfish, which can't come close to the true sole in flavor and texture. But there's no reason to despair. Any sole enrobed in my caringly innovative sauces becomes ecstatically delicious—as you'll discover for yourself when you enjoy this recipe and the one that follows.

1½ pounds lemon sole or gray sole
     fillets, cut into serving pieces
     Juice of ½ lime
1 tablespoon minced fresh basil or 2
   teaspoons dried sweet basil
   leaves, crushed
4½ teaspoons corn oil
1 small onion, minced
1 rib celery, minced
4 large fresh mushrooms, washed,
   dried, trimmed, and sliced
1 large clove garlic, minced
1 large shallot, minced
¼ cup red wine
¼ cup Rich Chicken Stock (page 94)
   or Jiffy Fish Stock (page 95)
1 small bay leaf
4 dashes ground red (cayenne)
   pepper
   Minced fresh parsley

1. Wash fish and pat dry with paper toweling. Rub with lime juice on both sides and sprinkle with minced basil, pressing into fish. Place in a dish. Cover with plastic wrap and let stand for at least 30 minutes before cooking.

2. Heat 2¼ teaspoons oil in large nonstick skillet until hot. Add vegetables, garlic, and shallot. Sauté until lightly browned. Transfer to dish.

3. Heat balance of oil in skillet and sauté fish for 2 minutes on one side. Turn. Sauté for 1 minute.

4. Return mixture of browned vegetables, garlic, and shallot to skillet. Add wine, stock, bay leaf, and ground red pepper. Bring to simmering point. Cover and simmer for 5 minutes.

5. Remove bay leaf. Serve fillets immediately, spooned with vegetable-thick sauce and sprinkled with parsley.

Yield: Serves 4

CAL	F	P:S	SOD	CAR	CHO	PRO
203.5	6.5	3.9:1	169	11	94.5	30

Creamy Curried Sole

1½ pounds fresh lemon sole fillets, cut into serving pieces
2 tablespoons fresh lime juice
¼ teaspoon sweet (unsalted) 100 percent corn oil margarine, for casserole
¼ cup dry vermouth, warmed
1 tablespoon minced celery
2 large cloves garlic, minced
2 shallots, minced
6 dashes ground red (cayenne) pepper
2 tablespoons minced fresh parsley
½ to ¾ cup Jiffy Fish Stock (page 95)
1½ teaspoons each corn oil and sweet (unsalted) 100 percent corn oil margarine
4 teaspoons unbleached flour
1 tablespoon curry powder (no salt or pepper added)
¼ teaspoon dried thyme leaves, crushed

¼ cup evaporated skim milk (¼ percent milkfat)
2 cups just-cooked rice (see note page 65)

1. Rinse fish and wipe dry with paper toweling. Pour lime juice into bowl. Add fish to bowl, turning to coat. Let stand, covered, at room temperature for 30 minutes, turning once.

2. Drain fish. Discard lime juice. Arrange in margarine-greased casserole. Pour vermouth over fish. Sprinkle with celery, garlic, shallots, ground red pepper, and 1 tablespoon of the parsley. Cover and bake in preheated 400°F oven for 12 to 15 minutes, depending on thickness of fillets. Fish should flake easily when tested with fork.

3. With slotted spatula, transfer fish to plate. Cover loosely with waxed paper to keep warm. Strain cooking liquid into measuring cup. Add enough fish stock to equal 1 cup.

4. Combine and heat oil and margarine in saucepan until hot. Add flour. Cook and stir over medium-high heat for 1 minute. Add measured liquid, a little at a time, while beating with wire whisk. Pour in exuded juices from fish.

5. Add curry powder and thyme, blending well. Gradually whisk in milk. Sprinkle with balance of parsley. Remove from heat.

6. Flake fish with fork into 1-inch pieces. Add to sauce. Stir. Heat just to simmering point.

7. Spoon equal amounts of rice onto individual warmed serving plates. Cover with fish and sauce. Serve immediately.

Yield: Serves 4

Serving Suggestion: This dish is best enjoyed alone as a main course. Broccoli Bisque (page 90) would make a delightful first course.

CAL	F	P:S	SOD	CAR	CHO	PRO
334	6	2.8:1	165.5	33.5	96.5	34

Fillet of Gray Sole with Mushrooms

The art of fish cookery begins *be-fore* you start to cook. You can't make a successful dish unless the fish is fresh. Test fillets (or steaks) for freshness by looking at them—they must be moist and close-textured; smelling them— they should have very little or no odor; and by feeling them—they should bounce back when pushed by your finger. The only test you can make on plastic-wrapped supermarket fillets (or steaks) is the eye test: the fish must look firm, not limp, and the date stamped on the package must be the same as the date of purchase. Start with *fresh* gray sole, follow this recipe with tender loving care, and you can turn any fish hater into a fish lover in one lovely forkful. That's how I converted my husband.

  4 *gray sole fillets (1½ pounds)*
  2 *teaspoons each fresh lemon and lime juice*
  ½ *pound fresh mushrooms, washed, dried, trimmed, and sliced*
  1 *cup water*
  1 *tablespoon sweet (unsalted) 100 percent corn oil margarine plus ¼ teaspoon for baking pan*
  1 *large clove garlic, minced*
  2 *large shallots, minced*
1½ *teaspoons unbleached flour*
  2 *tablespoons dry vermouth*
  ¼ *cup Rich Chicken Stock (page 94) or Jiffy Fish Stock (page 95)*
  2 *teaspoons minced fresh parsley*
  ½ *teaspoon each dried chervil and tarragon leaves, crushed*
  6 *dashes ground red (cayenne) pepper)*
  2 *teaspoons grated no-fat Sap Sago cheese*
     About ½ cup evaporated skim milk (¼ percent milkfat)

1. Wash fillets and wipe dry with paper toweling. Put in a dish and sprinkle with juices. Let stand, covered, at room temperature for 30 minutes.

2. In heavy-bottomed saucepan, bring mushrooms and water to boil. Turn heat down, partially cover, and simmer for 7 minutes. Drain mushrooms, reserving cooking liquid. Measure out ½ cup liquid. Refrigerate balance for use in soups and sauces. Wipe out saucepan.

3. Heat 1 tablespoon margarine in saucepan until hot, taking care that it does not brown. Add garlic and shallots. Sauté for 2 minutes.

4. Sprinkle with flour. Cook and stir for 1 minute. Add vermouth and cook 1 minute. Whisk in reserved mushroom liquid, stock, herbs, ground red pepper, and cheese. Remove from heat.

5. Add only enough evaporated milk to thin down to medium-thick sauce.

6. Fold each fillet in half, tip to tip. Arrange in one layer in margarine-greased baking dish. Pour hot sauce over fish. Bake, uncovered, in pre-heated 400°F oven for 10 to 12 minutes. Fish should flake easily when tested with fork. Serve immediately.

Yield: Serves 4

CAL	F	P:S	SOD	CAR	CHO	PRO
204.5	4.5	2.1:1	156.5	7.5	95.5	32

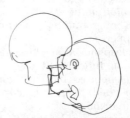

Dover Sole Paupiettes

Of all the soles, Dover sole is far and away the most delicious. A denizen of the English Channel, it is now flown fresh to quality fish markets in New York and, I should guess, to similar markets in other metropolises. The queen of British fish, it deserves regal treatment; and that's what I give it in this extravagant dish. Make it to impress those very special guests, and you won't have to fish for compliments.

For the stuffing:
⅔ cup cooked rice (see note page 65)
2 teaspoons corn oil
3 large fresh mushrooms, washed, dried, trimmed, and minced
1 large shallot, minced
1 clove garlic, minced
1 teaspoon minced fresh dill
⅛ teaspoon ground ginger
5 dashes ground red (cayenne) pepper
2 tablespoons Bread Crumbs (page 85)
3 water chestnuts, rinsed, drained, and coarsely chopped

For the paupiettes:
3 Dover soles (¾ pound each), filleted (for 6 fillets)
¼ teaspoon sweet (unsalted) 100 percent corn oil margarine, for casserole
1½ cup Jiffy Fish Stock (page 95), reduced to ¾ cup
1 clove garlic, coarsely chopped
2 shallots, coarsely chopped
1 cup canned tomatoes (no salt added), drained and chopped

For the sauce:
½ teaspoon curry powder (no salt or pepper added)
¼ teaspoon dried tarragon leaves, crushed

2 teaspoons arrowroot flour dissolved in 1 tablespoon cold water (optional)
2 tablespoons evaporated skim milk (¼ percent milkfat)

1. First prepare stuffing. Place cooked rice in bowl. Set aside.
2. Heat oil in nonstick skillet until hot. Sauté mushrooms, shallot, and garlic over medium-high heat until wilted but not browned, stirring constantly. Pour into bowl with rice. Add balance of stuffing ingredients. Blend.
3. To prepare paupiettes, wash fillets and wipe dry with paper toweling. Place mound of stuffing in center of each fillet. Fold ends over. Secure with toothpicks. Arrange 6 paupiettes in margarine-greased casserole in one layer.
4. In saucepan, combine stock, garlic, shallots, and tomatoes. Simmer for 2 minutes. Pour over paupiettes. Cover and bake in preheated 400°F oven for 10 minutes. With slotted spatula, transfer paupiettes to warm serving plate. Cover with waxed paper to keep warm.
5. Now prepare sauce. Pour cooking juices and solids into blender. Add curry powder and tarragon. Blend at high speed for 1 minute.
6. Pour mixture into saucepan. Dribble in only enough arrowroot mixture to thicken sauce lightly. Pour any exuded juice from serving plate into saucepan. Blend.
7. Add milk. Bring to simmering point. *Do not boil.*
8. Spoon sauce over paupiettes and serve, allowing 1½ paupiettes per serving.

Yield: Serves 4

Variation: Make your own rich Dover Sole Fish Stock. (See page 96.)

Note: Steps 1 through 3 may be completed in advance, and the paupiettes covered, and refrigerated. Remove from refrigerator 40 minutes before baking.

CAL	F	P:S	SOD	CAR	CHO	PRO
Stuffing:						
81	8.9	4.5:1	8	12	2	1
Paupiettes:						
100.5	1	1.8:1	79	5	47	15.5
Sauce:						
14	–	–	4	3	0.5	0.5

Bernard Meltzer's Poached Trout with Shrimp Sauce

Bernard Meltzer, the renowned host of the *What's Your Problem?* show (WOR, New York), is the most adored radio celebrity since Arthur Godfrey. He's a wonderful, warm human being, and a fine friend. Trout is his favorite food, and as a show of affection for him I created this nonpareil dish. Knowing Bernie, I'm certain he would want all his radio family (they number a million an hour) and the rest of the nation to share this treat with him.

For the poaching liquid and fish:
¾ cup Light Chicken Broth (page 95) or Jiffy Fish Stock (page 95)
¼ cup dry vermouth
2 cloves garlic, minced
2 shallots, minced
1 small onion, coarsely chopped
2 large fresh mushrooms, washed, dried, trimmed, and coarsely chopped
1 small bay leaf
1 teaspoon peeled and grated carrot
2 brook trout (about 1 pound each), filleted, skin left on

For the sauce:
1 tablespoon plus 1½ teaspoons corn oil
1 large shallot, minced
4 large fresh mushrooms, washed, dried, trimmed, and coarsely chopped
½ pound fresh shrimp, shelled, deveined, and coarsely chopped
8 dashes ground red (cayenne) pepper
1 tablespoon unbleached flour
⅔ cup evaporated skim milk (¼ percent milkfat)
1 teaspoon curry powder (no salt or pepper added)
1 tablespoon minced fresh parsley

1. Prepare poaching liquid first. Combine first 8 ingredients in large nonstick skillet. Bring to boil. Reduce heat to simmering. Cover and simmer for 5 minutes.
2. Add fillets, skin side down. Spoon with liquid. Bring to simmering point. Simmer for 10 minutes, spooning with liquid twice. With slotted spatula, transfer fish to warm serving plate. Cover with waxed paper to keep warm.
3. Strain contents of skillet into measuring cup, pressing out juices. If there's less than ¼ cup, add chicken or fish stock to equal ¼ cup. Set aside. Wash out skillet.
4. Now prepare sauce. Heat oil in skillet until hot. Spread shallot, mushrooms, and shrimp across skillet. Sprinkle with ground red pepper. Sauté over medium-high heat, stirring every few seconds, until shrimp turns light pink (about 2½ minutes).
5. Sprinkle flour over sautéed ingredients. Stir and cook for 1 minute.
6. Add reserved poaching liquid. Stir and cook for 30 seconds. Turn heat down. Add curry powder. Stir.
7. Gradually add milk to mixture, stirring constantly, until sauce reaches a medium-thick consistency. Bring sauce to simmering point. Pour over fish. Sprinkle with parsley and serve.

Yield: Serves 4

CAL	F	P:S	SOD	CAR	CHO	PRO
Poaching liquid and fish:						
141	2.5	1.5:1	70	5	27	12
Shrimp sauce:						
111.5	4	3.8:1	71	7.5	51.5	10.5

Poached Scrod with Creamy Sauce

A scrod is usually a young cod (it could be a young haddock). It's a bland and coarsely textured fish. But it is lean, and it can be transformed into a thing of joy by coddling it in a subtly seasoned court bouillon and bathing it in a luxurious sauce, as I've done here.

For the fish and court bouillon:
1½ pounds fresh scrod fillets, cut into
    serving pieces
⅓ cup dry vermouth or white wine
1 medium onion, thinly sliced
½ carrot, peeled and sliced
1 lemon slice
2½ cups water
1 rib celery with leaves, coarsely
    chopped
1 tablespoon peeled and minced
    fresh ginger
    Bouquet garni (1 sprig fresh
    parsley, 1 bay leaf, tied together
    with white thread)

For the creamy sauce:
1 teaspoon sweet (unsalted) 100
    percent corn oil margarine
2 teaspoons corn oil
1 large shallot, minced
1 tablespoon unbleached flour
½ teaspoon ground ginger
6 dashes ground red (cayenne)
    pepper
2 tablespoons minced fresh parsley
1 teaspoon minced fresh tarragon
    leaves or ½ teaspoon crushed
    dried tarragon leaves
¼ cup evaporated skim milk

1. First prepare fish and court bouillon. Wash fish and drain on paper toweling.

2. Combine balance of ingredients in poacher or stainless-steel pot large enough to hold fish in one layer.

3. When you use a poacher: Bring to boil. Reduce heat to simmering. Simmer for 15 minutes. Place fish on rack and lower into court bouillon. Return to boil. Reduce heat to simmering. Cover and simmer for 10 minutes. Remove fish from poacher. Cover to keep warm. Strain court bouillon; reserve ⅓ cup (see note page 31).

When you use a stainless-steel pot: Bring to boil. Reduce heat to simmering. Simmer for 15 minutes. Arrange fish in washed double layer of cotton cheesecloth. Fold cheesecloth around fish. Tie ends with white thread. Holding both tied ends, lower fish into simmering court bouillon. Return to boil. Reduce heat to simmering. Cover and simmer for 10 minutes. Remove fish. Unwrap cheesecloth and cover fish to keep warm. Strain court bouillon; reserve ⅓ cup (see note page 31).

4. Now prepare sauce. In heavy-bottomed saucepan, combine and heat margarine and oil until hot. Add shallot. Sauté for 1 minute.

5. Add flour. Cook for 1 minute, stirring constantly. Add reserved strained court bouillon. Beat with whisk until thickened and smooth. Whisk in spices, half of parsley, and the tarragon. Bring to simmering point.

6. Whisk while slowly adding milk. Bring just to simmering point.

7. Serve fish on warmed individual serving plates. Spoon with creamy sauce. Sprinkle with balance of parsley and serve immediately.

Yield: Serves 4

CAL	F	P:S	SOD	CAR	CHO	PRO
Fish and court bouillon:						
147.5	0.5	1.5:1	140	3.5	94.5	30.5
Sauce:						
78	7.5	4.2:1	5.5	2	–	0.5

Broiled Moist Porgies

Elsewhere in this section (page 34), I tell you how to test fish fillets or steaks for freshness. Here's how to test a whole fish. The eyes should be clear and bright, the scales should be snug against the body, and the gills (lift up the covering) should be red and clean. A fresh porgy will broil into a moist, smooth-fleshed fish. I've enchanced its natural flavor with sweet herbs and unsweetened pineapple chunks.

4 porgies (1 pound each), cleaned, head left on
¼ cup wine vinegar
2 tablespoons corn oil plus ¼ teaspoon for broiling pan
1 teaspoon fennel seeds, crushed
2 cloves garlic, coarsely chopped
1 tablespoon minced fresh parsley
¼ cup pineapple chunks packed in unsweetened pineapple juice, drained
6 dashes ground red (cayenne) pepper
Watercress sprigs and lemon wedges

1. Wash fish inside and out under cold running water. Dry with paper toweling. Place on plate. Make 3 to 4 diagonal gashes on each side of fish. Lightly oil broiling pan with ¼ teaspoon oil.
2. Combine vinegar, 2 tablespoons oil, and next 5 ingredients in blender. Purée at high speed for 30 seconds. Pour over both sides of fish, spooning into gashes and cavities. Let stand at room temperature for 30 minutes. Transfer to boiling pan.
3. Preheat broiler. Broil 2 to 3 inches from heat for 8 minutes. Turn carefully. Baste with sauce, and broil for 8 minutes.
4. Serve on warmed individual plates. Spoon with sauce, and garnish with watercress and lemon wedges.

Yield: Serves 4

CAL	F	P:S	SOD	CAR	CHO	PRO
287	13	3:1	130	1	1	36

Stewed Sea Bass

This is far and away the favorite fish among our Chinese-Americans, and it's easy to see why. The firm flesh of sea bass is delicately flavored, tender, and juicy; and it has the distinctive quality of absorbing seasonings and still remaining unmistakably sea bass. Its head and bones make delectable stock.

1 white sea bass (2½ pounds), filleted and skinned (reserve bones and head for stock)
2 tablespoons fresh lime juice
⅔ cup Jiffy Fish Stock (see note)
1 tablespoon each corn oil and Italian olive oil, combined
1 medium sweet green pepper, seeded and cut into ¼-inch slivers
1 medium leek, white part only, well washed and cut into ¼-inch slices
3 cloves garlic, minced
2 large shallots, minced
1 medium onion, coarsely chopped
½-inch slice fresh ginger, peeled and shredded
½ cup dry vermouth
2 medium fresh tomatoes, skinned, cored, and coarsely chopped
6 dashes ground red (cayenne) pepper
½ teaspoon each curry powder (no salt or pepper added) and crushed dried thyme leaves
Bouquet garni (1 sprig fresh parsley, 1 bay leaf, tied together with white thread)
Fresh parsley sprigs

1. Wash fillets and pat dry with paper toweling. Cut into 1½-inch pieces. Place in small bowl. Sprinkle with lime juice, turning to coat. Let stand for 30 minutes.

2. Make Jiffy Fish Stock from bones and head, following recipe on page 95. Set aside ⅔ cup and freeze balance.

3. Drain fish on paper toweling. Pat dry. Heat 1 tablespoon combined oils in nonstick skillet until hot. Add fish and sauté until lightly browned on both sides. Transfer to plate.

4. Heat balance of oil in waterless cooker or stainless-steel pot until hot. Add green pepper, leek, garlic, shallots, onion, and ginger. Sauté until wilted and mixture begins to turn golden brown.

5. Add vermouth. Bring to simmering point. Cook for 1 minute.

6. Add tomatoes, stock, spices, and bouquet garni. Bring to simmering point.

7. Add browned fish. Cover and simmer for 20 minutes. Remove bouquet garni and serve.

Yield: Serves 4

Serving Suggestions:

1. Prepare 8 ounces of your favorite pasta (made without salt or eggs). Serve on individual plates. Spoon with stew.

2. Prepare ¾ cup rice. Serve on individual plates. Spoon with stew.

3. Peel, dice (cut into ⅛- to ¼-inch cubes), and cook 3 medium potatoes in rapidly boiling water until tender but still firm. Drain well. Serve as a side dish on individual plates.

Note: The taste of this delicious stew is enhanced when stock is made from the fish's own bones and head. But if time is short, use the fish stock in your freezer and you'll still make a sumptuous dish.

CAL	F	P:S	SOD	CAR	CHO	PRO
194	20	2.5:1	34	13	61	23

Baked Red Snapper

How do you bring out the best in this masterpiece of a fish? Just prepare it with simple fresh ingredients, and its own distinctive delicate flavor will shine through. The key word in the preceding sentence is "fresh." And that word applies particularly to the fish.

1   red snapper (3 pounds), cleaned,
    head left on
3   sprigs fresh parsley
5   thin lemon slices
¾   teaspoon combined dried
    marjoram and rosemary leaves,
    crushed
8   dashes ground red (cayenne)
    pepper
5½ teaspoons corn oil
2   medium onions, thinly sliced
2   large cloves garlic, minced
4   large fresh mushrooms, washed,
    dried, trimmed, and sliced
2   medium tomatoes, skinned, cored,
    and coarsely chopped
¼   teaspoon sweet (unsalted) 100
    percent corn oil margarine, for
    baking pan
2   teaspoons apple cider vinegar
2   tablespoons each apple juice (no
    sugar added) and water

1. Wash fish under cold running water. Dry thoroughly inside and out with paper toweling. Tuck parsley sprigs into cavity. Secure with toothpicks or skewers.

2. Make several gashes on each side of fish. Rub with one of the lemon slices, then with herbs and ground red pepper.

3. Heat oil in nonstick skillet until hot. Sauté onions, garlic, and mushrooms for 3 minutes, taking care not to brown. Add tomatoes and cook for 2 minutes.

4. Grease baking pan with margarine. Pour into pan half of sautéed mix-

ture. Place fish on top of mixture. Spoon balance of mixture over fish.

5. In saucepan, combine vinegar, apple juice and water and bring to simmering point. Pour gently over fish.

6. Lay balance of lemon slices over fish. Cover tightly with aluminum foil. Bake in preheated 400°F oven for 25 minutes, basting once midway.

7. Transfer to warmed serving platter. Garnish with parsley. Serve individual portions at table.

Yield: Serves 4

CAL	F	P:S	SOD	CAR	CHO	PRO
215.5	3.5	3:1	130.5	7	98	40.5

Gingered Flounder with Lime Sauce

You never taste the ginger. It blends with a cornucopia of herbs and spices, vegetables and yogurt, chicken stock, fish stock, and wine to create a sauce with an utterly new taste. Spooned over the sweet-tasting flesh, it converts the humble flounder into a sumptuous dish.

1½ pounds fresh flounder fillets
     About ½ teaspoon ground ginger
1 tablespoon corn oil
1 small onion, minced
1 tablespoon minced sweet green
   pepper
2 teaspoons peeled and minced
   fresh ginger
½ rib celery, minced
2 fresh mushrooms, washed, dried,
   trimmed, and coarsely chopped
2 tablespoons fresh lime juice
¼ cup each Jiffy Fish Stock (page 95)
   and Rich Chicken Stock (page 94)
1 tablespoon minced fresh parsley
4 dashes ground red (cayenne)
   pepper

2 tablespoons low-fat plain yogurt
2 teaspoons dry sherry

1. Wash fish and pat dry with paper toweling. Cut into serving pieces. Sprinkle with ginger.

2. Heat oil over medium-high heat in large nonstick skillet. Add next 5 ingredients, spreading across skillet. Sauté for 1 minute. Place fillets over mixture and cook for 5 minutes. Turn and cook for 3 minutes.

3. Combine lime juice, stocks, parsley, and ground red pepper. Pour into skillet. Bring to simmering point. Reduce heat and cook for 3 minutes, spooning fish continually with sauce.

4. Push minced ingredients off fish into liquid. With slotted spoon, transfer fish to warmed serving plates. Cover with waxed paper to keep warm. Turn heat up under skillet and reduce liquid by one-third.

5. Pour into blender. Add whatever juices have been exuded by fish. Blend on high speed for 30 seconds. Pour back into skillet. Stir in yogurt. Heat to simmering point. *Do not boil.* Remove from heat.

6. Stir in sherry. Spoon over fish and serve.

Yield: Serves 4

CAL	F	P:S	SOD	CAR	CHO	PRO
200.5	5	3.3:1	167	6	96.5	31

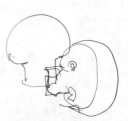

Fish Paella

The name *paella* is Spanish for the two-handled frying pan in which this popular dish is traditionally cooked and served. There's no difficulty understanding the need for two handles: the dish is that heavy. Here's a light version of a paella—assertively seasoned, enticingly aromatic, richly satisfying, and yet with a calorie count you can live with. *Olé!*

1½ cups water
¾ cup rice
2¼ teaspoons each corn oil and Italian olive oil, combined
4 large cloves of garlic, minced
1 tablespoon peeled and minced fresh ginger
1 medium onion, minced
2 large shallots, minced
2 tablespoons minced sweet green pepper
¼ cup red wine
¾ cup tomato purée (no salt added)
1 tablespoon tomato paste (no salt added)
½ cup Light Chicken Broth (page 95) or Rich Chicken Stock (page 94)
1 tablespoon minced fresh parsley
½ teaspoon each dried thyme leaves, crushed, and curry power (no salt or pepper added)
6 dashes ground red (cayenne) pepper
1 pound scrod or flounder fillets
¼ teaspoon ground ginger
2 teaspoons unbleached flour
¼ teaspoon corn oil, for casserole

1. Bring water to rolling boil in saucepan. Add rice and cook, partially covered, over medium-high heat until all liquid is absorbed. Set aside, uncovered.

2. Heat 2¼ teaspoons combined oils in nonstock skillet until hot. Add garlic, fresh ginger, onion, shallots, and green pepper. Sauté for 2 minutes, stirring constantly. Do not brown.

3. Add wine. Cook for 1 minute over medium-high heat.

4. Combine tomato purée, tomato paste, and broth or stock. Add to skillet. Bring to simmering point. Sprinkle in herbs and spices. Stir. Pour mixture into bowl. Wipe out skillet.

5. Wash fish and pat dry with paper toweling. Rub with ground ginger. Cut into 1½-inch pieces. Dust lightly with flour.

6. Heat balance of oil in skillet until hot. Sauté fish on both sides until golden brown (about 3 minutes). Do not overcook.

7. Arrange rice and fish in alternate layers in lightly oiled 1¾-quart casserole. Cover and bake in preheated 400°F oven for 20 minutes. Serve.

Yield: Serves 4

CAL	F	P:S	SOD	CAR	CHO	PRO
284.5	6.5	2.8:1	111.5	41	63	24.5

Chicken

Delicate Tarragon Chicken I

Did you ever hear anybody call an herb "romantic"? Well, that's what I call tarragon. It's the candlelight-and-roses of flavoring. Delicate and delicious, it transforms any meat, poultry, fish, or vegetable dish into a love affair. Here it creates tender moments that will linger long in your memory.

2 *chicken legs with thighs (1¼ pounds), skinned legs separated from thighs*
2 *whole chicken breasts, boned and skinned, (1¼ pounds boned weight)*
¼ *cup tarragon vinegar (page 99)*
2 *cups Light Chicken Broth (page 95)*
2 *large shallots, minced*
2 *large cloves garlic, minced*
4 *dashes ground red (cayenne) pepper*
½ *teaspoon Dijon mustard (no salt added)*
1 *large sprig fresh parsley*
1 *teaspoon dried tarragon leaves, crushed*
   Lettuce leaves
   Watercress sprigs and sliced pimientos

1. Wash chicken under cold running water and pat dry with paper toweling. Place in narrow waterless cooker or stainless-steel pot.
2. In jar, combine shallots, garlic, ground red pepper, mustard, and parsley. Shake to blend. Pour over chicken. Bring to boil. Boil, uncovered, for 2 minutes, removing scum that rises to top. Add tarragon leaves. Lower heat, cover tightly, and simmer for 30 minutes, turning twice. Turn off heat. Let chicken stand in pot, partially covered, for 20 minutes.
3. With slotted spoon, transfer chicken to covered bowl. Pour cooking liquid into jar for Delicate Tarragon Chicken II. Refrigerate both, tightly covered, until cold.
4. Serve chicken cold, arranged on crisp lettuce leaves, garnished with watercress and pimientos.

Yield: Serves 4

CAL	F	P:S	SOD	CAR	CHO	PRO
314	5.5	0.9:1	195	4.5	150	56.5

Delicate Tarragon Chicken II

1 *recipe Delicate Tarragon Chicken I, except lettuce leaves, watercress and pimientos*
2 *teaspoons arrowroot flour dissolved in 2 teaspoons water*
2 *teaspoons minced fresh parsley*

1. Discard any fat from top of cold cooking liquid (step 3, Delicate Tarragon Chicken I). Pour liquid into heavy-bottomed saucepan. Add cold chicken and reheat slowly.
2. Transfer chicken to serving plate. Cover to keep warm. Pour liquid into blender and blend for 30 seconds.
3. Add milk and blend again for 15 seconds. Pour back into saucepan.
4. Reheat to simmering point. Dribble in just enough dissolved arrowroot flour to make a medium-thick sauce. Pour over chicken. Sprinkle with parsley and serve.

Yield: Serves 4

CAL	F	P:S	SOD	CAR	CHO	PRO
334	5.5	0.9:1	198	8.5	151	57.5

Roast Chicken with Mushroom Sauce

I'm often asked, "How can you possibly roast a chicken with the skin removed? Where's the taste to come from?" It doesn't come from the fat in the skin, that's for certain. (Without skin, the chicken is at least 25 percent less fatty.) Here the taste comes from herbs and spices, a touch of lime juice, and a coating of yogurt (which also acts as a protective skin while the chicken is in the oven). Fact is, skinless chicken, treated in the various ways I've invented (the secrets are revealed in the recipes in this section), is far more tasty than chicken with the skin left on.

For the chicken:
1 broiling chicken (3 pounds),
    skinned, wing tips removed
2¼ teaspoons each corn oil and
    Italian olive oil, combined
¼ teaspoon each dried rosemary
    and thyme leaves, crushed
1 tablespoon fresh lime juice
½ cup low-fat plain yogurt
¼ cup water, plus more if necessary
    Minced fresh parsley

For the sauce:
¼ pound fresh mushrooms, washed,
    dried, trimmed, and sliced
¾ cup water
½ teaspoon ground ginger
2 large shallots, minced
3 tablespoons medium-dry sherry
⅓ cup evaporated skim milk (¼
    percent milkfat)
    Ground red (cayenne) pepper to
    taste
2 teaspoons arrowroot flour
    dissolved in 1 teaspoon cold water

1. Wash chicken inside and out under cold running water and pat dry with paper toweling.
2. Combine oils, dried herbs, and lime juice. Spoon and rub over bird and into cavity. Let stand at room temperature for 1 hour; or cover and refrigerate for several hours, removing from refrigerator 1 hour before roasting.
3. Truss bird. Place on rack in shallow roasting pan. Cover with aluminum foil. Roast in preheated 350°F oven for 30 minutes.
4. Uncover bird. Spread with 2 tablespoons yogurt. Add ¼ cup water to pan. Return to oven, covered, and roast 15 minutes. Uncover again and spread with balance of yogurt. Baste with pan juices. (If pan juices have evaporated, add ¼ cup water to pan. Stir around pan; then baste.) Re-cover and roast for 15 minutes.
5. While chicken is roasting, start preparation of sauce. Combine mushrooms, water, ginger, and shallots in small saucepan. Bring to boil. Cover partially and simmer for 5 minutes. Strain into bowl, reserving mushroom mixture.
6. Remove chicken from oven. Transfer to carving board. Cover to keep warm. Remove rack from pan. Place pan on top of stove over medium-high heat. Add sherry and strained mushroom liquid. Cook until liquid is reduced by one-third, scraping to loosen browned particles. Strain into clean saucepan. Add reserved mushroom mixture. Reheat to simmering point. Slowly add milk, whisking continuously. Add several dashes ground red pepper to taste.
7. Dribble in only enough arrowroot mixture to thicken sauce lightly.
8. Cut bird into serving pieces. Spoon with half of sauce. Sprinkle with parsley. Serve balance of hot sauce in sauceboat.

Yield: Serves 4

CAL	F	P:S	SOD	CAR	CHO	PRO
Chicken:						
281	13	1.7:1	94.5	2	96.5	37
Sauce:						
41.5	–	–	14.5	7.5	1	2

Chicken with Creamy Cranberry Sauce

Lovely to look at (it's a delicate pink), delicious to eat (it's slightly sweet and tart), and quick-and-easy to make, this novel combination of chicken with, of all things, cranberries, is among my most praised creations. Here cranberries move up from the side-dish category into the main course—and earn their right to stay there. A tonic for the person who has tasted everything.

2 tablespoons corn oil
2 large cloves garlic, minced
2 large shallots, minced
1 medium onion, minced
6 dashes ground red (cayenne) pepper
2 whole chicken breasts, boned and skinned (1½ pounds boned weight), each breast cut in half
½ teaspoon each dried sage and thyme leaves, crushed
1 sweet, crisp apple, such as Washington State, peeled, cored, and diced
½ cup fresh cranberries
⅓ cup Rich Chicken Stock (page 94)
½ cup apple juice (no sugar added)

1. Heat oil in nonstick skillet until hot. Add garlic, shallots, and onion, spreading across skillet. Sprinkle with ground red pepper. Sauté for 2 minutes, turning and spreading across skillet again.

2. Wash chicken breasts under cold running water and pat dry with paper toweling. Lay on top of sautéed mixture. Sauté on each side over medium-high heat until lightly browned (about 3½ minutes).

3. Sprinkle with dried herbs. Add apple. Stir and sauté for 1 minute.

4. Add balance of ingredients. Bring to simmering point. Reduce heat. Cover and simmer for 30 minutes, turning twice. Turn off heat. Let stand, covered, for 5 minutes.

5. With slotted spoon, remove chicken to warmed serving plate. Cover to keep warm. Pour contents of skillet into blender. Purée for 1 minute (see note). Pour back into skillet and reheat briefly. Pour over chicken and serve immediately.

Yield: Serves 4

Note: Because no thickeners are added to the sauce, it must be puréed just before serving.

CAL	F	P:S	SOD	CAR	CHO	PRO
345	9.5	3.3:1	120	83	84	40.5

Dorris Lee's Orange-Juniper Chicken

Dorris Lee is the extraordinary woman who recently updated Evelyn Wood's speed-reading program. She is as clever in the kitchen as she is with words—and the proof is this delectable bird, accented with the warm pungency of the juniper berry and the sweetness of orange juice concentrate. Speed-read the recipe if you can, but don't speed-eat the dish; it's just too wonderful not to savor with deliberate slowness.

1 *broiling chicken (3 pounds), skinned, wing tips removed*
4 *ounces partially thawed frozen orange juice concentrate (no sugar added)*
2 *tablespoons fresh lemon juice*
2 *tablespoons juniper berries, crushed*
1 *teaspoon ground ginger*
8 *dashes ground red (cayenne) pepper*
2 *large cloves garlic, minced*
1 *tablespoon corn oil*
1 *tablespoon minced fresh parsley or fresh Chinese parsley leaves*

1. Wash chicken inside and out under cold running water and pat dry with paper toweling. Place in bowl.
2. Prepare marinade by combining balance of ingredients in jar, shaking well.
3. Pour marinade over chicken, spooning some into cavity. Cover and refrigerate for 6 hours or more. (The longer the chicken is marinated, the more orangy the taste.) Remove from refrigerator 1 hour before cooking.
4. Drain chicken, reserving marinade. Place chicken on rack in shallow roasting pan. Cover loosely with aluminum foil. Roast in preheated 375°F oven for 20 minutes. Uncover. Spoon with half of marinade. Re-cover and roast another 25 minutes. Pour balance of marinade over chicken. Re-cover and return to oven for 10 minutes. Baste. Roast, uncovered, for 5 minutes.
5. Cut into serving pieces and serve.

Yield: Serves 4

Variation: Cut raw skinned broiling chicken into serving pieces. Marinate. Broil in broiler following directions for Broiled Lime Chicken (page 156).

CAL	F	P:S	SOD	CAR	CHO	PRO
297.5	9	2:1	108.5	14.5	94.5	37

Chicken with Broccoli

Do you remember the *New Yorker* cartoon in which the spoiled rich kid served broccoli by the butler screams, "I say it's spinach—and I say the hell with it." Actually, broccoli is an elegant and delicate vegetable—when it's not overcooked. When it is, it becomes mushy, the color turns a dull yellow-green, and the flavor becomes overpowering and unpleasant. In this happy marriage with subtly marinated chicken breasts, legs, and thighs, the quick-cooked broccoli turns a brilliant jade green (the sign of perfect cooking), and emerges with a texture and flavor that puts it in a class with that jewel of vegetables, asparagus.

2 small whole chicken breasts,
  boned and skinned (1¼ pounds
  boned weight), each breast cut in
  half
2 small chicken legs with thighs,
  skinned (about 1 pound skinned
  weight), legs separated from
  thighs
2 tablespoons fresh lime juice
1 bunch fresh broccoli (2 medium
  stalks)
2 teaspoons each corn oil and
  Italian olive oil, combined
½ teaspoon dried tarragon leaves,
  crushed
3 large cloves garlic, minced
1 medium onion, minced
1 tablespoon peeled and shredded
  fresh ginger
1 tablespoon wine vinegar
1 cup Light Chicken Broth (page 45)
8 dashes ground red (cayenne)
  pepper
1 tablespoon minced fresh parsley
⅓ cup evaporated skim milk (¼
  percent milkfat)
1 tablespoon arrowroot flour
  dissolved in 1 tablespoon cold
  water
3 tablespoons medium-dry sherry

1. Wash chicken under cold running water and pat dry with paper toweling. Place in bowl. Sprinkle with lime
juice, turning to coat. Cover and let
marinate at room temperature for 1
hour.

2. Cut away stalks of broccoli beginning 2 inches below flowerets. Use
floweret sections only, reserving cut-
away stalks for soups or stock. Drop
broccoli into large pot of briskly boiling
water. Cook for 1½ minutes after water
begins to boil again. Drain in colander.
Rinse under cold running water to stop
cooking action. Set aside.

3. Drain chicken. Pat dry with paper toweling. Heat half of oil in large
nonstick skillet until hot. Sauté chicken
on one side for 3 minutes. Pour off any
exuded juices. Sprinkle with tarragon,

turn, and sauté for 2 minutes. Transfer
to plate. Wipe out skillet.

4. Heat balance of oil in skillet.
Sauté garlic, onion, and ginger over medium-high heat until wilted but not
brown. Add vinegar. Cook 1 minute.
Add broth, ground red pepper, and
parsley. Bring to simmering point. Return chicken to skillet and spoon with
sauce. Cover and simmer for 25 minutes, turning once midway and again
when finished. Let stand, covered,
in sauce for 5 minutes. With slotted
spoon, transfer chicken to warmed
serving dish. Cover to keep warm.

5. Add milk to sauce, stirring and
cooking over medium heat for 1 minute,
taking care not to boil.

6. Dribble in only enough arrowroot mixture to thicken sauce lightly.
Add sherry and stir.

7. Add broccoli and cook, uncovered, until heated through.

8. Pour sauce and broccoli over
chicken, coating chicken well and distributing broccoli in a neat, eye-pleas-
ing pattern. Serve immediately.

Yield: Serves 4

CAL	F	P:S	SOD	CAR	CHO	PRO
318.5	10.5	1.7:1	208	13	151	59

Coriander Chicken

Coriander, a favorite spice seed
in the Near East since biblical times,
seems to have the taste of anise, cumin,
and oranges. Here it blends beautifully
into a symphony of spices, herbs, and
fruit juices to accent a dish that could
be the highlight of a dinner in Cairo or
Beirut.

¼ cup each fresh orange juice and
  unsweetened pineapple juice
1 tablespoon fresh lime juice
½ teaspoon cardamom seeds,
  crushed

2 teaspoons coriander seeds,
   crushed
6 dashes ground red (cayenne)
   pepper
2 dashes ground cloves
1 broiling chicken (3 pounds), cut
   into serving pieces, skinned
1 tablespoon corn oil
1 large clove garlic, minced
2 tablespoons minced fresh parsley

1. Combine and blend first 6 ingredients in bowl to make marinade.

2. Wash chicken under cold running water and pat dry with paper toweling. Add chicken to marinade, turning to coat. Cover. Let marinate for 2
hours or more, turning occasionally.

3. Drain chicken, reserving marinade. Pat lightly with paper toweling.
Heat oil in nonstick skillet until moderately hot. Add garlic and chicken.
Sauté for 10 minutes, turning chicken
once midway.

4. Add reserved marinade and
parsley. Bring to simmering point.
Cover tightly and simmer for 40 minutes. Turn off heat and let stand, partially covered, for 20 minutes.

5. Cook, uncovered, over medium-
high heat for 5 minutes, turning chicken
twice, until chicken browns and juices
become syrupy. Serve immediately.

Yield: Serves 4

CAL	F	P:S	SOD	CAR	CHO	PRO
252.5	9	2:1	86	5.5	94.5	36

First Fall Stew

October afternoon. Leaves turning
golden brown. A touch of Jack Frost in
the air. The sky clear with wisps of
winter-warning clouds. And my dear
husband pleading, "Isn't it time for the
First Fall Stew?" So into the kitchen,
and onto the table with this potpourri
of tender chicken and garden-fresh
vegetables. "First Fall Stew, huh?" Har-
old, toughest of critics, says tasting it. "I
think anybody will fall in love with it."

1 chicken (3 pounds), cut into 8
   pieces, skinned, wing tips
   removed
½ teaspoon each ground ginger and
   crushed dried thyme leaves
2 tablespoons grated no-fat Sap
   Sago cheese
⅓ cup Matzoh Crumbs (page 85)
8 dashes ground red (cayenne)
   pepper
2 tablespoons corn oil
1 small onion, minced
2 large cloves garlic, minced
½ medium sweet green pepper,
   seeded and cut into 1¼-inch
   slivers
1 tablespoon apple cider vinegar
2 medium carrots, peeled and cut
   into 1½-inch slivers
8 small red-skinned potatoes, or 2
   medium Idaho potatoes, peeled
   and cut into 2-inch chunks
½ cup 1-inch-cubed yellow turnip
2 medium tomatoes, skinned, cored,
   and cut into 1-inch chunks
¼ cup each grape juice (no sugar
   added) and Rich Chicken Stock
   (page 94)

1. Wash chicken inside and out under cold running water and pat dry
with paper toweling. Rub with ginger
and thyme.

2. Combine cheese, crumbs, and
ground red pepper. Spread on plate.

Roll chicken in mixture, shaking off excess.

3. Heat 1 tablespoon oil in nonstick skillet until hot. Sauté chicken until lightly browned on all sides. Transfer to narrow waterless cooker or stainless-steel pot.

4. Heat balance of oil in skillet until hot. Sauté onion, garlic, and green pepper until wilted but not browned.

5. Add vinegar. Cook for 1 minute.

6. Add balance of ingredients and bring to boil. Pour over chicken. Bring to simmering point. Cover pot tightly and simmer for 50 minutes, turning chicken and stirring twice.

7. Transfer to tureen or deep covered serving bowl and serve.

Yield: Serves 4

CAL	F	P:S	SOD	CAR	CHO	PRO
375	8	4.4:1	144	22.5	94.5	43

Poached Chicken with Spicy Sauce

Not spicy as in torrid chili. But spicy as in gentle, warming, flavorful. Bathed in a subtle wine sauce, here is a chicken dish utterly new in flavor, but certain to become an oft-repeated favorite. Add this bonus: just 45 minutes from start to finish.

For the chicken:
2 cups water
1 thin lemon slice
½ rib celery, diced
1 large clove garlic, minced
2 shallots, minced
½ carrot, peeled and diced
4 fresh mushrooms, washed, dried, trimmed, and thinly sliced
½ cup peeled and diced white turnip
Bouquet garni (1 sprig fresh parsley, 1 bay leaf, tied together with white thread)
2 whole chicken breasts, boned and skinned (1½ pounds boned weight), each cut in half

For the sauce:
⅓ cup red wine
2 tablespoons minced fresh parsley
2 teaspoons tomato paste (no salt or pepper added)
1 teaspoon chili con carne seasoning (no salt added)
½ teaspoon dry mustard
6 dashes ground red (cayenne) pepper

1. Poach chicken first. Combine all ingredients except chicken in waterless cooker or stainless-steel pot. Bring to boil. Lower heat, cover, and simmer for 10 minutes.

2. Add chicken. Bring to slow boil and boil, uncovered, for 5 minutes, removing any scum that rises to top. Reduce heat to simmering, cover, and simmer for 20 to 25 minutes. (Cooking time will vary with thickness of chicken.) Uncover and let cool for 5 minutes.

3. With slotted spoon, transfer chicken to bowl and cover.

4. Prepare sauce. Turn heat up under pot and reduce liquid by half. Let cool for a few minutes. Remove bouquet garni. Pour contents of pot into blender and purée for 1 minute. Measure out ⅓ cup and reserve for sauce. (See serving suggestions at end of recipe for uses for balance of purée.) Pour reserved purée into heavy-bottomed saucepan.

5. In bowl, combine and blend wine with 1 tablespoon parsley and balance of sauce ingredients. Gradually whisk mixture into purée.

6. Place saucepan over low heat. Add chicken, turning to coat. Bring mixture to simmering point. Cook, uncovered, for 5 to 10 minutes, turning

chicken and spooning with sauce until well coated and heated through.

7. Transfer to serving plate. Sprinkle with balance of parsley and serve.

Yield: Serves 4

Variation: Replace one of the chicken breasts with 2 small chicken legs and thighs.

Serving suggestions for balance of purée:

1. Slowly reheat and spoon over steamed broccoli, carrots, cauliflower, potatoes, fish, or rice.

2. Use as base for soup. Slowly reheat purée together with ¼ cup nonfat liquid milk or evaporated skim milk. Pour into 2 soup bowls, sprinkle with minced parsley, and serve.

CAL	F	P:S	SOD	CAR	CHO	PRO
Chicken:						
203	2	0.6:1	127.5	5.5	86	40
Sauce:						
21	–	–	27	5	–	1
Variation:						
228	5	0.9:1	133.5	5.5	110	40

Martini Chicken

Mix gin and vermouth, and you get a martini. Mix this gin-accented chicken with this vermouth-flavored sauce, and you get a Martini Chicken. Don't worry about the alcoholic content, because there isn't any. All of it vaporizes in cooking. What remains are the intriguing combinations of herbs in these liquors. These combinations can't be duplicated any other way because they're carefully guarded trade secrets. Don't have a martini *before*

dinner; have a Martini Chicken *for* dinner.

For the chicken:
2   whole chicken breasts, boned and skinned (1½ pounds boned weight), pounded to ¼-inch thickness
¼   cup fresh lemon juice
1   tablespoon dry gin
3   large cloves garlic
1   tablespoon peeled and shredded fresh ginger
½   cup Bread Crumbs (page 85)
3   tablespoons toasted wheat germ (no sugar added)
2½ teaspoons each corn oil and Italian olive oil, combined

For the sauce:
1   teaspoon each corn oil and sweet (unsalted) 100 percent corn oil margarine
2   teaspoons unbleached flour
3   tablespoons dry vermouth
½   cup Light Chicken Broth (page 95)
1½ teaspoons each minced fresh parsley and dill, combined
4   dashes ground red (cayenne) pepper
¼   cup evaporated skim milk (¼ percent milkfat)

1. Wash chicken breasts and pat dry with paper toweling. Combine lemon juice, gin, garlic, and ginger in bowl. Add chicken and marinate, covered, for at least 2 hours.

2. Drain chicken. Strain marinade, reserving liquid. Set aside.

3. Combine crumbs with wheat germ, blending well. Spread over plate. Dip chicken into crumb mixture, coating lightly on both sides.

4. Heat 2¼ teaspoons combined oils in nonstick skillet until hot. Sauté chicken until golden brown on one side. Transfer chicken to plate.

5. Heat balance of oil in skillet. Sauté chicken for 5 minutes on other side. Total cooking time should not exceed 10 minutes.

6. While chicken is cooking, prepare sauce. Heat combined oil and margarine in saucepan until hot. Add flour and cook 1 minute, stirring constantly. Add vermouth and cook 1 minute.

7. Combine strained reserved marinade with broth. Add to saucepan a little at a time, whisking constantly. Add herbs and ground red pepper. Stir.

8. Add milk in a steady stream, whisking continuously. Heat until barely simmering. *Do not boil.*

9. Arrange chicken on warmed individual serving plates. Spoon with sauce and serve.

Yield: Serves 4

Note: Hearty French Bread (page 77) makes particularly delicious crumbs for this dish.

CAL	F	P:S	SOD	CAR	CHO	PRO
Chicken:						
263.5	7.7	2.9:1	112	14	84	42
Sauce:						
49	2	3.3:1	8	5.5	1	2

Chicken with Puréed Leek

St. David is the patron saint of the Welsh, and without leeks in the cawl (Welsh for "stew") no St. David's Day dinner would be authentic. Here's my very modern version of the national dish that makes all good Welshmen stand up and sing *Land of My Fathers*. The leeks are puréed, and the distinctive flavor of this sophisticated member of the garlic family is orchestrated with a medley of gourmet herbs and spices. Don't wait for St. David's Day (March 1) to enjoy this unusual delight.

1 whole chicken breast, boned and skinned (1½ pounds boned weight), cut into 4 pieces
2 small chicken legs with thighs, skinned (about 1 pound skinned weight), legs separated from thighs
4½ teaspoons fresh lemon juice
4½ teaspoons corn oil
1 large leek, white part only, well washed and minced
2 large cloves garlic, minced
1 tablespoon peeled and minced carrot
1 tablespoon each minced fresh dill and parsley, combined
¼ teaspoon each dried thyme and sage leaves, crushed
6 dashes ground red (cayenne) pepper
⅓ cup dry vermouth
½ cup Rich Chicken Stock (page 94)
3 whole cloves
½ teaspoon dry mustard dissolved in 1 teaspoon water
¼ cup evaporated skim milk (¼ percent milkfat)

1. Wash chicken under cold running water and pat dry with paper toweling. Place in bowl. Sprinkle with lemon juice. Let stand for 15 minutes, then pat dry with paper toweling.

2. Heat oil in nonstick skillet until moderately hot. Sauté leek, garlic, and carrot for 2 minutes. Add chicken and sauté for 3 minutes on each side.

3. Add fresh and dried herbs and ground red pepper. Sauté for 1 minute. Add vermouth. Cook for 30 seconds.

4. Add stock, cloves, and mustard. Bring to simmering point. Cover and simmer gently for 30 minutes, turning every 10 minutes. Turn off heat. Spoon sauce over chicken. Cover partially and let stand for 10 minutes.

5. With slotted spoon, transfer chicken to warmed serving plate. Cover to keep warm.

6. Turn up heat under skillet and

reduce liquid by half. Pour reduced liquid and vegetables into blender. Blend on high speed for 30 seconds. Add milk. Blend for 30 seconds more. Pour back into skillet and reheat briefly to simmering point. *Do not boil.*

7. Spoon sauce over chicken and serve immediately.

Yield: Serves 4

CAL	F	P:S	SOD	CAR	CHO	PRO
268	7	1.8:1	0.5	10	109.5	42

Chestnut Chicken

When I was a small girl, the first signal of the winter holidays was the mouth-watering aroma of roasting chestnuts wafting from street vendors' stands. But in adolescence and young womanhood, I shunned these delectable morsels, fearing the bulges in the wrong places they would bring to my figure. What wasted years! There are only 14 calories in a chestnut, and a mere 0.1 milligram of fat, most of it polyunsaturated. There are ample supplies of fresh chestnuts in supermarkets from November through December, and you can obtain the canned variety (be sure there's no sugar added) in gourmet shops all year round. Why not preview the winter holidays in July (or any other time of year) with this heart-warming delight?

2 *whole chicken breasts, boned and skinned (1½ pounds boned weight), each breast cut in half*
2 *small chicken legs with thighs (1¼ pounds), skinned, legs separated from thighs*

2 *large cloves garlic, finely minced*
2 *teaspoons Italian olive oil*
1 *teaspoon ground ginger*
2 *tablespoons fresh lemon juice*
3 *teaspoons corn oil*
1 *medium onion, minced*
3 *large fresh mushrooms, washed, dried, trimmed, and sliced*
2 *tablespoons dry vermouth*
½ *cup Rich Chicken Stock (page 94)*
⅓ *cup tomato purée (no salt added)*
6 *dashes ground red (cayenne) pepper*
½ *teaspoon cuminseed, crushed*
1 *tablespoon minced fresh parsley*
¾ *cup canned unsweetened chestnuts, drained and halved (see note)*

1. Wash chicken under cold running water and pat dry with paper toweling. Combine garlic, olive oil, ginger, and lemon juice in bowl large enough to accommodate chicken. Add chicken, turning to coat. Cover and marinate for 1 hour at room temperature.

2. Remove chicken from marinade. Discard marinade. Pat lightly with paper toweling, leaving intact remnants of garlic left on chicken.

3. Heat 1½ teaspoons corn oil in nonstick skillet until hot. Add chicken and sauté until lightly browned on both sides. Transfer to plate. Wipe out skillet.

4. Heat balance of oil in skillet until hot. Add onion and mushrooms. Sauté until lightly browned.

5. Add vermouth. Cook for 1 minute. Add stock, tomato purée, ground red pepper, and cuminseed, stirring to blend.

6. Return browned chicken to skillet. Add parsley and turn chicken to coat. Bring to simmering point. Cover and simmer for 20 minutes.

7. Add chestnuts, stirring and distributing evenly in skillet. Re-cover and simmer for 15 minutes. Turn heat off. Baste. Let stand, covered, for 20 min-

utes. (Sauce will thicken naturally.) Reheat and serve very hot.

Yield: Serves 6

Note: Imported salt-free canned chestnuts, available in gourmet shops, are excellent. If raw chestnuts are available in your local markets (they usually are around Thanksgiving and Christmas), by all means whisk them into your shopping cart. Here's how they're cooked:

Make a cut on flat side of each nut. Place in small saucepan. Add water to cover. Bring to rolling boil and cook for 1 minute. Pour off water, and reserve. Let nuts cool until you can handle them. Peel off shell and brown inner skin. Store in refrigerator with cooking water to cover for 3 to 4 days. In this recipe, add chestnuts to mixture as chicken is returned to skillet. One-half pound unshelled chestnuts yields about 1¼ cups shelled.

CAL	F	P:S	SOD	CAR	CHO	PRO
324	11	1.8:1	105	18.5	99.5	41

Chicken Jubilee

A jubilee is an occasion of general joy. Gather the family around this I've-never-tasted-anything-so-good-before chicken dish, highlighted by potato-y Jerusalem artichokes, and have a jubilee.

1 broiling chicken (3 pounds), skinned and cut into serving pieces
1 lemon wedge
8 Jerusalem artichokes, peeled
3 tablespoons unbleached flour
1 tablespoon each corn oil and Italian olive oil, combined
1 medium onion, minced
2 large cloves garlic, minced
2 shallots, minced
2 tablespoons minced sweet green pepper
½ teaspoon each ground cinnamon and crushed dried rosemary leaves
6 dashes ground red (cayenne) pepper
1 cup canned tomatoes (no salt added), chopped
½ cup Light Chicken Broth (page 95)
1 tablespoon minced fresh parsley

1. Wash chicken under cold running water and pat dry with paper toweling. Rub with lemon wedge. Place chicken in bowl. Squeeze all juice from lemon over chicken. Let stand covered for at least 30 minutes.
2. Cut each artichoke into 4 pieces. Parboil for about 10 minutes. Drain. Set aside.
3. Dredge chicken in flour, shaking off excess.
4. Heat 1 tablespoon combined oils in nonstick skillet until hot. Add chicken and sauté on both sides until lightly browned. Transfer to plate.
5. Heat balance of oil in skillet until hot. Sauté onion, garlic, shallots, and

green pepper until mixture just begins to brown. Sprinkle with cinnamon, rosemary, and ground red pepper. Stir to blend.

6. Add tomatoes, broth, parsley, and artichokes. Bring to simmering point. Cover and simmer over very low heat for 45 minutes, basting and turning chicken and artichokes twice.

7. Remove from heat and let stand, covered, for 5 minutes before serving.

Yield: Serves 4

CAL	F	P:S	SOD	CAR	CHO	PRO
347	7	2.5:1	116	39.5	94.5	39

Crisp Sautéed Chicken with Quick Pineapple Sauce

The secret of the crispness is a breading of matzoh crumbs and my flavorful bread crumbs. The secret of the sauce is evaporated skim milk. And a just-so blend of herbs and spices is the secret of this dish's deliciousness.

For the chicken:
2 whole chicken breasts, boned and skinned (1¼ pounds boned weight), each cut in half
¼ cup evaporated skim milk (¼ percent milkfat)
1 teaspoon curry powder (no salt or pepper added)
6 dashes ground red (cayenne) pepper
⅓ cup Bread Crumbs (page 85)
2 tablespoons Matzoh Crumbs (page 85)
2 teaspoons no-fat grated Sap Sago cheese
1 teaspoon juniper berries, crushed

½ teaspoon dried savory leaves, crushed
2 tablespoons corn oil
2 large cloves garlic, minced
2 shallots, minced
Fresh parsley sprigs

For the sauce:
1 cup canned pineapple chunks packed in unsweetened pineapple juice, drained but ¼ cup juice reserved, at room temperature
¼ cup evaporated skim milk (¼ percent milkfat)
½ teaspoon curry powder (no salt or pepper added)
3 dashes ground cloves
1 teaspoon fresh lemon juice
4 dashes ground red (cayenne) pepper

1. Wash chicken under cold running water and pat dry with paper toweling.

2. Combine milk, curry powder, and ground red pepper in small bowl. In separate shallow bowl, combine crumbs and cheese, blending well.

3. Dip chicken into liquid mixture and then into crumbs, turning to coat.

4. Combine juniper berries and savory leaves. Sprinkle and press mixture into both sides of coated chicken.

5. Heat 1 tablespoon oil in nonstick skillet until hot. Add garlic and shallots. Sauté for 30 seconds. Place chicken breasts on top of mixture and sauté until golden brown (about 5 minutes).

6. Heat balance of oil in skillet. Sauté chicken on second side for 5 minutes. Turn again and sauté for 5 minutes; then turn once more and sauté for another 5 minutes.

7. While chicken is sautéing, prepare sauce. Place all ingredients for sauce in blender and blend for 30 seconds. Pour into saucepan and heat. Do not boil.

8. Transfer chicken to warmed serving platter. Garnish with parsley.

Pour sauce into sauceboat and serve along with chicken.

Yield: Serves 4

Variation: Chicken is delicious, too, without sauce. Garnish with fresh orange slices.

CAL	F	P:S	SOD	CAR	CHO	PRO
Chicken:						
258.5	9	3.6:1	120	13	85	35.5
Sauce:						
47	–	–	23	9	1	1.5
1 thin orange slice:						
4	–	–	–	1	–	–

Chicken Velouté

Cook this simply prepared dish quickly, dress it in a lovely herbaceous sauce, eat it as soon as it comes out of the skillet—and you'll experience a velvety delight as smooth on the tongue as it is pleasing to the eye. Our guests gather around the table well in advance to savor that evanescent just-out-of-the skillet flavor.

2 whole chicken breasts, boned and skinned (1½ pounds boned weight), each breast cut in half
1 tablespoon each corn oil and sweet (unsalted) 100 percent corn oil margarine
⅓ cup Rich Chicken Stock (page 94)
2 tablespoons dry sherry
1 large shallot, minced
2 large cloves garlic, minced
2 tablespoons minced fresh basil or 1 teaspoon crushed dried sweet basil leaves
6 dashes ground red (cayenne) pepper
½ cup evaporated skim milk (¼ percent milkfat)
2 teaspoons fresh lemon juice

1. Wash chicken under cold running water and pat dry with paper toweling. Flatten between two pieces of waxed paper to uniform thickness.

2. Heat oil and margarine in large nonstick skillet until moderately hot. Add chicken and sauté for 3 to 4 minutes on each side. Watch heat so that chicken does not brown or overcook. Transfer to warmed serving plate. Cover to keep warm.

3. Add stock, sherry, shallot, and garlic to skillet. Cook over medium-high heat until reduced and syrupy.

4. Add basil and ground red pepper, stirring to blend. Gradually whisk in milk.

5. Cook over low heat, just under boiling point, until lightly thickened (about 3 minutes).

6. Stir in lemon juice. Spoon sauce over warm chicken and serve immediately.

Yield: Serves 4

CAL	F	P:S	SOD	CAR	CHO	PRO
284	8.5	2.7:1	127	4.5	88.5	42.5

Curried Chicken with Tomatoes

Basic to all curry powders are ground red (cayenne) pepper, coriander, cumin, fenugreek, and turmeric; and it's this concoction that gives curry its special taste. Other spices are often added, and curries range from the torrid and pungent to the warm and mild. The curry powder I use (you can get it in most supermarkets) is on the mild side. Here it's employed to add an intriguing flavor to an otherwise All-American chicken-tomato stew.

2 whole chicken breasts, boned and skinned (1½ pounds boned weight), each breast cut in half
½ teaspoon ground ginger
8 dashes ground red (cayenne) pepper
4½ teaspoons corn oil
2 large cloves garlic, minced
1 small rib celery, minced
1 small onion, minced
2 shallots, minced
3 large fresh mushrooms, washed, dried, trimmed, and sliced
1 small sweet green pepper, cut into ½-inch slivers
2 medium ripe tomatoes, skinned, cored, and chopped
¼ cup each dry vermouth and Rich Chicken Stock (page 94)
½ teaspoon each dried rosemary leaves and cuminseed, crushed
1 tablespoon curry powder (no salt or pepper added)

1. Wash chicken and pat dry with paper toweling. Sprinkle with ginger and ground red pepper.
2. Heat 2¼ teaspoons oil in non-stick skillet until hot. Add chicken, and brown lightly on both sides. Transfer to dish.
3. Heat balance of oil until hot. Add garlic, celery, onion, shallots, mushrooms, and green pepper. Sauté until lightly browned.
4. Add tomatoes. Cook for 1 minute.
5. Add vermouth and cook for 1 minute. Add stock, rosemary, cuminseed and curry powder. Bring to simmering point. Return chicken to skillet. Cover and simmer gently for 25 minutes, turning once midway.

6. Turn off heat. Uncover partially and let stand for 15 minutes. Reheat for 2 minutes. Serve.

Yield: Serves 4

CAL	F	P:S	SOD	CAR	CHO	PRO
264	5.5	3:1	148.5	9	84	41

Chicken Dumpling Stew

If you're in Austria, Poland, Hungary, or Czechoslovakia, or most anywhere in Central Europe, you're certain to be regaled by dumplings. These boiled balls of deliciousness, made with small amounts of wheat flour (I use cornmeal as well), lift stews, no matter how delicious to begin with, to a new level of taste appeal. Light as air, my subtly flavored dumplings are a special treat for the diet-conscious food lover: only 52.5 calories a dumpling, and just 3.5 milligrams of sodium.

For the chicken stew:
1 broiler (3 pounds), skinned and cut into quarters
4 cups water
1 whole leek, well washed and coarsely chopped, or 1 whole green onion, coarsely chopped
½ rib celery, minced
1 small onion, coarsely chopped
3 large cloves garlic, minced
2 large fresh mushrooms, washed, dried, trimmed, and sliced
1 tablespoon apple cider vinegar
½ teaspoon dried thyme leaves, crushed
¼ teaspoon dried sage leaves, crushed
6 dashes ground red (cayenne) pepper
  Bouquet garni (2 fresh dill sprigs and 1 bay leaf, tied together with white thread)

For the dumplings:
  1 tablespoon corn oil
  1 egg white plus ½ egg yolk
  1 large clove garlic, minced
  1 small scallion, minced
  1 tablespoon minced fresh dill
  ¼ teaspoon each dried sage and
    thyme leaves, crushed
  6 dashes ground red (cayenne)
    pepper
  ¼ cup yellow cornmeal
  ¼ cup each evaporated skim milk (¼
    percent milkfat) and liquid nonfat
    milk, combined
  ⅔ cup unbleached flour
  2½ teaspoons low-sodium baking
    powder

1. Prepare chicken stew first. Place chicken and water in waterless cooker or stainless-steel pot. Bring to boil. Reduce heat to slow boil and cook for 10 minutes, removing scum that rises to top.

2. Add balance of ingredients for stew. Cover partially and simmer gently for 1 hour.

3. With slotted spoon, remove chicken from stewing liquid and place in bowl. Pour stewing liquid into another bowl. Cover and refrigerate chicken and stewing liquid until well chilled. Remove chicken from bones and cut into 1-inch pieces. Cut away any hardened fat from the stewing liquid. Pour stewing liquid into wide pot. Bring to simmering point over low heat.

4. While stew is heating, prepare dumplings. Place oil, egg white, and ½ egg yolk in bowl. Beat well with fork. Add garlic, scallion, dill, dried herbs, and ground red pepper and blend. Add cornmeal, beating constantly. Stir in milk. In a separate bowl, combine flour with baking powder. Add to mixture a little at a time until all liquid is absorbed.

5. Drop 12 spoonfuls of dumpling mix into simmering stew. Cover partially and simmer for 12 minutes. Stew will thicken and dumplings will puff up. With slotted spoon, remove dumplings to serving bowl. Cover to keep warm.

6. Add chicken to stew and simmer only until chicken is heated through. Pour stew and chicken over dumplings and serve immediately.

Yield: Stew and chicken serves 4, 2 to 3 dumplings per portion

CAL	F	P:S	SOD	CAR	CHO	PRO
Chicken:						
233	6	0.6:1	92	5.5	99	37
Per dumpling:						
52.5	1.5	3.8:1	3.5	8.3	11	2

Vegetables, Grains, and Pasta

Elegant Duxelles

Want quick, true mushroom flavor? Have duxelles on hand, and your wish is instantly granted. This is a mushroom preparation that has a week's refrigerator life, and it can also be frozen. I use it as a flavoring for stuffing, sauces, vegetables, and main courses—and, by itself or blended with other delectables, as a 10-rated spread. My basic magical ingredient for Elegant Duxelles is my own chicken stock.

2 tablespoons corn oil
¾ pound fresh mushrooms, washed, dried, trimmed, and minced
1 large whole scallion, minced (see note 2)
1 large clove garlic, minced
½ teaspoon dried chervil leaves, crushed
1 tablespoon minced fresh parsley
8 dashes ground red (cayenne) pepper
¼ cup Rich Chicken Stock (page 94)

1. Heat oil in nonstick skillet until hot. Add mushrooms, scallion, and garlic and sauté over medium-high heat for 5 minutes, stirring and turning every minute. Volume will reduce, and mushrooms will release their juices.
2. Sprinkle with chervil, parsley, and ground red pepper. Stir to blend. Continue sautéing until all liquid evaporates.
3. Add stock and sauté until all liquid evaporates (about 5 minutes). Let cool.
4. Pour into jar and refrigerate, or turn into freezeproof container and freeze.

Yield: 1 cup

Notes:
1. Shelf life of refrigerated duxelles is 5 to 7 days. Frozen duxelles will last 2 to 3 months.
2. Two large shallots, minced, may be substituted for scallion.

CAL	F	P:S	SOD	CAR	CHO	PRO
Per tablespoon:						
22.5	1.5	4.4:1	4.5	1	–	1
Per cup:						
359	27.6	4.4:1	74	18.4	–	11.6

Braised Cucumbers

A dieter's delight (they're 96 percent water), cucumbers, usually eaten raw or pickled, can be marinated, boiled, sautéed, baked and stuffed, and braised. In preparing my braised cucumbers, I eschew briny commercial bouillon. Instead I simmer them in a spiced, herbaceous salt-free broth of my own invention. Kirby cucumbers, which I recommend, are short and knobby, and are far more flavorful than the more familiar longer variety.

1¾ pounds Kirby cucumbers, peeled, cut into quarters lengthwise
1 tablespoon fresh lemon juice
2 teaspoons corn oil
2 large scallions, coarsely chopped
1 large shallot, minced
2 cloves garlic, minced
1 tablespoon dry vermouth
½ teaspoon ground ginger
4 dashes ground red (cayenne) pepper
1 tablespoon minced fresh dill (see note)
¼ cup Rich Chicken Stock (page 94)

1. Remove as many seeds from cucumbers as possible. Place cucumbers in large bowl. Sprinkle with lemon juice and let stand for 10 minutes.
2. Heat oil in nonstick skillet until hot. Add scallions, shallot, and garlic and sauté briefly until wilted.
3. Add vermouth and cook on high heat for 1 minute. Add ginger, pepper, dill, and stock. Bring to simmering point.
4. Drain cucumbers and add to skillet. Cover and simmer until tender (about 15 minutes), basting frequently.

Yield: Serves 6

Note: Do not replace fresh dill with dried dill (it's too high in sodium).

When fresh dill isn't available, substitute fresh tarragon, parsley, or basil.

CAL	F	P:S	SOD	CAR	CHO	PRO
58	2.5	4.1:1	17.5	8	–	2.5

My Ratatouille

There are five basic ingredients in the classic ratatouille: tomatoes, eggplant, green pepper, zucchini, and olive oil. In my lighter version of this popular Gallic stew, I eliminate zucchini and mix olive oil with corn oil (more of the healthful polyunsaturated fat that way). I also use a mélange of spices and herbs that are lighter on the tongue than the originals. Result: a dish you can consume with light hearted enjoyment. Only 110 calories per serving!

1 tablespoon each corn oil and
   Italian olive oil, combined
1 eggplant (12 ounces to 1 pound),
   washed, dried, and cut into 1-inch
   cubes
3 large cloves garlic, minced
1 medium onion, thinly sliced
1 small sweet green pepper, seeded
   and minced
¼ pound fresh mushrooms, washed,
   dried, trimmed, and thickly sliced
3 tablespoons dry vermouth
3 large fresh tomatoes, skinned and
   coarsely chopped
¼ cup tomato purée (no salt added)
2 tablespoons tomato paste (no salt
   added)
½ cup minced fresh basil
½ teaspoon dried thyme leaves,
   crushed
8 dashes ground red (cayenne)
   pepper

1. Heat iron skillet over medium-high heat until hot. Add 1 tablespoon combined oils. Sauté eggplant 2 minutes, stirring constantly.

2. Add balance of oil to skillet. Sauté garlic, onion, green pepper, and mushrooms, stirring constantly for 3 minutes.

3. Add vermouth. Cook for 1 minute.

4. Combine tomatoes, tomato purée, and tomato paste. Add to skillet. Stir in basil, thyme, and ground red pepper. Bring to simmering point.

5. Reduce heat, cover tightly and simmer for 20 minutes. Turn off heat and let stand for 10 minutes. Reheat before serving.

Yield: Serves 4

Variation: Substitute 2 tablespoons minced fresh parsley for basil and 1 tablespoon crushed juniper berries for thyme leaves.

Alternate cooking method: After all ingredients are combined (step 4), turn mixture into lightly oiled 1½-quart casserole, cover, and bake in preheated 375°F oven for 30 minutes.

CAL	F	P:S	SOD	CAR	CHO	PRO
110	2.6	2.8:1	26	18	–	3

Variation: No appreciable difference

Make-Ahead Vegetables in a Crock

Just what the title says (see serving suggestion). What it doesn't say is just how out-of-this-worldish this otherwise ordinary combination of potatoes, carrots, and yams becomes when enriched with my extraordinary mélange of herbs and spices.

½ cup peeled and cubed yellow
     turnip (½-inch cubes)
2 medium Idaho potatoes, peeled
     and cut into ½-inch cubes
1 medium yam, peeled and cut into
     ½-inch cubes
1 tablespoon apple juice (no sugar
     added)
1 tablespoon corn oil
1 large clove garlic, minced
2 shallots, minced
½ teaspoon dried chervil leaves,
     crushed
½ teaspoon aniseed, crushed
8 dashes ground red (cayenne)
     pepper
1½ teaspoons each combined minced
     fresh parsley and dill
2 tablespoons low-fat plain yogurt
½ teaspoon sweet (unsalted) 100
     percent corn oil margarine, for
     crocks

1. Bring saucepan of water to rolling boil. Add turnip and cook, uncovered, for 10 minutes. Add cubed Idahos and yam, and cook for 10 minutes more. Drain. Return to saucepan. Add apple juice, and mash.
2. Add balance of ingredients except yogurt and blend. Stir in yogurt.
3. Turn into 4 margarine-greased ovenproof crocks. Bake in preheated 400°F oven for 20 minutes. Serve immediately.

Yield: Serves 4

Serving suggestion: This slightly sweet dish (which can be prepared early in the day for the evening meal) is a perk-up accompaniment to simply broiled meats and chicken.

CAL	F	P:S	SOD	CAR	CHO	PRO
204	6	3.7:1	40	17.5	2	4.5

Gingered Potatoes

Hurray for the potato! The number of cooking varieties are endless, and for weeks on end, you need never eat the same version twice until you get that irresistible urge to return to one of your favorites. Here's one of mine. For the skeptical dieter, may I remind you that a medium-sized white potato contributes only 80 to 100 calories, an almost negligible amount of fat, no cholesterol, and just a miserly amount of sodium.

3 potatoes (about 1¼ pounds),
     peeled, cubed, cooked until
     tender, and drained
3 tablespoons evaporated skim milk
     (¼ percent milkfat)
1 tablespoon corn oil
2 large cloves garlic, minced
2 large shallots, minced
1 teaspoon peeled and minced fresh
     ginger
2 large mushrooms, washed, dried,
     trimmed, and coarsely chopped
1 teaspoon apple cider vinegar
¼ teaspoon each dried thyme and
     rosemary leaves, crushed
1½ teaspoons each combined minced
     fresh parsley and dill
6 dashes ground red (cayenne)
     pepper
1¼ teaspoons ground ginger
2 teaspoons medium-dry sherry
¼ teaspoon sweet (unsalted) 100
     percent corn oil margarine, for
     casserole

1. Place warm drained potatoes in bowl. Mash with fork or electric beater. Add milk and blend.

2. Heat oil in nonstick skillet until hot. Sauté garlic, shallots, minced ginger, and mushrooms until wilted but not browned.

3. Add vinegar. Cook for 30 seconds.

4. Pour skillet mixture into mashed potatoes. Sprinkle with herbs and spices; blend. Stir in sherry.

5. Pile potatoes into margarine-greased 1-quart ovenproof casserole. Bake, uncovered, in preheated 400°F oven for 15 to 20 minutes. Top should be lightly browned.

Yield: Serves 4

CAL	F	P:S	SOD	CAR	CHO	PRO
136	3.5	4.4:1	11.5	23	1	3

Pretty Potato Balls

Potato dishes are often works of art, as witness Potatoes Anna, Duchesse potatoes, Lyonnaise potatoes, and *pommes soufflées* among others. My contribution to the gallery is pure pop art. These pretty sculptured balls are meant to be enjoyed by all.

2 Idaho potatoes (about 1 pound), peeled and cut into 1-inch cubes
1 tablespoon corn oil

2 large shallots, minced
1 large clove garlic, minced
2 tablespoons minced onion
3 large fresh mushrooms, washed, dried, trimmed, and coarsely chopped
6 dashes ground red (cayenne) pepper
¼ teaspoon each ground ginger and crushed dried thyme leaves
1 teaspoon minced fresh dill
¼ cup buttermilk (no salt added)
2 tablespoons toasted wheat germ (no sugar added)
¼ teaspoon sweet (unsalted) 100 percent corn oil margarine, for baking pan

1. Place potatoes in saucepan. Cover with water. Boil, uncovered, until tender but not oversoft (about 12 minutes). Drain. Return to saucepan. Toss over high heat for a few seconds until potatoes are dry. Mash with fork or masher.

2. Heat oil in nonstick skillet until hot. Sauté shallots, garlic, onion and mushrooms until wilted but not browned, turning often. Combine with mashed potatoes.

3. Sprinkle with spices and herbs. Mash to blend. Stir in buttermilk.

4. Shape mixture into 8 balls. Roll in wheat germ. Place in margarine-greased baking pan.

5. Bake in preheated 400°F oven for 10 minutes. Then roll 2 or 3 times and bake until balls are lightly browned all over.

Yield: Serves 4

Variations:

1. Substitute ½ teaspoon chili con carne seasoning (no salt or pepper added) for 1 teaspoon fresh dill.

2. Evaporated skim milk (¼ percent milkfat) may be substituted for buttermilk.

3. Two tablespoons sesame seeds, pressed gently into the balls, may be substituted for wheat germ.

CAL	F	P:S	SOD	CAR	CHO	PRO
128	4	4.4:1	13	20	–	4

Variation 1: No appreciable difference

Variation 2:

135	4	4.4:1	12.5	19	1	3.5

Variation 3:

125.5	3.5	4:1	13	18.5	–	3

Pink Panther Potatoes

Because they're pink. And because they're as vivacious as the Pink Panther.

2 each small Idaho potatoes and yams (total weight 1½ pounds), peeled, cubed, and cooked until tender
1 tablespoon corn oil
½ teaspoon ground ginger
6 dashes ground red (cayenne) pepper
3 dashes ground cloves
½ teaspoon ground cinnamon
¼ teaspoon chili con carne seasoning (no salt or pepper added)
2 large shallots, minced
½ teaspoon dried sweet basil leaves, crushed
2 teaspoons minced fresh parsley or dill
2 tablespoons apple juice (no sugar added)
2 tablespoons low-fat plain yogurt
½ teaspoon sweet (unsalted) 100 percent corn oil margarine, for crocks

1. Place cooked potatoes in bowl. Add oil and spices. Mash until smooth.
2. Add shallots, herbs, and apple juice; stir. Stir in yogurt.
3. Pile into 4 margarine-greased crocks. Bake in preheated 400°F oven for 20 minutes. Mixture will puff up. Serve immediately.

Yield: Serves 4

Note: Potatoes may be prepared ahead of time, piled into crocks, and refrigerated. Bring to room temperature before baking.

CAL	F	P:S	SOD	CAR	CHO	PRO
185	5	3.6:1	31.5	31.5	2	4

Potato-Mushroom Mélange

Two of my favorite vegetables combine with my own magical Light Chicken Broth and a small cornucopia of herbs and spices to produce this vegetable wonder. Note for scholars only: Strictly speaking, mushrooms aren't vegetables. They're a fungus. But just imagine replying to your spouse's "What's for dinner?" with, "Oh, just some fungus." In my kitchen, mushrooms are vegetables—and they're going to stay that way.

1½ pounds baking potatoes (about 3 potatoes), peeled and cut into 1-inch chunks
1 cup Light Chicken Broth (page 95)
4½ teaspoons corn oil
¼ pound fresh mushrooms, washed, dried, trimmed, and sliced
1 large onion, quartered and thinly sliced
3 large cloves garlic, minced
1 large shallot, minced
½ teaspoon each dried rosemary and thyme leaves, crushed
6 dashes ground red (cayenne) pepper
½ teaspoon ground ginger
¼ teaspoon caraway seeds, lightly crushed

1. In small saucepan, combine potatoes with broth and enough water to cover. Bring to boil. Reduce heat to simmering. Cover and simmer until almost tender (about 10 minutes). Drain and cool. Reserve cooking liquid for soups, stocks, and sauces.

2. Heat 2¼ teaspoons oil in nonstick skillet until hot. Sauté mushrooms over medium-high heat for 4 minutes, turning constantly. Remove to bowl.

3. Add balance of oil to skillet. Sauté onion, garlic, and shallot until lightly browned. Sprinkle with herbs. Stir.

4. Add potatoes. Sprinkle with ground red pepper, ginger, and caraway seeds. Sauté for 5 minutes, turning continuously.

5. Add sautéed mushrooms. Stir to combine all ingredients and sauté until well heated.

Yield: Serves 4

CAL	F	P:S	SOD	CAR	CHO	PRO
180	5	4.4:1	21	28	–	5.5

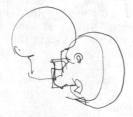

Sautéed Green Tomatoes

These unripe tomatoes, dipped in sweet milk, sprinkled with sweet herbs, then coated with flavorful bread crumbs, come to your table tasting more like sweet and tart potatoes than tomatoes. Sautéed green tomatoes have been a passion of my husband's ever since he was a boy, but he enjoys my healthful version even better. They

could become one of your favorites, too.

4 medium green tomatoes, cored
¼ cup evaporated skim milk (¼ percent milkfat)
1 teaspoon dried tarragon leaves, crushed
6 dashes ground red (cayenne) pepper
¼ cup Bread Crumbs (page 85)
2¼ teaspoons each corn oil and Italian olive oil, combined
3 large shallots, minced
1 large clove garlic, minced

1. Place tomatoes on side, cut in half.

2. Combine milk with tarragon and ground red pepper. Dip tomatoes into milk, then into crumbs, coating well.

3. Heat combined oils in nonstick skillet until hot. Add shallots and garlic. Sauté for 30 seconds. Add tomatoes and sauté on both sides until golden brown, turning 3 or 4 times. Serve immediately.

Yield: Serves 4

CAL	F	P:S	SOD	CAR	CHO	PRO
109	7	3.2:1	13	13	1	2.5

Stuffed Acorn Squash

This variety of winter squash was eaten green by the American Indians (the word "squash" comes from the Massachusetts Indian word as-quash which means, as you've already guessed, "eaten green"). But just the thought of eating a raw green squash turns me green. Here I fill it with an herbaceous bread-and-apple stuffing, and bake it to tenderness. A bit on the sweet side, it's a splendid foil for pungent dishes. (As is another winter squash, butternut squash, which is prepared to perfection in the recipe that follows.)

2 acorn squash (1¼ pounds each)
1 tablespoon corn oil
2 tablespoons minced onion
1 large shallot, minced
½ teaspoon apple cider vinegar
1 tablespoon peeled and coarsely grated carrot
2 slices lightly toasted rye bread (page 79) or whole-wheat bread (page 68), broken into small pieces
1 tart green apple, peeled, cored, and coarsely chopped
2 tablespoons minced fresh basil
½ teaspoon each ground ginger and crushed aniseed
6 dashes ground red (cayenne) pepper

1. Wash and dry squash. Cut in half. Remove seeds and pulp. Turn stem and blossom ends so that halves stand upright. Stand in shallow baking dish.

2. Heat oil in nonstick skillet until hot. Sauté onion and shallot for 2 minutes.

3. Add vinegar. Cook for 1 minute.

4. Add balance of ingredients, stirring to blend. Spoon into squash cavities.

5. Add ½ inch boiling water to baking dish. Cover with aluminum foil. Bake in preheated 400°F oven for 45 to 50 minutes.

Yield: Serves 4

Note: If you can't get fresh basil, don't substitute dried basil (there's a quantum difference in taste). Instead, replace basil with equal amounts of fresh tarragon, parsley, or dill.

CAL	F	P:S	SOD	CAR	CHO	PRO
226.5	4	4.2:1	7.5	36.5	–	5.5

Mashed Butternut Squash

2 pounds butternut squash
1 tablespoon sweet (unsalted) 100 percent corn oil margarine
2 large shallots
2 teaspoons fresh lime juice
½ teaspoon aniseed, crushed
8 dashes ground red (cayenne) pepper
2 teaspoons minced fresh parsley
1 teaspoon honey (optional)

1. Peel squash with swivel-bladed peeler. Cut in half lengthwise. Scoop out seeds and pulp. Cut into 1-inch cubes. Place in heavy-bottomed saucepan. Add enough water barely to cover. Bring to boil. Cover partially and slow-boil until tender but not oversoft (about 15 minutes). Drain. Return to saucepan. Cook briefly over medium-high heat, shaking pan, until excess liquid evaporates. Remove to bowl. Mash. Wipe out saucepan.

2. Heat margarine in saucepan until melted. Do not brown. Add squash, lime juice, aniseed, ground red pepper, and parsley. Stir to blend.

3. Taste. Add honey, if desired, stirring well. Serve very hot.

Yield: Serves 4

CAL	F	P:S	SOD	CAR	CHO	PRO
73	3	2.5:1	7	4.5	–	1
With honey:						
78	3	2.5:1	7	5.5	–	1

Sunday Beans

CAL	F	P:S	SOD	CAR	CHO	PRO
310	6	3.2:1	69	40	27	16

With Baby White beans: No appreciable difference
With turkey:

317	0.5	2.6:1	89	40	28	16.5

Beans have been the basis of mouth-watering cassoulets, stews, rice dishes, and soups in many of the great cuisines of the world. What lover of American food, for example, doesn't feel the salivary juices flow at just the mention of Boston baked beans, or Southern black bean soup, or Western-style chili? My haute cuisine of health can also boast of great bean dishes, and here's one of them. (You'll find another, Three-Way Black Bean Soup, on page 87.) It will make any day of the week taste like Sunday.

1 cup Great Northern or Baby
  White beans, soaked overnight in
  water to cover
¾ cup Rich Chicken Stock (page 94)
1 recipe Tomato-Mushroom Sauce
  (page 96), heated
1 cup diced cooked chicken or
  turkey
  Minced fresh parsley

1. Drain beans. Place in heavy-bottomed saucepan. Add stock and enough water to cover. Bring to simmering point. Cover partially and simmer until tender (45 to 50 minutes). Remove from heat. Let stand, covered. in cooking liquid.
2. Add chicken or turkey to hot sauce. Simmer briefly until heated through. If sauce becomes too thick, thin down with small amount of bean liquid.
3. Drain beans. Pour into serving bowl. Pour sauce over beans. Sprinkle with parsley and serve.

Yield: Serves 4

Serving suggestion: For a complete, satisfying meal, serve with Tomatoes Grand Hotel (page 132) or mixed green salad.

It-Goes-with-Everything Sautéed Rice

As readers of my other books know, I prefer each grain of rice to stand on its own, and not stick to its partners to form a gummy mess (see note). It's only these sturdy but tender rice individuals that sauté to perfection. The title delivers what it promises. There's no main dish that can't be enhanced when accompanied by this gently spiced side dish.

2¼ teaspoons each corn oil and
  Italian olive oil, combined
2 large cloves garlic, minced
1 large shallot, minced
½ small sweet red pepper, seeded
  and minced
4 large fresh mushrooms, washed,
  dried, trimmed, and sliced
1½ cups slightly undercooked rice,
  cooled (see note)
¼ teaspoon ground ginger
6 dashes ground red (cayenne)
  pepper
½ teaspoon dried tarragon leaves,
  crushed
2 teaspoons tarragon vinegar (page
  99)
¼ cup Light Chicken Broth (page 95)
  or Rich Chicken Stock (page 94)
1 tablespoon minced fresh parsley

1. Heat combined oils in nonstick skillet until hot. Add garlic, shallot, sweet red pepper, and mushrooms.

Sauté over medium-high heat until very lightly browned.

2. Add rice. Stir to blend.

3. Sprinkle with spices and tarragon. Stir. Add vinegar and cook for 30 seconds.

4. Add broth. Stir and cool until mixture is heated through.

5. Turn into warmed serving dish. Sprinkle with parsley and serve.

Yield: Serves 4

Variation: Substitute 2 tablespoons Elegant Duxelles (page 56) for fresh mushrooms when adding rice in step 2.

Note: Be sure to follow directions on box of rice so that it is cooked to individual-kerneled perfection.

CAL	F	P:S	SOD	CAR	CHO	PRO
141.5	5	2.9:1	12	21	–	2.5
Variation:						
144	5	2.9:1	11.5	21	–	2.5

Sublime Couscous

There are many marvelous replacements (on occasion) for potatoes, and to my taste this rolled and steamed hard-wheat product is the most heavenly of all. Taste this feather-light dish just once, and you'll understand why it's the national dish of Morocco and Algeria and adored by the multitudes in Saudi Arabia and Egypt as well. My two healthful versions (Couscous with Mushrooms follows) use my own salt-free chicken broth instead of the traditional salt-laden bouillon, as well as a most non-Mideastern bevy of ingredients including, of all things, apple juice. In restaurants, couscous is usually served under heaps of mushy stewed meats and vegetables. Here's your chance to taste it au naturel—naturalized for American tastes.

¾ cup uncooked couscous (see note)
About 1½ cups warm Light
Chicken Broth (page 95)

1. Place couscous in bowl. Sprinkle with ⅓ cup broth. Moisten evenly by stirring with fork. Let stand for 2 to 3 minutes.

2. For this step, use a couscoussiere, or devise your own steamer as follows: Half-fill the bottom of a double-boiler with water. Fit a strainer into pot so that rim of strainer is held in place by rim of pot. Line strainer with moistened cheesecloth or small, loose-stranded cotton dish towel.

3. Spoon dampened couscous into cheesecloth. Cover tightly. Bring water to boil. Steam for 15 minutes.

4. Remove cover. Sprinkle with ⅓ cup broth. Stir with fork to separate grains. Re-cover and steam for 15 minutes. Repeat the sprinkling, steaming, and stirring process 3 additional times. Total cooking time is 1 hour. Couscous should be very light and fluffy.

5. Serve as a side dish with meat, fish, or poultry. If main dish is served with sauce, pour portion of sauce over couscous.

Yield: Serves 4

Note: Uncooked couscous is available in ethnic markets, specialty shops, and some supermarkets. For name of a reliable mail-order house, see page 177.

CAL	F	P:S	SOD	CAR	CHO	PRO
57.5	–	–	9	10	–	4.5

Couscous with Mushrooms

⅔ cup uncooked couscous (see note page 65)
⅓ cup apple juice (no sugar added)
1 cup Light Chicken Broth (page 95)
4½ teaspoons corn oil
1 large shallot, minced
¼ pound fresh mushrooms, washed, dried, trimmed, and sliced
½ teaspoon ground ginger
6 dashes ground red (cayenne) pepper
1 tablespoon minced fresh basil (see note)

1. Pour couscous in bowl. Sprinkle with apple juice. Moisten evenly by stirring with fork, then let stand for 3 minutes.

2. Follow balance of cooking directions for Sublime Couscous (page 65).

3. Five minutes before couscous has finished steaming, heat oil in nonstick skillet until hot. Sauté shallot and mushrooms over medium-high heat until lightly browned, stirring constantly.

4. Spoon cooked couscous into warmed serving bowl. Add sautéed mixture. Sprinkle with ginger, ground red pepper, and basil. Toss gently. Serve immediately.

Yield: Serves 4

Note: Fresh herbs taste better than dried herbs in this dish. If fresh basil is not available, substitute 1 tablespoon minced fresh tarragon or dill.

CAL	F	P:S	SOD	CAR	CHO	PRO
99	3.5	4.5:1	13	3	–	4

Vermicelli with Creamy Sauce

Yes, you can eat pasta while you're shedding weight or keeping it rock-steady. Ounce for ounce, there's not much difference between the calorie content of approved pasta and that of my low-calorie breads. By "approved," I mean containing no eggs or salt; and there's a rich variety of such pastas available in your supermarkets, including the vermicelli in this recipe and the spaghetti in the recipe that follows. What adds calories to most pasta dishes is the sauce, but my creamy sauce for vermicelli and my exquisite mushroom sauce for spaghetti are as poor in calories as they are rich in taste. Enjoy!

2¼ teaspoons each corn oil and Italian olive oil, combined
3 large cloves garlic, minced
1 large shallot, minced
1 leek, white part only, well washed and minced
½-inch slice fresh ginger, peeled and shredded
1 small sweet red pepper, seeded and cut into ¼-inch slivers
½ teaspoon each dried thyme and tarragon leaves, crushed
¼ teaspoon aniseed, crushed
⅓ cup dry vermouth
½ cup Rich Chicken Stock (page 94)
8 dashes ground red (cayenne) pepper
¼ cup apple juice (no sugar added)
1 tablespoon tomato paste (no salt added)
8 ounces enriched vermicelli (no salt added)
⅓ cup evaporated skim milk (¼ percent milkfat)
1 tablespoon minced fresh parsley

1. Heat combined oils in nonstick skillet until hot. Add garlic, shallot,

leek, ginger, and sweet red pepper. Sauté for 5 minutes over medium-high heat, stirring often. Do not allow to brown.

2. Sprinkle with dried herbs and aniseed. Add vermouth and cook for 1 minute.

3. Combine stock, ground red pepper, apple juice, and tomato paste. Add to skillet, stirring to blend. Bring to simmering point. Reduce heat. Cover and simmer for 30 minutes.

4. Fifteen minutes before sauce is finished, bring pot of water to rolling boil. Add vermicelli and cook for 8 to 10 minutes. Do not overcook. Drain. Transfer to serving plate.

5. Gradually add milk to simmering sauce. *Do not boil.*

6. Pour sauce over vermicelli, sprinkle with parsley, and serve.

Yield: Serves 4

CAL	F	P:S	SOD	CAR	CHO	PRO
321.5	6	2.9:1	19.5	56	1.5	10

Velvet Spaghetti with Mushroom Sauce

2¼ teaspoons each corn oil and Italian olive oil, combined
2 tablespoons minced sweet green pepper
3 large cloves garlic, minced
2 large shallots, minced
½ pound fresh mushrooms, washed, dried, trimmed, and sliced
½ teaspoon each dried thyme and sweet basil leaves, crushed
6 dashes ground red (cayenne) pepper
2 tablespoons red wine

⅓ cup Rich Chicken Stock (page 94)
1 teaspoon tomato paste (no sugar added)
1 tablespoon fresh lemon juice
8 ounces enriched spaghetti (no salt added)
½ cup evaporated skim milk (¼ percent milkfat)
1 tablespoon minced fresh parsley
2 teaspoons no-fat grated Sap Sago cheese

1. Heat combined oils in nonstick skillet until hot. Sauté green pepper, garlic, shallots, and mushrooms for 5 minutes, stirring often.

2. Sprinkle with dried herbs and ground red pepper. Stir to blend. Add wine and cook for 1 minute.

3. Combine stock with tomato paste and lemon juice. Stir into mixture. Simmer for 30 minutes, stirring twice.

4. Fifteen minutes before sauce is finished, bring pot of water to a rolling boil. Add spaghetti. Boil for 8 to 10 minutes, stirring often. Do not overcook.

5. Gradually add milk to simmering sauce. *Do not boil.*

6. Pour sauce over spaghetti. Sprinkle with parsley and Sap Sago cheese and serve.

Yield: Serves 4

CAL	F	P:S	SOD	CAR	CHO	PRO
312.5	6	4.2:1	28.5	52	4.5	12

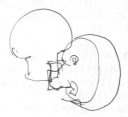

Breads

Light Whole-Wheat Bread

Lightness is not the only unusual quality of this exciting whole-wheat bread. You've never tasted a whole-wheat bread like it, because whole wheat is combined with unbleached flour and a soupçon of rye flour to create a new kind of whole-wheat taste altogether. And buttermilk (remember, despite its name, it's low, low, low in fat) adds its distinctive twang.

2　tablespoons dry yeast or 2　premeasured packages
3　cups whole-wheat flour
2　cups unbleached flour
½　cup rye flour
½　teaspoon ground cinnamon
1　tablespoon aniseed, crushed
1　cup apple juice (no sugar added)
½　cup water
2　tablespoons honey
2　tablespoons corn oil plus ½　teaspoon for bowl
1　teaspoon freshly grated orange rind, preferably from navel orange
¾　cup buttermilk (no salt added), at room temperature
½　teaspoon sweet (unsalted) 100 percent corn oil margarine, for pans

1. In large mixing bowl, combine yeast, 1 cup whole-wheat flour, 1 cup unbleached flour, all of rye flour, cinnamon, and aniseed.

2. Heat apple juice, water, honey, 2 tablespoons oil, and orange rind until warm (105° to 115°F). Pour over dry ingredients and beat with wooden spoon for 2 minutes; or use electric mixer at medium speed for 1 minute.

3. Add buttermilk and continue beating until well blended.

4. Add all of remaining whole-wheat flour and all but ½ cup of remaining unbleached flour, ½ cup at a time, beating after each addition. When dough becomes too difficult to handle with wooden spoon, scoop up and turn onto lightly floured board. Knead until smooth and elastic, using balance of flour, if necessary, to make a smooth and elastic dough.

5. Shape dough into ball. Drop into lightly oiled fairly straight-sided bowl, turning to coat. Cover tightly with plastic wrap and let rise at room temperature (70° to 80°F) until doubled in bulk (1 hour to 1 hour 15 minutes).

6. Punch dough down, pressing out bubbles. Shape into large loaf. Transfer to board and cut into 3 equal pieces. Shape into loaves. Place in small (7⅜- x 3⅝- x 2¼-inch) loaf pans, lightly greased with margarine. Cover with waxed paper and let rise for 1 hour.

7. Place all three pans on cookie sheet. (They're easier to handle this way.) Bake in preheated 375°F oven for 40 minutes.

8. Transfer loaves from loaf pans to cookie sheet. Return to oven and bake for 5 minutes more. Finished loaves should be crispy to the touch and produce a hollow sound when tapped on the bottom with knuckles.

9. Remove from oven and cool completely on rack before slicing.

Yield: 3 loaves, 20 slices (⅜-inch each) per loaf

CAL	F	P:S	SOD	CAR	CHO	PRO
Per slice:						
44.5	0.5	4.1:1	2	9	–	3.5

Beige Bread

What does "beige" taste like? The essence of fruit. And no wonder, because apple juice, orange rind, and grape juice are ingredients in this novel creation. Actually, the name derives from the color, imparted by the grape juice and a small amount of whole-wheat flour. And a plus—the loaves are health-fortified with wheat germ.

2 tablespoons dry yeast or 2
   premeasured packages
¼ cup nonfat dry milk
6 to 6½ cups unbleached flour
1 cup whole-wheat flour
1 tablespoon aniseed, crushed
½ cup unsweetened grape juice
¼ cup apple juice (no sugar added)
1¾ cups water
1 tablespoon corn oil plus ½
   teaspoon for bowl
1 tablespoon honey
1 teaspoon freshly grated orange
   rind, preferably from navel orange
¼ cup toasted wheat germ (no sugar
   added)
½ teaspoon sweet (unsalted) 100
   percent corn oil margarine for
   pans and waxed paper
1 egg white mixed with 1 tablespoon
   water

1. In large bowl of electric mixer, combine yeast, milk, 1 cup unbleached flour, all of whole-wheat flour, and aniseed.

2. In saucepan, combine grape juice, apple juice, water, 1 tablespoon oil, honey, and orange rind. Heat until warm (105° to 115°F). Pour over dry ingredients. Beat on medium speed of electric mixer for 3 minutes.

3. Add wheat germ and 5 cups of unbleached flour to bowl, ½ cup at a time, beating with wooden spoon after each addition. When dough becomes too difficult to beat with wooden

spoon, scoop up and turn onto lightly floured board. Knead, adding enough of balance of flour to make a smooth and elastic dough.

4. Shape dough into ball. Drop into lightly oiled fairly straight-sided bowl, turning to coat. Cover tightly with plastic wrap, and let rise at room temperature (70° to 80°F) until more than doubled in bulk.

5. Punch dough down, pressing out bubbles. Transfer to board and cut into 3 equal pieces. Shape into loaves. Place in small (7⅝- x 3⅝- x 2¼-inch) loaf pans lightly greased with margarine. Cover loosely with margarine-greased waxed paper. Let rise until well above sides of pans.

6. Brush loaves with egg white mixture and bake in center section of preheated 375°F degree oven for 40 minutes.

7. Remove bread from pans. Place back in oven, directly on rack, for 5 minutes. Loaves should be golden brown and produce a hollow sound when tapped on the bottom with knuckles.

8. Remove from oven. Let cool completely on rack before slicing.

Yield: 3 loaves, 20 slices (⅜-inch each) per loaf

Note: For easier handling, all three pans may be placed on cookie sheet and baked.

CAL	F	P:S	SOD	CAR	CHO	PRO
Per slice:						
59	0.5	4:1	4	13.5	–	2.5

Sourdough Whole-Wheat Bread

In the rough-and-ready days of the gold rushes in California and Alaska, grizzled prospectors huddled around their campfires to make flapjacks, biscuits, and breads with a yeastless leavener (no yeast on the wild, wild frontiers). That leavener was sourdough (hence the name "sourdoughs" for the prospectors of those golden days). Sourdough, an aromatic brew of flour, water, and benign bacteria, is step one in the making of a sourdough bread. Today there are many different kinds of sourdough starters, but mine may be the most unusual of all. This is probably the only bread that retains the very special tart flavor and aroma—the true sourness—so prized by the "sourdoughs" of old.

For the Half-and-Half Starter:
 1 tablespoon dry yeast or 1
    premeasured package
 1 cup whole-wheat flour
 1 cup unbleached flour
 1 tablespoon nonfat dry milk
2¼ cups warm water (105° to 115°F)

1. Prepare starter 3 days ahead. Start by combining first 4 ingredients in bowl. Add water. Stir to blend.
2. Cover tightly with plastic wrap and let stand at room temperature (70° to 80°F) for 3 days. Mixture will become bubbly, rise and fall, and develop a slightly sour aroma.
3. After using starter, replenish with an amount of water-flour mixture equal to the volume used. Example: When you use 1 cup of starter, pour balance of starter into bowl, add 1 cup each flour and warm water, stir to blend, and cover with plastic wrap. Let stand at room temperature until bubbly. Stir down. Pour into jar and refrigerate.
Note: To keep starter alive, use at least once a week, replenishing in accordance with step 3. If not used within that period, pour off half of starter and replenish.

For the bread:
 1 cup Half-and-Half Starter
1½ cups warm water (105° to 115°F)
 2 cups plus 2 tablespoons
    unbleached flour
 1 tablespoon dry yeast or 1
    premeasured package
 ½ cup apple juice (no sugar added)
 1 teaspoon honey
 1 tablespoon aniseed, crushed
 4 cups whole-wheat flour
 ½ teaspoon corn oil, for bowl
 ½ teaspoon sweet (unsalted) 100
    percent corn oil margarine, for
    pans and waxed paper

1. The night before baking, combine in mixing bowl starter, 1 cup water, and 1 cup unbleached flour, stirring to blend. Cover tightly with plastic wrap.
2. Next day, combine in small bowl 2 tablespoons flour and yeast. In saucepan, combine apple juice, balance of water, and honey. Heat until warm (110° to 115°F). Pour half of liquid over yeast and flour. Stir to blend. Let stand for 7 minutes.
3. Stir down mixture prepared the night before. Sprinkle with aniseed. Add balance of warmed liquid. Beat with wooden spoon.
4. Add foamy yeast mixture and stir.
5. Add 2 cups whole-wheat flour and balance of unbleached flour, blending well with wooden spoon. Cover and let stand for 3 minutes.
6. Add 1½ cups whole-wheat flour and beat with wooden spoon. When dough becomes too difficult to handle with spoon, turn onto lightly whole-wheat-floured board and knead, adding enough of balance of flour until dough is smooth and elastic (see note 1). (The combination of starter and whole-wheat flour produces a slightly sticky, but very pliable, dough. But most of the

stickiness disappears when the dough is well kneaded.)

7. Shape dough into ball. Drop into fairly straight-sided lightly oiled bowl. Cover tightly with plastic wrap and let rise at room temperature (70° to 80°F) until doubled in bulk (about 1½ hours).

8. Punch dough down. Transfer to board and knead briefly. Cut into 3 equal pieces. Shape into loaves. Place in 3 small (7⅜- x 3⅝- x 2¼-inch) loaf pans, lightly greased with margarine. Cover with waxed paper that has been greased lightly with margarine. Let rise until doubled in bulk (well over sides of pans).

9. Bake in preheated 375°F oven for 45 minutes.

10. Remove bread from pans. Loaves should be golden brown and crispy to the touch. Test doneness by tapping bottom of loaf with knuckles. The loaf is done when you hear a hollow sound. If not done, place back in oven directly on rack for 5 minutes.

11. Remove from oven and let cool completely on rack before slicing.

Yield: 3 loaves, 20 slices (⅜-inch each) per loaf

Notes:

1. When using a dough hook, start after dough becomes too difficult to handle with wooden spoon. Knead for 7 minutes after dough has cleaned sides of bowl and has clung to dough hook. Stop machine. Knead for 2 minutes by hand. Continue with recipe.

2. Because this bread contains no oil and very little honey, it tastes best on the first and second days. To preserve that just-baked taste, anticipate the amount of bread you'll be using the first two days and freeze the balance on baking day.

CAL	F	P:S	SOD	CAR	CHO	PRO
Starter (per cup):						
243	1.4	4:1	10.5	50.5	–	10.5
Bread (per slice):						
46	0.5	4.4:1	1	10	–	1.5

Chewy Oatmeal Bread

Here's my modern version of an old-fashioned loaf, complete with an irresistible aroma. The modern touch? Just the right amount of spices and natural sweeteners to drive old-fashioned salt and sugar out of fashion. One slice, crisply toasted, is a waker-upper at breakfast time and a steady source of energy throughout the morning.

 2 tablespoons dry yeast or 2 premeasured packages
⅓ cup nonfat dry milk
 1 cup whole-wheat flour
3¾ cups unbleached flour
¼ cup toasted wheat germ (no sugar added)
½ teaspoon each ground cinnamon and ginger
 1 tablespoon aniseed, crushed
 1 cup old-fashioned rolled oats
 1 teaspoon freshly grated orange rind, preferably from navel orange
1½ cups water
¾ cup apple juice (no sugar added)
 1 tablespoon sweet unsalted 100 percent corn oil margarine plus ½ teaspoon for pans and waxed paper
 1 tablespoon corn oil plus ¼ teaspoon for bowl
 1 tablespoon dark honey, such as buckwheat
 1 teaspoon nonfat liquid milk

1. In large mixing bowl, combine yeast, dry milk, all of whole-wheat flour, 1 cup unbleached flour, wheat germ, spices, and aniseed.

2. In another bowl, combine rolled oats and orange rind.

3. In saucepan, combine water, apple juice, 1 tablespoon each margarine and oil, and honey. Heat until warm (105° to 115°F). Pour half of warmed mixture over oats–orange rind mixture,

stirring to moisten. Add other half to dry yeast mixture and beat with wooden spoon for 1 minute. Cover yeast mixture and let stand for 5 minutes.

4. Add moistened oats-orange rind mixture to yeast mixture and beat with wooden spoon until blended.

5. Add all but ½ cup of balance of unbleached flour, ½ cup at a time, beating with wooden spoon after each addition. When dough becomes too difficult to handle with wooden spoon, turn onto lightly floured board and knead, adding enough of balance of flour to make a smooth and elastic dough. (If you have a dough hook, start putting it to work for you the moment your wooden spoon stops working for you; see note 1, page 71.)

6. Shape dough into ball. Drop into lightly oiled, fairly straight-sided bowl, turning to coat. Cover tightly with plastic wrap and let rise at room temperature (70° to 80°F) until more than doubled in bulk (about 1½ hours).

7. Punch dough down. Transfer to board and knead briefly. Cut into 3 equal pieces. Shape into loaves. Grease 3 small (7⅜- x 3⅝- x 2¼-inch) loaf pans with margarine. Lightly grease with margarine a sheet of waxed paper large enough to cover pans; cover loosely. Let rise until doubled in bulk.

8. Bake in preheated 375°F oven for 40 minutes, brushing midway with milk, taking care that it does not drip down the sides of pan.

9. Remove bread from pans. Test for doneness by tapping bottoms of loaves with knuckles. You should hear a hollow sound when done. If not done, place loaves in oven directly on rack and bake for 5 minutes more. Loaves should be crisp and lightly browned on all sides.

10. Remove from oven, place on rack, and brush again with milk. Let cool thoroughly before slicing.

Yield: 3 loaves, 20 slices (⅜-inch each) per loaf.

CAL	F	P:S	SOD	CAR	CHO	PRO
Per slice:						
49	1	4.3:1	4	9	–	2

Easy No-Knead Buckwheat Bread

When you're pressed for time and you still can't do without a homemade loaf, here's the bread for you. Kneading time is eliminated, but there's no loss of flavor. Buckwheat, because it's an herb, not a grain, imparts an intriguingly delightful herbaceousness. Save time, and savor a bread that's devoid of clichés.

¾ cup water
¼ cup apple juice (no sugar added)
¼ cup evaporated skim milk (¼ percent milkfat)
1 teaspoon honey
½ teaspoon freshly grated orange rind, preferably from navel orange
½ teaspoon cardamom seeds, crushed
1 tablespoon dry yeast or 1 premeasured package
2¼ cups unbleached flour
¼ cup buckwheat flour
¼ teaspoon corn oil, for bowl
¼ teaspoon sweet unsalted 100 percent corn oil margarine, for casserole
3 teaspoons white cornmeal

1. In saucepan, combine water, apple juice, milk, honey, orange rind, and cardamom seeds. Heat until warm (105° to 115°F).

2. Place yeast in bowl of electric mixer. Pour warmed liquid over yeast and stir until dissolved. Let stand for 2 minutes.

3. Add 1 cup unbleached flour and all of buckwheat flour. Beat at medium speed for 1 minute. Stop machine. Scrape sides of bowl. Beat at high speed for 2 minutes. Scrape sides of bowl again.

4. Add balance of flour, a little at a time, stirring with wooden spoon, then working with hands only until all flour is absorbed and dough can be shaped easily into a soft ball.

5. Lightly oil fairly straight-sided bowl. Drop dough into bowl, turning to coat. Cover tightly with plastic wrap. Let rise at room temperature (70° to 80°F) until doubled in bulk (about 1½ hours).

6. Grease 1½-quart casserole with margarine. Sprinkle 2 teaspoons of cornmeal on bottom and around sides of casserole, shaking out excess. Punch dough down, squeezing out all bubbles. Shape into ball. Place in casserole. Cover with plastic wrap. Let rise until doubled in bulk (about 40 minutes). Sprinkle with balance of cornmeal.

7. Bake in preheated 400°F oven for 25 minutes.

8. With blunt knife, loosen bread around sides of casserole. Remove from casserole. Cool completely on rack before slicing.

Yield: 1 loaf, 14 slices (½-inch each), each slice cut in half

Notes:

1. This coarse-textured bread tastes best sliced ½-inch thick.

2. Because no oil is added to this loaf, it tastes best on the day it is made. Preserve the fresh-baked taste by cutting unused balance of bread into ½-inch slices, reassembling into long shape, wrapping in aluminum foil, and freezing. Then whenever you want fresh-tasting bread, flip off a slice and pop it into your toaster.

CAL	F	P:S	SOD	CAR	CHO	PRO
Per half-slice:						
51.5	0.5	3.5:1	3	10.5	–	2

Light-as-Air Challah

Challah, a traditional holiday bread in the Jewish home, is a favorite among all bread lovers. But egg- and butter-rich, and sugar laden, this delicacy is on the forbidden list of calorie-watchers everywhere. Not my version. Made only with healthful ingredients, my challah matches the cakelike crumb, the sweetness, and the eggy consistency of the original. Warning: The ecstatically tantalizing aroma wil have your neighbors flocking to your door. Better prepare an extra loaf. Or more.

5 to 5½ cups unbleached flour
1½ tablespoons dry yeast or 1½ premeasured packages
½ teaspoon ground cinnamon
1 teaspoon low-sodium baking powder
1 cup water
½ cup unsweetened pineapple juice
2 teaspoons finely grated fresh orange rind, preferably from navel orange
3 tablespoons plus ½ teaspoon honey
1 large whole egg
¼ cup corn oil plus ½ teaspoon for bowl and waxed paper
½ teaspoon sweet (unsalted) 100 percent corn oil margarine, for cookie sheets
1 egg white mixed with 1 teaspoon water
2 teaspoons each poppy seeds and sesame seeds

1. In large bowl, combine 2 cups flour and yeast.

2. In another bowl, combine 3 cups flour, cinnamon, and baking powder. Stir to blend. Set aside.

3. In saucepan, combine water, pineapple juice, orange rind, and 3 tablespoons honey. Heat until warm

(105° to 115°F). Pour over yeast-flour mixture and beat with wooden spoon for 1 minute. Cover and let stand for 30 minutes.

4. Stir down. Beat egg and ¼ cup oil in cup with fork until blended; then add to batter. Mix with wooden spoon until smooth.

5. Add flour mixture from step 2 to batter, ½ cup at a time, beating well with wooden spoon after each addition. Dough will be sticky until all flour has been added and absorbed. When dough becomes too difficult to handle with wooden spoon, turn onto lightly floured board and knead, using balance of flour if necessary, until dough is smooth and elastic and no longer sticky. (You'll find this dough soft, pliable, and most responsive to your hands.)

6. Shape dough into ball. Place in large, fairly straight-sided bowl, greased with ¼ teaspoon oil. Turn dough to coat, then cover tightly with plastic wrap and let rise at room temperature (70° to 80°F) until more than double in bulk (about 1½ hours).

7. Punch dough down. Transfer to board and knead briefly, squeezing out bubbles (they'll crackle). Shape into ball and return to bowl. Cover and let rise again for 1½ hours.

8. Repeat the punching-down and kneading process. Remove to board and cut into 6 equal pieces. Cover with waxed paper and let rest on board for 5 minutes.

9. Shape each piece into slender 14-inch-long ropes. For each loaf, lay 3 ropes alongside each other. Starting at the middle, braid ropes down to ends, taking care not to leave spaces between ropes. Pinch ends together.

10. Lightly grease two 11½- x 15½-inch jelly-roll pans with margarine. With spatula, carefully transfer braided dough to cookie sheets. Cover with lightly oiled waxed paper and let rise at room temperature.

11. Combine ½ teaspoon honey with egg white mixture, beating with fork to blend. Brush over loaves, taking care that liquid does not drip onto cookie sheets. Sprinkle one loaf with poppy seeds and the other with sesame seeds. Bake in preheated 350°F oven for 45 minutes, reversing rack position of pans midway so that both loaves are baked evenly.

12. Remove loaves from oven. Remove from pans and let cool thoroughly on rack before slicing.

Yield: 2 braided loaves, 24 slices (½-inch each) per loaf

CAL	F	P:S	SOD	CAR	CHO	PRO
Per slice:						
65	1.5	3.4:1	3	11.5	5	2

Potato Braids

The texture of this bread is different from any other. It's substantial as a potato, yet as light as a soufflé. It rises like a dream and toasts to perfection. Simply stated, it's in a class by itself.

1 medium potato, peeled and cubed
2½ cups water
    About ½ cup apple juice (no sugar added)
1 teaspoon honey
1 tablespoon corn oil plus ¼ teaspoon for bowl
2 tablespoons (sweet) unsalted 100 percent corn oil margarine plus ¾ teaspoon for pans and waxed paper
1½ teaspoons aniseed, crushed
6 dashes ground red (cayenne) pepper
¼ teaspoon ground cinnamon
1 tablespoon dry yeast or 1 premeasured package
7 to 7¼ cups unbleached flour
¼ cup rye flour

1 *tablespoon white cornmeal*
1 *egg white beaten with 1*
tablespoon water
1½ *teaspoons each poppy seeds and*
sesame seeds

1. Place potato and water in saucepan. Boil until tender. Drain, reserving liquid (about 1½ cups).

2. Mash potatoes. Add 1¼ cups reserved potato liquid and blend. Let cool.

3. Add enough apple juice to balance of reserved potato liquid to make ¾ cup. Pour into saucepan. Add honey, 1 tablespoon oil, 2 tablespoons margarine, aniseed, and spices. Stir and heat until warm (105° to 115°F).

4. Place yeast in large mixing bowl. Pour warm mixture over yeast and stir to dissolve. Stir in mashed potato mixture.

5. Add ¾ cup unbleached flour and all of rye flour. Beat with wooden spoon until smooth. Cover with plastic wrap. Let stand for 45 minutes.

6. Stir down. Add all but ¼ cup of unbleached flour, ½ cup at a time, beating with wooden spoon after each addition. When dough becomes too difficult to be handled with wooden spoon, turn out on board, which has been sprinkled with balance of flour, and knead until smooth and elastic.

7. Shape dough into ball. Drop into fairly straight-sided lightly oiled bowl, turning to coat. Cover tightly with plastic wrap and let rise at room temperature (70° to 80°F) until more than doubled in bulk (about 1½ hours).

8. Punch down dough, kneading out bubbles. Shape into loaf about 12 inches long. Cut in half lengthwise. Then cut each half into 3 pieces. Cover with waxed paper and let rest for 3 minutes.

9. Roll each piece into a 14-inch-long rope. For each loaf, lay 3 ropes side by side on board. Braid ropes from middle to ends, pinching ends together.

10. Lightly grease two 11½- x 15½-inch jelly-roll pans with ½ teaspoon margarine. Sprinkle with cornmeal, tilting pans from side to side to coat surface evenly. Shake out excess cornmeal. Carefully lift loaves off board and place in center of pans. Rub 2 sheets of waxed paper lightly with balance of margarine. Place, greased side down, over loaves. Let rise for 1 hour at room temperature (70° to 80°F). Brush lightly with egg mixture, taking care that liquid doesn't drip into pans. Sprinkle 1 loaf with poppy seeds and the other with sesame seeds.

11. Bake in preheated 375°F oven for 40 minutes, reversing rack position of pans in oven midway, so that breads are baked evenly. Remove from oven and cool completely on rack before slicing.

Yield: 2 braided loaves, 30 slices (½-inch each) per loaf

Note: For more center and less crust, bake into 2 round loaves; increasing baking time to 45 minutes. Loaves will be light and high.

CAL	F	P:S	SOD	CAR	CHO	PRO
Per slice:						
60	1	3.2:1	2	10	–	2

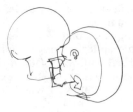

Italian Bread—My Style

This is a bold variation on the classic Italian loaf. Adventurously, I've added coriander, pineapple juice, and orange rind to impart an ever-so-slight sweetness. The result is a bread as distinctive as it is delicious. The long crunchy and light loaves are ideal for stuffings and bread crumbs. *Pane dolce* for the *la dolce!*

1 tablespoon dry yeast or 1
    premeasured package
6 to 6¼ cups unbleached flour
½ cup whole-wheat flour
1 tablespoon toasted coriander
    seeds, crushed (see note 1)
1 teaspoon ground cardamom
2 cups water
½ cup unsweetened pineapple juice
2 teaspoons freshly grated orange
    rind, preferably from navel orange
1 tablespoon honey (optional)
¼ teaspoon corn oil for bowl
¾ teaspoon sweet (unsalted) 100
    percent corn oil margarine, for
    loaf pans and waxed paper
2 teaspoons white cornmeal
1 large egg white beaten with 1
    tablespoon water
1 tablespoon sesame seeds

1. In large mixing bowl, combine yeast, 2 cups unbleached flour, all of whole-wheat flour, coriander seeds, and cardamom.

2. In saucepan, combine water, pineapple juice, orange rind, and honey. Heat until warm (105° to 115°F).

3. Pour warm mixture over dry ingredients. Beat with wooden spoon until yeast is dissolved and flour absorbed. Cover with plastic wrap and let stand for 10 minutes.

4. Add all but ¼ cup unbleached flour, ½ cup at a time, beating after each addition with wooden spoon. When dough becomes too difficult to be handled with wooden spoon, turn onto very lightly floured board, and knead, using balance of flour if necessary, to make a smooth and elastic dough. You'll find the dough soft, pliable, and a delight to the touch. (Or use a dough hook; from this point on, it works marvelously well; see note 1, page 71).

5. Shape dough into ball. Place in fairly straight-sided lightly oiled bowl, turning to coat. Cover tightly with plastic wrap and let rise at room temperature (70° to 80°F) until more than doubled in bulk (about 2 hours).

6. Punch dough down, squeezing out bubbles (they'll crackle). Transfer to board and knead briefly. Cut into 4 equal parts. Cover and let rest for 5 minutes.

7. Roll each piece of dough into a slender loaf 14 inches long. Grease four 14-inch French loaf pans with ½ teaspoon margarine. Sprinkle pans with cornmeal and tilt from side to side to distribute evenly. Place each loaf in pan.

8. With sharp razor or serrated knife, slash each loaf diagonally 4 times. Grease a large sheet of waxed paper with balance of margarine. Place, greased side down, over pans, tucking in ends of paper to prevent dough from drying out. Let rise at room temperature until dough just touches waxed paper.

9. Gently remove paper. Brush loaves with egg white mixture. Sprinkle with sesame seeds. Let rise, uncovered, until dough reaches well above sides of pans.

10. Bake in preheated 450°F oven for 15 minutes. Reduce heat to 375°F. Bake for 20 minutes.

11. Slide loaves out of pans. Place back in oven, directly on rack. Bake for an additional 5 minutes. Loaves should be well browned. Test for doneness by thumping loaves with knuckles. A hollow sound indicates the loaves are done.

12. Remove from oven. Let cool thoroughly on rack before slicing.

Yield: 4 large loaves, 14 slices (1-inch each) per loaf

Notes:
1. Here's how to toast coriander seeds: Heat skillet until hot. Add seeds, shaking around in skillet for 2 minutes. Crush toasted seeds using mortar and pestle.
2. Because no shortening is used, bread will remain fresh for just one day. Should some bread remain after baking day, wrap tightly in plastic wrap, then in aluminum foil. When ready to use, freshen by removing wraps, rewrapping in aluminum foil and baking in preheated 375°F oven for 15 minutes; then open foil and let cool for 2 minutes before slicing.

CAL	F	P:S	SOD	CAR	CHO	PRO
Per slice:						
49.5	–	–	1.5	10.5	–	2
With honey:						
50.5	–	–	1.5	11.5	–	2

Hearty French Bread

Prepare this light, golden-crusted bread for an enticing accompaniment to creamy full-bodied soups, such as my Broccoli Bisque (page 90) or Purée of Lentil Soup (page 92). Toast some, too, for croutons; and blend some for the most delicious crumbs. Or devour slices with your favorite food, or simply as is. This is one of my most popular breads.

2 tablespoons dry yeast or 2 premeasured packages
1¼ cups warm water (105° to 115°F)
7 to 7¼ cups unbleached flour
¼ cup toasted wheat germ (no sugar added)
1 cup whole-wheat flour
2 tablespoons toasted coriander seeds, crushed (see note 1, page 77)
½ teaspoon aniseed, crushed
½ teaspoon ground cinnamon
½ cup each water and apple juice (no sugar added)
¼ teaspoon corn oil, for bowl
¾ teaspoon sweet (unsalted) 100 percent corn oil margarine, for pans and waxed paper
4 teaspoons white cornmeal
1 egg white mixed with 1 tablespoon water

1. Pour yeast into large bowl of electric mixer. Add ¾ cup water and beat with fork to dissolve. Add ½ cup unbleached flour and stir. Cover with plastic wrap and let stand at room temperature (70° to 80°F) for 30 minutes. Mixture will become bubbly.
2. In another bowl, combine wheat germ, whole-wheat flour, 5 cups unbleached flour, coriander seeds, aniseed, and cinnamon. Stir to blend.
3. In saucepan, combine balance of water and apple juice. Heat until warm (105° to 115°F). Pour into yeast mixture and stir.
4. Add half of flour mixture to yeast mixture and stir with wooden spoon until all flour is absorbed. Add balance of flour mixture and beat with wooden spoon until flour is moistened. Scoop up and turn onto lightly floured board and knead, adding all but ½ cup of balance of flour, until smooth and elastic. (The same procedure applies when you use a dough hook; see note 1, page 71.)
5. Shape dough into ball. Drop into fairly straight-sided lightly oiled bowl, turning to coat. Cover tightly with plastic wrap. Let rise at room temperature

(70° to 80°F) until more than doubled in bulk (about 1½ to 2 hours).

6. Punch dough down. Transfer to very lightly floured board and knead briefly by hand. (This dough will remain slightly sticky.) Cut into 4 equal pieces. Cover with waxed paper and let rest for 3 minutes.

7. Roll each piece of dough into a slender loaf 12 inches long. Grease four 14-inch French loaf pans with ½ teaspoon margarine. Sprinkle with cornmeal, shaking out excess. Lay loaves in pans.

8. With sharp razor or serrated knife, slash each loaf diagonally 4 times. Grease a large sheet of waxed paper with balance of margarine. Place waxed paper, greased side down, over pans, tucking in ends of paper to prevent dough from drying out. Let rise at room temperature until dough just touches waxed paper.

9. Gently remove paper. Brush loaves with egg white mixture. Sprinkle with sesame seeds. Let rise, uncovered, until dough reaches well above sides of pans.

10. Bake in preheated 450°F oven for 10 minutes. Reduce heat to 400°F and bake for 10 minutes. Shift loaves around in oven. Reduce heat to 375°F and bake for 12 to 15 minutes. Loaves should be crisp and golden brown.

11. Remove bread from pans. Tap bottom of loaves with knuckles. If you hear a hollow sound, the bread is done. If not, place undone loaves back in oven directly on rack and bake for an additional 5 minutes.

12. Remove from oven. Let cool thoroughly on rack before slicing.

Yield: 4 loaves, 17 to 18 slices (1-inch each) per loaf

Variation: This recipe can also produce golden-brown crusty rolls. Each quarter of dough will make 12 round rolls. Here's how:

1. Cut one-quarter of dough into 12 pieces. (Balance of dough will make 3 loaves.) Tuck edges of each piece to form a rough ball, one part of which is fairly smooth and the other puckered. Squeeze puckers together to hold and refine shape of ball.

2. Place balls, puckered part down, onto 2 cookie sheets that have been greased with ½ teaspoon margarine, then sprinkled with 1 tablespoon white cornmeal and the excess shaken out. Arrange balls in 4 parallel rows of 3 rolls each. Brush with egg white mixture. Cover loosely with waxed paper and let rise for 20 minutes.

3. Brush again with egg white mixture. Do not re-cover. Let stand until puffed up and doubled in bulk (about 1 hour). Sprinkle with 2 teaspoons poppy and sesame seeds. Bake in preheated 425°F oven for 10 minutes. Reduce heat to 400°F. Bake 10 minutes more, or until golden brown. Transfer to rack and let cool before serving.

Yield: 12 rolls

CAL	F	P:S	SOD	CAR	CHO	PRO
Per slice:						
48	0.5	3.5:1	1.5	8.5	–	2
Per roll:						
76	1	3.5:1	2	13.5	–	3.5

Fennel Rye Bread

This is a semidark bread with a strong rye flavor, enhanced by the aromatic herbaceousness of fennel. It's a great keeper, and its flavor improves with age. On the third day after baking, it remains as moist as on the first day, and it's even more flavorful. No problem about rising with this rye bread, because ¾ cup gluten flour acts as a rising booster.

2 tablespoons dry yeast or 2
  premeasured packages

3 to 3¼ cups unbleached flour
2½ cups dark rye flour (see notes)
1 tablespoon fennel seeds, lightly
  crushed
½ cup apple juice, no sugar added
1¼ cups water
1 tablespoon buckwheat honey
1 tablespoon corn oil plus ¼
  teaspoon for bowl
⅛ teaspoon ground red (cayenne)
  pepper
2 teaspoons freshly grated orange
  rind, preferably from navel orange
½ cup low-fat plain yogurt, at room
  temperature
¾ cup gluten flour
½ teaspoon sweet (unsalted) 100
  percent corn oil margarine, for
  pan and waxed paper
2 teaspoons white cornmeal

1. In large mixing bowl, combine yeast, 1 cup each unbleached and rye flours, and fennel seeds.

2. In saucepan, combine apple juice, water, honey, oil, ground red pepper, and orange rind. Heat until warm (105° to 115°F). Pour over dry ingredients. Beat with wooden spoon for 1 minute. Cover with plastic wrap and let stand for 15 minutes.

3. Stir down. Add yogurt and beat with wooden spoon to blend.

4. Add balance of rye flour, gluten flour, and 2 cups of unbleached flour, ½ cup at a time, beating with wooden spoon after each addition. When dough becomes too difficult to be handled with wooden spoon, scoop up and turn onto lightly floured board (or use your dough hook from this point on; see note 1, page 71), and knead until smooth and elastic. (This is a sticky dough due to the moisture in the rye flour.) Add balance of unbleached flour (¼ cup) only if necessary to reduce stickiness. This dough will become much smoother and easier to handle after the first rising.

5. Pour warm water into fairly straight-sided bowl. Empty and dry well. Coat lightly with oil.

6. Form dough into ball. Drop into bowl, turning to coat. Cover tightly with plastic wrap and let rise at room temperature (70° to 80°F) until doubled in bulk (about 1½ hours).

7. Punch dough down. Knead briefly in bowl. Transfer to board and cut in half. Shape into 2 round loaves.

8. Grease 11½- x 15½-inch cookie sheet with ¼ teaspoon margarine. Sprinkle with cornmeal, shaking out excess. Place loaves in opposite corners of baking sheet. Grease a sheet of waxed paper with balance of margarine. Place over loaves, greased side down. Let rise until doubled (about 1 hour).

9. Bake in preheated 375°F oven for 40 minutes. Test for doneness by tapping bottom of loaves with knuckles. Loaves are fully baked when you hear a hollow sound. Brush with cold water.

10. Let cool on rack before slicing.

Yield: 2 loaves; each quarter loaf makes 8 uneven slices (1/2-inch each)

Notes:
1. Dark rye flour is available in ethnic markets and grain stores. (It's also available by mail order. See page 177 for details.)

2. Although dark rye flour produces a richer bread than medium rye flour, medium rye flour may be used in this recipe.

CAL	F	P:S	SOD	CAR	CHO	PRO
Per slice:						
46	0.5	3.9:1	1.5	8.5	–	2

Aromatic Rye

If there were a society of rye bread lovers, this bread could become its symbol. It's so strongly rye-flavored! (A good deal of credit goes to the starter.) And as all great rye breads should be, it's impeccably textured for sandwiches. A good keeper to boot. And revel in the aromatic blend of herbaceous tastes, which sets it apart from all other ryes.

> 2 tablespoons dry yeast or 2 premeasured packages
> 3 cups rye flour
> 2 cups unbleached flour
> 1 teaspoon each fennel seeds and caraway seeds, crushed
> 1¼ cups apple juice (no sugar added)
> 1 tablespoon corn oil plus ½ teaspoon for bowl
> 1 tablespoon freshly grated orange rind, preferably from navel orange
> 1 cup Half-and-Half Starter (page 70)
> ½ cup gluten flour
> 2 teaspoons white cornmeal

1. In large mixing bowl, combine and stir yeast, 1 cup each rye flour and unbleached flour, and seeds.

2. In saucepan, combine apple juice, 1 tablespoon oil, and orange rind. Heat until warm (105° to 115°F). Pour into dry ingredients. Beat with wooden spoon for 2 minutes or use electric mixer at medium speed.

3. Add starter and beat for 2 minutes more. Cover tightly with plastic wrap and let stand for 20 minutes.

4. Stir down. Add gluten flour, balance of rye flour, and ½ cup unbleached white flour. Beat with wooden spoon. When dough becomes too difficult to handle with spoon, turn onto lightly floured board and knead. Add enough of balance of unbleached flour (½ cup) to make a smooth and elastic dough. (A dough hook does a splendid kneading job at this point; see note 1, page 71.)

5. Shape dough into ball. Drop into fairly straight-sided warmed, lightly oiled bowl. Cover tightly with plastic wrap. Let rise at room temperature (70° to 80°F) until doubled in bulk (about 1 hour 15 minutes).

6. Punch dough down. Transfer to board and knead for 1 minute. Divide dough in half. Shape into 2 round loaves. Rub 11½- x 15-inch cookie sheet very lightly with oil. Sprinkle with cornmeal. Place loaves in opposite corners. Cover with waxed paper and let rise until doubled in bulk (about 1 hour 15 minutes).

7. Brush with warm water. Bake in preheated 375°F oven for 45 minutes, brushing midway with water and again when loaves are done. Tap bottom of loaves with knuckles. Loaves are fully baked when you hear a hollow sound.

8. Cool on rack before slicing.

Yield: 2 loaves, each quarter loaf makes 8 slices (½-inch each)

Note: This bread will keep exceptionally well for 4 days at room temperature when wrapped tightly in plastic wrap and aluminum foil.

CAL	F	P:S	SOD	CAR	CHO	PRO
Per slice:						
42	0.5	4.3:1	0.5	7.7	–	2

Mystery Bread

Anybody who has read my books knows that my favorite kitchen time is breadmaking time. It's fun! This bread in particular is a fun bread. I challenge its admirers to identify the ingredients; not even the most experienced breadmakers can. Small amounts of buckwheat and whole-wheat flours combined with unbleached flour, fruit juices, and cinnamon blend so perfectly that the ingredients remain a mystery. Try it and you'll see what I mean. (I hope you make breadmaking as much a fun part of your life as it is of mine.)

2 tablespoons dry yeast or 2
  premeasured packages
¼ cup nonfat dry milk
2 teaspoons aniseed, crushed
5 to 5½ cups unbleached flour
½ cup apple juice (no sugar added)
¾ cup unsweetened pineapple juice
1¼ cups water
2 teaspoons freshly grated orange
  rind, preferably from navel orange
½ teaspoon ground cinnamon
1 teaspoon honey (optional)
1 tablespoon corn oil plus ½
  teaspoon for bowl
½ cup each whole-wheat flour and
  buckwheat flour
½ teaspoon sweet (unsalted) 100
  percent corn oil margarine, for
  pans

1. In large mixing bowl, combine yeast, milk, aniseed, and 2 cups unbleached flour.

2. In saucepan, combine juices, water, orange rind, cinnamon, honey, and 1 tablespoon oil. Heat until warm (105° to 115°F). Pour over dry ingredients. Beat with wooden spoon for 1 minute. Cover with plastic wrap and let stand for 10 minutes.

3. Add whole-wheat flour, buckwheat flour, and all but ½ cup of balance of unbleached flour, ½ cup at a time, beating with wooden spoon after each addition. After adding 4½ cups of flour, dough will become difficult to beat with wooden spoon. Scoop up and turn onto lightly floured board and knead, adding balance of flour, if necessary, to make a smooth and elastic dough.

4. Shape dough into ball. Drop into lightly oiled, fairly straight-sided bowl, turning to coat. Cover tightly with plastic wrap and let rise at room temperature (70° to 80°F) until doubled in bulk (about 1 hour 15 minutes).

5. Punch dough down. Transfer to board and cut into 3 equal parts. Cover with waxed paper and let dough rest for 5 minutes.

6. Roll each piece out into a 7- x 12-inch rectangle. Starting with short end, roll up tightly, tucking in sides and pressing seam to hold. Place, seam side down, in 3 small (7⅜- x 3⅝- x 2¼-inch) loaf pans greased with margarine. Cover with plastic wrap and let rise at room temperature until doubled in bulk (about 1 hour).

7. Gently remove plastic wrap. Bake in preheated 375°F oven for 40 minutes.

8. Remove bread from pans. Place back in oven directly on rack and bake for 5 minutes more. Loaves should be crispy and golden brown. Let cool thoroughly on rack before slicing.

Yield: 3 loaves, 20 slices (⅜-inch each) per loaf

CAL	F	P:S	SOD	CAR	CHO	PRO
Per slice:						
50	0.5	3.9:1	4	10	–	2
With honey: No appreciable difference						

Cracked-Wheat Surprise

Close your eyes and take a bite. Is it a cake? A bread? What is it? It's a lovely surprise for bread aficionados with a sweet tooth. This blend of cracked wheat, spices, fruit juices, and other delectables makes it a perfect bread for you to enjoy at breakfast, teatime, or any time you crave a sweet.

¼ cup uncooked cracked-wheat
  cereal (no salt or sugar added)
¾ cup unsweetened pineapple juice
½ cup water
2 tablespoons honey
2 tablespoons corn oil
½ teaspoon each ground cinnamon
  and ginger
1 tablespoon dry yeast or 1
  premeasured package
2 tablespoons buckwheat flour
½ cup low-fat plain yogurt, at room
  temperature
1 teaspoon freshly grated orange
  rind, preferably from navel orange
4 to 4¼ cups unbleached flour
½ teaspoon sweet (unsalted) 100
  percent corn oil margarine, for
  pan and waxed paper
2 teaspoons evaporated skim milk

1. Place cracked wheat in small
bowl. In saucepan, combine pineapple
juice, water, honey, oil, and spices.
Bring to boil and pour over cracked
wheat. Stir. Let stand until cooled
down to warm (105° to 115°F).

2. Place yeast and buckwheat flour
in mixing bowl. Pour cracked wheat
mixture over yeast and flour. Beat with
wooden spoon for 1 minute. Cover and
let stand for 15 minutes.

3. Stir down. Add yogurt and orange rind. Beat with wooden spoon until blended.

4. Add all but ½ cup unbleached
flour, ½ cup at a time, beating with
wooden spoon after each addition.
When dough becomes too difficult to be
handled with wooden spoon, turn onto
lightly floured board and knead, using
just enough of balance of flour until
dough is smooth and elastic. Shape into
ball.

5. Lightly grease a 10-inch metal
pie pan with margarine. Place ball of
dough in center and press down until
dough almost touches the sides. Lightly
grease a long sheet of waxed paper
with margarine and place it over pan,
greased side down. Let stand at room
temperature (70° to 80°F) until doubled
in bulk (about 1½ hours).

6. Brush dough lightly with milk,
taking care it does not drip down sides
of pan. Bake in center of preheated
375°F oven for 45 minutes.

7. Remove bread from oven. Place
pan on rack and let cool for 10 minutes.
With blunt knife, loosen bread around
sides of pan. Remove from pan and
let cool on rack for 1½ hours before
slicing. Cut carefully, from center out-
ward, into 1-inch wedges.

Yield: 30 wedges (1-inch each), each
wedge cut in half

Variation: For rolls, shape dough into
30 high, round balls. Arrange on 11½- x
15½-inch cookie sheets (12 rolls will fit
on 1 cookie sheet), which have been
greased with margarine and lightly
sprinkled with cornmeal. Brush with
milk. Bake in preheated 375°F oven for
20 to 25 minutes.

CAL	F	P:S	SOD	CAR	CHO	PRO
Per half wedge:						
43	1	4:1	2	8	–	0.5
Per roll:						
86	2	4:1	4	16	–	1

Double Twist: English Muffins and English Muffin Bread

Here are a baker's dozen muffins, English style—crunchy when pulled apart (never cut) and toasted—plus a good-sized loaf that toasts to perfection. Marvelous for breakfast in either form; and the muffins make a superlative hamburger bun. One great difference between my English muffins and the commercial variety: mine contain 9 milligrams of sodium a muffin; the commercial variety contains 293! You'll never miss the salt.

⅓ cup yellow cornmeal plus 2
   tablespoons
1 cup thick buttermilk (no salt
   added), at room temperature
2 tablespoons dry yeast or 2
   premeasured packages
1 teaspoon aniseed, crushed
½ teaspoon each ground ginger and
   cinnamon
1 cup whole-wheat flour
3¾ to 4 cups unbleached flour
⅔ cup apple juice (no sugar added)
½ cup water
2 tablespoons sweet (unsalted) 100
   percent corn oil margarine plus ¼
   teaspoon for pan
1 tablespoon honey (optional)
½ teaspoon corn oil, for rising bowl
   and waxed paper

1. Combine ⅓ cup yellow cornmeal and buttermilk in bowl. Stir well to blend and set aside.

2. In mixing bowl, combine yeast, aniseed, spices, and ½ cup each whole-wheat and unbleached flours.

3. In saucepan, heat apple juice, water, margarine, and honey until warm (105° to 115°F). Pour over dry ingredients in mixing bowl. Beat with wooden spoon for 2 minutes or with electric mixer for 1 minute.

4. Gradually beat in buttermilk mixture. Add balance of whole-wheat flour and all but ¼ cup unbleached flour, ½ cup at a time, and beat until all flour is absorbed. When dough becomes too difficult to be handled with wooden spoon, start using your dough hook (see note 1, page 71) or turn onto lightly floured board and knead until smooth and elastic, adding only enough of balance of flour to make a nonsticky dough. The dough is a delight to handle.

4. Shape dough into ball. Place dough in fairly straight-sided, lightly oiled bowl, turning to coat. Cover tightly with plastic wrap and let rise at room temperature (70° to 80°F) until more than doubled in bulk (about 1½ hours).

5. Punch dough down. Transfer to board and knead briefly, squeezing out bubbles. Cut dough in half. Shape 1 piece into loaf. Place in margarine-greased loaf pan (8½ x 9 x 2½ inches). Cover with lightly oiled sheet of waxed paper. Let rise until doubled in bulk (about 1 hour).

6. Meanwhile, on very lightly floured board, roll out other half of dough to a thickness of ⅜ inch. Sprinkle sheet of waxed paper with 1 tablespoon cornmeal. Cut into rounds with 3-inch cookie cutter. Re-roll scraps and cut into rounds. Lay rounds on waxed paper. Repeat until all dough is used up. Sprinkle rounds with balance of cornmeal. Cover loosely with another sheet of waxed paper, and let rise until light and doubled (45 to 60 minutes, not longer).

7. When loaf has doubled in bulk, bake in preheated 375°F oven for 40 minutes. Remove from pan. Place back in oven directly on rack for 5 minutes. Remove from oven. Cool thoroughly on rack before slicing.

8. Heat 2 nonstick skillets until hot. With spatula, very gingerly transfer

risen muffins to skillets. Bake for 2 minutes on each side, taking care not to scorch. Turn down heat to medium, and bake on each side for 6 to 7 minutes, shifting muffins around skillet so they bake uniformly. Remove from skillet and place on racks. Split (don't cut) in half and toast.

Yield: 1 loaf, 23 slices (⅜-inch each); 13 to 14 muffins

CAL	F	P:S	SOD	CAR	CHO	PRO
Per half muffin:						
95	1.5	3.2:1	4.5	18	–	3.5
With honey:						
97.5	1.5	3.2:1	4.5	18.5	–	3.5
Bread, per half slice:						
58	1	3.2:1	2.5	10.5	–	2
With honey:						
59.5	1	3.2:1	2.5	11	–	2

Sitar Bread

The sitar is a Hindu guitar that makes exotically beautiful music. This bread was named by a devotee of Hindu cuisine who exclaimed that my loaf made music just as exotically beautiful. Not an Indian bread, this mild pink-and-tan loaf is redolent of the flavors of two of India's favorite spices, cumin and curry. It is so irresistibly delicious that it would be a shame to enjoy it any way except *au naturel*.

2 tablespoons dry yeast or 2 premeasured packages
2 cups dark rye flour (see notes page 79)
3½ to 3¾ cups unbleached flour
½ teaspoon each cuminseed and caraway seeds, crushed
¼ cup toasted wheat germ (no sugar added)
1½ cups tomato juice (no salt added)

¾ cup water
1 tablespoon corn oil plus ¼ teaspoon for bowl
1 tablespoon sweet (unsalted) 100 percent corn oil margarine plus ¼ teaspoon for cookie sheet
1 tablespoon honey
½ teaspoon ground cinnamon
1 teaspoon curry powder (no salt or pepper added)
8 dashes ground red (cayenne) pepper
1 tablespoon white cornmeal
1 egg white mixed with 1 teaspoon water
1 tablespoon caraway seeds

1. In large mixing bowl, combine and stir yeast, 1 cup each rye flour and unbleached flour, cuminseed, caraway seeds, and wheat germ.

2. In saucepan, combine tomato juice, water, 1 tablespoon oil, 1 tablespoon margarine, honey, and spices. Heat until warm (105° to 115°F). Pour over dry ingredients. Beat with wooden spoon or electric mixer for 2 minutes.

3. Add balance of rye flour and all but ½ cup of balance of unbleached flour, adding ½ cup at a time and beating with wooden spoon after each addition. At this point, you can knead by hand or with a dough hook (which does a splendid job; see note 1, page 71). When kneading by hand, turn dough onto very lightly floured board, adding balance of flour if necessary to make a soft, nonsticking dough.

4. Shape into ball. Drop into lightly oiled, fairly straight-sided bowl, turning to coat. Let rise at room temperature (70° to 80°F) for 1 hour.

5. Punch dough down. Re-cover and let rise again until doubled in bulk.

6. Punch dough down and knead briefly on board. Cut into 2 equal pieces; shape into 2 balls. Very lightly rub 11½- x 15½-inch cookie sheet with margarine. Sprinkle with cornmeal, shaking off excess. Place loaves on opposite corners.

7. Brush loaves with egg white mixture. Cover loosely with waxed paper and let rise until double in bulk (about 1 hour).

8. Brush again with egg white mixture. Sprinkle with caraway seeds. Bake in preheated 375°F oven for 40 minutes. Test for doneness by tapping bottom of loaves with knuckles. They're fully baked when you hear a hollow sound.

9. Let loaves cool on rack for at least 1½ hours before slicing. Delicious served slightly warm.

Yield: 2 loaves; each quarter loaf makes 8 uneven slices (½-inch each)

CAL	F	P:S	SOD	CAR	CHO	PRO
Per slice:						
42	15	3.8:1	2	10.5	–	2

Bread Crumbs

I never throw away a "crumb" of bread. I use day-old or fresh bread for stuffing and crumbs. Any of my breads can easily be converted into crumbs. The kind of bread you use for crumbs will affect the flavor of your finished recipe. So try the same recipe often using different bread crumbs.

8 ⅜-inch slices bread

1. Cut slices into ½-inch cubes. Spread on cookie sheet and bake in preheated 425°F oven for 10 minutes, turning once with spatula. Cool.

2. Transfer to blender and blend on high speed for 1 minute.

3. Pour into glass jar. Cool. Cover and store in refrigerator.

Yield: 1 cup

Variation: Prepare 6 slices of bread according to step 1. Add ¼ cup toasted wheat germ (no sugar added) and blend on high speed of blender for 10 seconds. Yield: 1 cup

CAL	F	P:S	SOD	CAR	CHO	PRO
Per cup:						
396	–	–	12	82	–	16
Per tablespoon:						
25	–	–	1	5	–	1
Variation (per cup):						
407	3	4.1	10	74.5	–	21
Variation (per tablespoon):						
25.5	–	–	0.5	4.5	–	1.5

Matzoh Crumbs

Matzoh crumbs may be substituted for bread crumbs in many recipes. The result is lighter-tasting food. I usually combine matzoh crumbs with toasted wheat germ for added flavor.

4 plain matzohs (no salt, shortening, or eggs added)

1. Break matzohs into pieces. Blend, half at a time, in blender until fine.

2. Store in glass jar in refrigerator.

Yield: 1 cup

Variation: Prepare 3 matzohs according to step 1. Add ¼ cup toasted wheat germ (no sugar added) and blend on high speed of blender for 10 seconds. Yield: 1 cup

CAL	F	P:S	SOD	CAR	CHO	PRO
Per cup:						
384	–	–	12	84	–	12
Per tablespoon:						
24	–	–	1	5	–	–
Variation (per cup):						
390	3	4.1	10	76	–	18
Variation (per tablespoon):						
26.5	–	–	0.5	5	–	1.5

Soups

Thick and Hearty Beef-Vegetable Soup

With only 125 calories a portion? Sure! It's just another example of what you can do when you base your cuisine on healthful ingredients. Only 40 milligrams of sodium, too.

½ pound lean beef, wiped with
   paper toweling, cut into ½-inch
   cubes
2 cups water
1 tablespoon tarragon vinegar (page
   99)
2 cups Rich Chicken Stock (page 94)
½ rib celery, minced
1 small onion, minced
1 small sweet green pepper, seeded
   and cut into ½-inch pieces
¼ cup peeled and ½-inch-diced
   yellow turnip
4 cloves garlic, minced
   Bouquet garni (1 sprig fresh
   parsley, 1 bay leaf, tied together
   with white thread)
½ cup broken whole-wheat
   spaghetti or enriched spaghetti
1 cup canned tomatoes (no salt
   added)
2 teaspoons tomato paste (no salt
   added)
½ teaspoon each dried thyme leaves,
   crushed, and chili con carne
   seasoning (no salt or pepper
   added)
¼ cup red wine

1. Place meat and water in waterless cooker or stainless-steel pot. Bring to boil. Cook, uncovered, for 5 minutes, removing scum that rises to top.
2. Add vinegar. Cook for 1 minute.

3. Add stock, vegetables, garlic, and bouquet garni. Bring to simmering point. Cover and simmer for 1 hour.
4. Add balance of ingredients. Bring to simmering point. Cover and simmer for 30 minutes. Stir. Let stand, covered, for 10 minutes. Remove bouquet garni and serve.

Yield: Serves 6

CAL	F	P:S	SOD	CAR	CHO	PRO
125	3	0.3:1	40	11.5	25	13

Creamy Chicken Soup

Why not make a comparison test? Taste a canned creamed chicken soup, then taste mine. It will start you on your own back-to-nature movement. The canned variety, not in the same taste-class as my natural soup, is a chemist's nightmare of polysyllabic additives doused in brine. I often wonder if a real chicken has ever been within miles of the manufacturer's kettles. Why settle for the ersatz when this satiny-smooth delight is so easy to prepare?

1 small chicken breast, skinned,
   bone in (¾ pound)
1 whole chicken leg with thigh,
   skinned (½ pound)
3 cups water
1 medium onion, coarsely chopped
1 small leek, white part only, well
   washed and coarsely chopped

3 large cloves garlic, minced
½ rib celery, diced
½ carrot, peeled and diced
4 large fresh mushrooms, washed,
    dried, trimmed, and coarsely
    chopped
1 small potato, peeled and diced
    (about ½ cup)
½ cup peeled and diced white turnip
2 tablespoons minced fresh parsley
½ teaspoon each ground ginger and
    crushed thyme leaves
8 dashes ground red (cayenne)
    pepper
    Small bouquet garni (1 sprig fresh
    parsley, 1 bay leaf, tied together
    with white thread)
⅓ cup evaporated skim milk (¼
    percent milkfat)
2 teaspoons medium-dry sherry
    (optional)

1. Place first 11 ingredients plus 1 tablespoon parsley in waterless cooker or stainless-steel pot. Bring to boil. Lower heat to slow boil and cook, uncovered, for 5 minutes, removing scum that rises to top.

2. Add ginger, thyme, ground red pepper, and bouquet garni. Turn heat down to simmering. Cover and simmer for 45 minutes. Uncover partially and let soup cool in pot for 30 minutes.

3. With slotted spoon, transfer chicken to carving board. Slice chicken from bones. Cut into bite-sized pieces. Place in bowl. Set aside.

4. Turn heat up under pot to slow boil and reduce liquid for 5 minutes. Let cool for a few minutes. Remove bouquet garni. Pour into blender and purée for 1 minute. Rinse out pot. Pour puréed soup back into pot.

5. Stir in evaporated milk and chicken. Reheat slowly to simmering point. Do not boil. Stir in optional sherry.

6. Pour into soup plates, sprinkle with balance of parsley, and serve.

Yield: Serves 6

Variation: Soup may be prepared without milk, in which case include the sherry, stirring in just before serving.

CAL	F	P:S	SOD	CAR	CHO	PRO
147	6	1:1	91.5	9.5	50	61.5

With sherry: No appreciable difference
Without milk:

142	6	1:1	88	9	50	61

Three-Way Black Bean Soup

The first way is a traditional vegetable soup, raised to a new taste level; the second way, an excitingly untraditional purée; and the third way, a hearty variation of the basic soup for confirmed beef eaters. Any way, here's a robust and filling soup that's fit for a regal repast.

¾ cup dried unsalted black beans
2¼ teaspoons each Italian olive oil
    and corn oil, combined
1 large leek, white part only, well
    washed and coarsely chopped
½-inch slice fresh ginger, peeled and
    shredded
3 large cloves garlic, minced
1 small carrot, peeled and cut into
    ¼-inch cubes
½ rib celery, minced
1 teaspoon dried thyme leaves,
    crushed
8 dashes ground red (cayenne)
    pepper
2 teaspoons wine vinegar
⅓ cup peeled white or yellow turnip
    cut into ¼-inch cubes
1½ cups each Rich Chicken Stock
    (page 94) and water
1 teaspoon curry powder (no salt or
    black pepper added)
1 teaspoon chili con carne
    seasoning (no salt added)
2 tablespoons medium-dry sherry

First way:
1. Wash and drain beans. Place in waterless cooker or stainless-steel pot. Add water to cover. Bring to boil, partially covered; cover tightly and let stand for 2 hours. Drain beans, reserving liquid. Wipe out pot.
2. Heat oils in iron skillet until hot. Add leek, ginger, garlic, carrot, and celery. Sauté over medium-high heat until lightly browned.
3. Sprinkle with thyme and ground red pepper. Stir and cook for 1 minute. Add vinegar. Cook for 1 minute.
4. Pour into waterless cooker or stainless-steel pot. Add beans, turnip, stock, water, and spices. Bring to simmering point. Cover tightly and simmer for 1½ to 2 hours, stirring often. Beans should be tender yet firm when fully cooked.
5. Add sherry. Stir to blend. Serve.

Second way:
1. Follow steps 1 through 4. Pour soup into blender and purée until smooth. Pour back into pot.
2. Add sherry. Reheat and serve.

Third way:
1. Follow steps 1 through 3.
2. Place small beef bone and ¼ pound lean cubed beef in separate pot. Add water to cover. Bring to boil and cook for 2 minutes. Pour contents of pot into colander. Rinse meat and bone under cold running water.
3. Include parboiled meat and bone in step 4 and continue with recipe.

Yield: First way: Serves 4 as main dish, 6 as first course
Second way: Serves 6
Third way: Serves 4 as main dish, 6 as first course

CAL	F	P:S	SOD	CAR	CHO	PRO
First way (main dish):						
283	14	2.8:1	53.5	31	–	9.5
First way (first course):						
188	9.5	2.8:1	35.5	20.5	–	6.5
Second way: No appreciable difference						
Third way (main dish):						
329.5	16.5	2.8:1	89	31	19	15.5
Third way (first course):						
219	11	2.8:1	45	25.5	3	9

Fish Chowder— Manhattan Style

Chowder, that hearty soup thick with luscious edibles, is as American as New England, where in fact it originated. There are two rival fish chowders, Boston and Manhattan; but as far as I'm concerned, there's no contest: I'll take Manhattan. (I like the tomatoes, so absent in the Back Bay version.) My Manhattan chowder is as sophisticated as a book announcement party at Simon & Schuster, and just as zingy with excitement. (By the way, did you know the word "chowder" derives from the French *chaudière* which means "large pot"? It comes as a surprise to me, too. I always thought that "chowder" came from our American Indian heritage.)

1 pound fresh cod fillet (1 thick slice)
1 carrot, peeled and cut into ¼-inch cubes
⅓ cup peeled white turnip cut into ½-inch cubes
1 medium potato, peeled and cut into ½-inch cubes
1 cup canned tomatoes (no salt added)
1½ cups each Jiffy Fish Stock (page 95) and water
2 teaspoons curry powder (no salt or pepper added)
⅛ teaspoon ground red (cayenne) pepper
¾ teaspoon combined dried thyme and rosemary leaves, crushed
2 tablespoons minced fresh parsley
2 tablespoons corn oil

3 cloves garlic, minced
1 rib celery, coarsely chopped
2 tablespoons minced sweet green
   pepper
4 large fresh mushrooms, washed,
   dried, trimmed, and coarsely
   chopped
1 medium onion, minced
¼ cup dry vermouth

1. Wash fish under cold running water and dry with paper toweling. Cut into 1-inch chunks. Set aside.

2. Combine next 9 ingredients in kettle. Bring to simmering point. Cover tightly and simmer for 15 minutes.

3. While vegetables are simmering, heat oil in nonstick skillet until hot. Sauté garlic, celery, green pepper, mushrooms, and onion, stirring, until wilted. Push to side of skillet.

4. Add fish chunks. Sauté for 3 minutes, turning often. Combine fish with vegetable mixture.

5. Add vermouth. Stir and cook over high heat for 1 minute.

6. Pour contents of skillet into kettle. Stir. Bring to simmering point. Cover and simmer for 15 minutes. Serve.

Yield: Serves 6

CAL	F	P:S	SOD	CAR	CHO	PRO
144.5	5	4.4:1	83	10	42	14.5

Purée of Cauliflower Soup

If, as Mark Twain once remarked, "Cauliflower is cabbage with a college education," it earns its Ph.D. in this soup. Helping it get its advanced degree are ingredients you never saw in a cauliflower soup recipe before: evaporated skim milk, curry, cream of wheat, and much more. Reading the recipe is as much fun as savoring the soup—almost.

1 medium head cauliflower
1 slice lemon
1 tablespoon corn oil
3 cloves garlic, minced
2 shallots, minced
1 small onion, minced
½ rib celery, minced
2 teaspoons apple cider vinegar
2½ cups Rich Chicken Stock (page 94)
½ cup tomato juice (no salt added)
1 teaspoon regular cream of wheat
1 teaspoon dried sweet basil leaves,
   crushed
⅛ teaspoon ground red (cayenne)
   pepper
½ teaspoon curry powder (no salt or
   pepper added)
⅓ cup nonfat liquid milk
¼ cup evaporated skim milk (¼
   percent milkfat)

1. Choose a crisp, snow-white cauliflower. Cut away tough outer leaves and stalk. Separate into flowerets. Wash. Set aside.

2. Fill large kettle with 1 inch water. Add lemon slice. Bring to rolling boil. Add flowerets, flower side down, and boil, uncovered, for 5 minutes. Pour contents of pot into colander. Drain. Discard lemon slice. Wipe out pot.

3. Heat oil in pot until very warm. Sauté garlic, shallots, and onion until wilted but not browned.

4. Add vinegar. Cook for 1 minute. Add stock and tomato juice. Bring to boil. Sprinkle with cream of wheat and stir.

5. Add cauliflower. Bring to boil. Sprinkle with basil and spices. Turn heat down to simmering. Cover and simmer for 15 minutes. (Cooking time will vary with the size and freshness of flowerets. Do not overcook.) Uncover and let cool in pot for 10 minutes.

6. Pour mixture into blender, half at a time, and purée until smooth. Pour purée back into pot.

7. Add milks. Heat to simmering point. *Do not boil.* Serve immediately.

Yield: Serves 6

CAL	F	P:S	SOD	CAR	CHO	PRO
92.5	3	3.9:1	40.5	15.5	2	7.5

Broccoli Bisque

A bisque, as who doesn't know, is a creamed soup. And broccoli, that brilliantly dark green delight, has been extolled as the aristocrat of vegetables by Greek and Italian gastronomes for more than 2,000 years. Combine broccoli and bisque, and you have the *crème de la crème* of vegetable soups.

1 bunch fresh broccoli (2 large stalks)
4½ teaspoons corn oil
¼ cup minced onion
3 large cloves garlic, minced
2 large shallots, minced
1 tablespoon tarragon vinegar (page 99)
2 cups Light Chicken Broth (page 95)
1 cup water
2 tablespoons grated carrot
1 teaspoon regular cream of wheat
1 tablespoon curry powder (no salt or pepper added)
4 dashes ground red (cayenne) pepper
1 teaspoon dried chervil, crushed
2 teaspoons medium-dry sherry
½ cup evaporated skim milk (¼ percent milkfat)

1. Cut away and discard tough bottom ends of broccoli stalks. Then cut close to flowerets. Peel away thick skin from stalks. Cut stalks into ½-inch cubes. Set aside.

2. Heat oil in waterless cooker or stainless-steel pot until hot. Sauté onion, garlic, and shallots until wilted but not browned. Add broccoli and sauté for 1 minute.

3. Add vinegar. Cook for 1 minute. Add broth, water, and carrot. Bring to rolling boil. Sprinkle with cream of wheat. Stir vigorously.

4. Add curry powder, ground red pepper, and chervil. Turn heat down to simmering. Cover partially and simmer for 12 minutes. Partially cool.

5. Pour into blender, half at a time, and purée until smooth. Pour into bowl.

6. Stir in sherry. Whisk in milk. Serve well chilled.

Yield: Serves 6

Variations:
1. For an enticing side dish, increase cream of wheat to 2 teaspoons. Soup will be thick. Serve well chilled with meat, fish, or poultry.
2. For a canapé spread, combine 3 tablespoons puréed soup with 3 mashed hard-boiled egg whites, ¼ cup minced onion, and 2 teaspoons minced fresh parsley. Spread on 3 thin slices of any of my breads (pages 68–85). Cut each slice into thirds.

CAL	F	P:S	SOD	CAR	CHO	PRO
102	3.5	4.4:1	37	10.5	2	7
Variation 1:						
106.5	3.5	4.4:1	39	11.5	2	10.5
Variation 2 (per canapé):						
20	–	–	18.5	2.5	1.5	2.5

Potato and Mushroom Soup I

The Greeks called mushrooms *bromo theon,* "the food of the gods." What else, then, to use but mushrooms to transform a prosaic potato potage into a heavenly delight? And what's even better, I've transformed it into *two* heavenly delights (Potato and Mushroom Soup II follows this recipe).

¾ pound fresh mushrooms, washed, dried, trimmed, quartered, and sliced
1½ cups water
1 tablespoon tarragon vinegar (page 99)
2 medium potatoes, peeled and cut into ½-inch cubes
1 small carrot, peeled and cut into ½-inch cubes
½ rib celery, minced
4½ teaspoons corn oil
1 small onion, minced
1 green onion or 2 large shallots, coarsely chopped
3 large cloves garlic, minced
1½ tablespoons unbleached flour
2 cups Light Chicken Broth (page 95) or Rich Chicken Stock (page 94)
½ teaspoon each dried tarragon leaves, crushed, and ground ginger
2 tablespoons minced fresh parsley
¼ cup evaporated skim milk (¼ percent milkfat)
6 dashes ground red (cayenne) pepper

1. Combine mushrooms, water, and vinegar in saucepan. Bring to simmering point. Cover partially and simmer for 5 minutes. Place strainer over waterless cooker or kettle. Pour contents of saucepan into strainer and drain liquid into cooker. Set mushrooms aside.

2. Add potatoes, carrot, and celery to mushroom liquid. Simmer, partially covered, for 12 minutes. Add mushrooms. Turn off heat.

3. Heat oil in nonstick skillet until hot. Add onion, green onion, and garlic. Sauté until wilted. Sprinkle with flour. Stir and cook for 1 minute.

4. Gradually add stock, continuing to stir, until liquid thickens. Pour into mushroom mixture.

5. Add tarragon, ginger, and parsley. Cover partially and simmer gently for 20 minutes.

6. Add evaporated milk, stirring to blend. Continue to cook over low heat until well heated. *Do not boil.* Add ground red pepper and serve.

Yield: Serves 6

CAL	F	P:S	SOD	CAR	CHO	PRO
110	4	4.1:1	28	15	0.5	5.5

Potato and Mushroom Soup II

2 tablespoons corn oil
2 leeks, white part only, well washed and minced
3 large cloves garlic, minced
1 small rib celery, minced
¼ pound fresh mushrooms, washed, dried, trimmed, and sliced
½ cup sliced tender cabbage leaves
1 teaspoon caraway seeds, crushed
1 tablespoon wine vinegar
¼ cup carrot, peeled and cut into ½-inch cubes
1 medium potato, peeled and cut into ½-inch cubes
¼ teaspoon each dried sage and thyme leaves, crushed
2 cups each Rich Chicken Stock (page 94) and water
½ cup apple juice (no sugar added)
8 dashes ground red (cayenne) pepper

1. Heat 1 tablespoon oil in nonstick skillet until hot. Sauté leeks, garlic, celery, and mushrooms until lightly browned, stirring often. Turn into bowl.

2. Heat balance of oil in skillet. Add cabbage. Sprinkle with caraway seeds. Sauté over medium-high heat until lightly browned.

3. Add vinegar. Cook for 1 minute. Turn into waterless cooker or stainless-steel pot.

4. Add balance of ingredients. Bring to simmering point. Simmer, uncovered, for 5 minutes, removing scum that rises to top. Cover partially and simmer for 1 hour.

5. Cover tightly. Let soup stand in pot for 20 minutes. Reheat, if necessary, before serving.

Yield: Serves 4

CAL	F	P:S	SOD	CAR	CHO	PRO
111.5	7	3.9:1	24	20	–	3

Purée of Lentil Soup

The potage that Esau swapped for his birthright (Gen. 25:29–34), Bible scholars now inform us, was actually made from lentils. Lovers of this tastiest (and one of the most nutritious) of all legumes will tell you Esau couldn't have made a better bargain. In the Near East, 'mjeddrah—"Essan's dish of lentils"—is still consumed with joy both in peasant households and in the opulent palaces of princes. Here is my version of 'mjeddrah, brought up to date with the magic of the blender.

1¼ cups lentils, washed
2 cups cold water
1 tablespoon corn oil
3 large cloves garlic, minced
2 teaspoons peeled and minced fresh ginger
1 small rib celery, coarsely chopped
2 leeks, white part only, well washed and minced
½ cup peeled and diced yellow turnip
1 tablespoon each wine vinegar and fresh lemon juice
2 cups each Rich Chicken Stock (page 94) and water
1½ teaspoons chili con carne seasoning (no salt or pepper added)
½ teaspoon dried thyme leaves, crushed
6 dashes ground red (cayenne) pepper
  Bouquet garni (1 sprig fresh parsley, 1 bay leaf, tied together with white thread)
1 tablespoon medium-dry sherry

1. Soak lentils in 2 cups cold water until all water is absorbed (about 3 hours).

2. Heat oil in kettle until hot. Add garlic, ginger, celery, and leeks. Sauté until tender but not brown. Add turnip and sauté for 1 minute.

3. Add vinegar and lemon juice. Cook over medium-high heat for 1 minute.

4. Add lentils and balance of ingredients except sherry. Bring to simmering point. Partially cover and simmer for 1 hour. Cover tightly and let stand for 1 hour.

5. Remove bouquet garni. Pour mixture into blender, half at a time, and purée until smooth. Pour back into pot. Stir in sherry. Reheat just before serving.

Yield: Serves 6

Note: We like our soup thick. If you prefer yours less thick, you may thin it down with a mixture of equal parts stock and water.

CAL	F	P:S	SOD	CAR	CHO	PRO
184.5	2.5	4:1	30	28	–	12

Thick 'n' Hearty Scotch Broth

The dour climate of Scotland demands warming food and drink, and Scottish people have responded to nature's challenge with two worldwide favorites, Scotch whisky and Scotch broth. The essential ingredient in both is barley. Here, that excellently nut-flavored cereal is combined with lamb and an un-Scotchlike extravagance of herbs, spices, and vegetables to make the richest Scotch broth you've ever tasted. Accompany it with a simple green salad, and enjoy a filling, nutritious, and unforgettable meal.

2 pounds lean lamb, cut from the
   leg, and 2 large lamb bones
5½ cups water
1 tablespoon corn oil
1 large onion, minced
3 large cloves garlic, minced
1 rib celery, minced
4 large fresh mushrooms, washed,
   dried, trimmed, and sliced
1 carrot, peeled and cut into ¼-inch
   cubes
1 cup peeled and diced yellow
   turnip (cut into ¼-inch cubes)
⅓ cup barley, washed
2 teaspoons wine vinegar
1 tablespoon tomato paste (no salt
   added)
½ teaspoon dried thyme leaves,
   crushed
6 dashes ground red (cayenne)
   pepper
1 teaspoon chili con carne
   seasoning (no salt or pepper
   added)
   Bouquet garni (3 sprigs fresh dill, 1
   bay leaf, tied together with white
   thread)

1. Wash meat under cold running water. Place in kettle. Add water and bring to boil. Let boil, uncovered, for 5 minutes, removing scum that rises to top. Turn heat down to simmering. Cover tightly, and simmer for 1 hour.

2. Pour meat and broth into fine-meshed strainer or chinois* with bowl underneath. Let broth cool. Skim fat (see note 2). Remove meat from bones. Cut into ½-inch pieces. Wash and dry kettle.

3. Heat oil in skillet until hot. Add onion, garlic, celery, and mushrooms. Sauté until wilted but not browned.

4. Add carrot, turnip, and barley. Stir and cook for 2 minutes. Add vinegar. Cook for 1 minute.

5. Return meat and broth to pot. Stir. Add tomato paste, thyme, ground red pepper, chili con carne seasoning, and bouquet garni. Bring to simmering point. Cover partially and simmer for 1½ hours.

6. Turn off heat. Let soup stand, tightly covered, for 10 minutes. Remove bouquet garni and reheat before serving.

Yield: Serves 6

Notes:

1. Leg of lamb is the leanest cut of lamb. I buy a whole leg of lamb, have my butcher cut a 3- to 4-pound shank end for roasting, and the balance into pieces for lamb stew and soup. The meat freezes very well, cooked and uncooked.

2. Step 1 may be prepared a day ahead. Broth and meat should be stored and refrigerated separately. Hardened fat is easily removed when broth is cold.

CAL	F	P:S	SOD	CAR	CHO	PRO
241	8.5	1.3:1	92	13.5	88	26.5

* A conical-shaped, fine-meshed metal sieve.

Stocks, Sauces, Condiments, and Marinades

STOCKS

Stocks are the very foundation—the French word for stock is, indeed, *fonds*—of gourmet cooking. They are highly concentrated clear broths—replete with the flavorful essences of chicken, meat, bones, or fish parts, as well as vegetables, herbs, and spices. They do wonders for sauces, soups, and gravies; and are virtually omnipresent in my meat, fish, and poultry dishes. An invigorating amount of stock can transmute the dullest vegetable or grain into a gastronome's dream. Stocks are easy to make, simmering away happily by themselves while you live your life. They're fat free, low in calories, and are a treasurehouse of nutrients.

In the recipes in this book, I employ a Rich Chicken Stock (recipe follows) and a Jiffy Fish Stock (page 95), supplemented by a Light Chicken Broth (a broth can be viewed as a less concentrated stock; page 95). They can be frozen; and a good idea is to store some of your stock in ice-cube trays, and pop out a cube whenever you need a couple of tablespoons of stock.

Rich Chicken Stock

3½ pounds chicken giblets (excluding liver), backs, and wings, or broiling chicken and giblets (3½ pounds), skinned and quartered
3 large cloves garlic, minced
1 medium onion, quartered
¼ cup peeled and cubed black radish (½-inch cubes)
⅓ cup peeled and cubed yellow turnip (½-inch cubes)
2 large scallions, well washed and cut into large pieces
1 large carrot, peeled and cut into 3 pieces
1 large rib celery, cut into 3 pieces
½ cup dry vermouth
4 large dill sprigs
1 large bay leaf
7 cups water

1. Combine all ingredients in waterless cooker or stainless-steel pot. Bring to rolling boil. Turn heat down to slow boil and cook, uncovered, for 10 minutes, removing scum that rises to top. Turn heat down to simmering. Cover partially and simmer for 2½ hours. Uncover. Let stock cool in pot.

2. Place fine-meshed strainer or chinois over bowl. Pour stock into strainer pressing solids to extract juices. Save whole pieces of chicken to use in salad; discard remaining solids. Pour stock into freezeproof containers. Cover tightly and refrigerate overnight. Remove hardened fat that rises to top.

3. Refrigerate some stock for use within a few days and freeze the balance.

Yield: About 5 cups

	CAL	F	P:S	SOD	CAR	CHO	PRO
Per cup:	53	–	–	21.5	5	–	8.5
Per tablespoon:	3.5	–	–	1.5	0.5	–	0.5

Light Chicken Broth

1 broiling chicken (3½ pounds),
    skinned and quartered
1 large carrot
1 medium onion
3 large cloves garlic
1 large rib celery with leaves
2 large fresh mushrooms
½ cup dry vermouth
2 large leeks, white part only, well
    washed
2 teaspoons peeled and minced
    fresh ginger
3 sprigs fresh parsley
1 bay leaf
7 cups water

1. Combine all ingredients in pot. Bring to boil. Cook, uncovered, for 10 minutes, removing scum that rises to top. Cover partially and simmer for one hour 15 minutes.

2. With slotted spoon, remove chicken from broth. Enjoy as is, or try my recipe for Dilled Chicken Mousse (page 144).

3. Place fine-meshed strainer or chinois over bowl. Pour balance of ingredients into strainer, pressing broth out of solids. Discard solids.

4. Transfer broth to freezeproof containers. Refrigerate overnight. Cut away and discard hardened fat from top of broth.

5. Refrigerate some of broth for use within a few days and freeze the balance.

Yield: About 6 cups

CAL	F	P:S	SOD	CAR	CHO	PRO
Per cup:						
44	–	–	18	4	–	7
Per tablespoon:						
3	–	–	1	–	–	0.5

Jiffy Fish Stock

2 pounds bones and heads of any
    white-fleshed fish
1 small onion, sliced
2 large cloves garlic, minced
2 large shallots, minced
½ - inch slice fresh ginger, peeled and
    shredded
1 small carrot, peeled and sliced
3 whole cloves
1 small bay leaf
3 cups water
⅓ cup dry vermouth
½ teaspoon dried thyme leaves

1. Wash fish bones and heads under cold running water. Place in narrow waterless cooker or stainless-steel pot. Add balance of ingredients except thyme. Bring to boil. Turn heat down to slow boil and cook for 3 minutes, removing scum that rises to top.

2. Add thyme. Cover tightly, turn heat down, and simmer for 30 minutes.

3. Place in fine-meshed strainer or chinois over bowl. Pour stock through strainer, pressing solids to remove all stock. Discard solids.

4. Refrigerate some stock for use within a day and freeze the balance.

Yield: 3 cups

CAL	F	P:S	SOD	CAR	CHO	PRO
Per cup:						
20	–	–	28	3	–	2
Per tablespoon:						
1	–	–	2	–	–	–

Rich Dover Sole Fish Stock

Bones from 3 Dover sole (¾ pound
  each), cut into 3-inch pieces
¼ teaspoon ground ginger
2 large fresh mushrooms, washed,
  dried, trimmed, and sliced
½ carrot, peeled and sliced
½ rib celery, sliced
1 large clove garlic, coarsely
  chopped
½ cup dry vermouth or white wine
  Bouquet garni (1 sprig each fresh
  parsley and dill, 1 bay leaf, tied
  together with white thread)
1¼ cups water

1. Lay bones in one layer in wide
kettle. Add balance of ingredients.
Bring to simmering point. Cover and
simmer for 30 minutes, pressing bones
down into kettle several times and removing scum that rises to top.

2. Place fine-meshed strainer or
chinois over bowl. Pour ingredients
into strainer, pressing out juices. Wash
out kettle. Return stock to kettle. Reduce over medium-high heat to ¾ cup.

Yield: ¾ cup

CAL	F	P:S	SOD	CAR	CHO	PRO
60	–	–	84.5	14	–	1
Per tablespoon:						
5	–	–	7	1	–	–

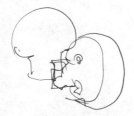

SAUCES

Sauces are to great food what de-
signer clothes are to beautiful women.
Virtually all of my sauces are made to
order for my dishes, and they fit like a
dream. But here are two off-the-rack
sauces that fit a variety of foods every
bite as well. They're my glamorous versions of the nation's most popular
sauce—tomato sauce.

Tomato-Mushroom Sauce

4½ teaspoons corn oil
2 medium onions, minced
3 large cloves garlic, minced
2 large shallots, minced
1 small rib celery, minced
1 small sweet green pepper, minced
1 tablespoon peeled and minced
  fresh ginger
¼ pound fresh mushrooms, washed,
  dried, trimmed, and thickly sliced
½ cup full-bodied red wine
½ cup Rich Chicken Stock (page 94)
1 cup canned tomatoes (no salt
  added), chopped
½ teaspoon each dried rosemary
  and thyme leaves, crushed
3 tablespoons tomato paste (no salt
  added)
4 dashes ground red (cayenne)
  pepper
  Bouquet garni (1 sprig each fresh
  parsley and dill, 1 bay leaf, tied
  together with white thread)

1. Heat 2¼ teaspoons oil in large
nonstick skillet until hot. Sauté onions,
garlic, shallots, celery, green pepper,
and ginger until wilted but not
browned. Push to side of skillet.

2. Add balance of oil. Sauté mushrooms for 2 minutes, or until barely cooked through.

3. Combine mushrooms with vegetables in skillet. Add wine and cook for 1 minute.

4. Add balance of ingredients. Bring to simmering point, cover partially, and simmer for 45 minutes. Let stand, covered, for 30 minutes before serving. Sauce will be very thick.

5. Discard bouquet garni. Slowly reheat sauce and serve.

Yield: About 2 cups

Variations:

1. Substitute dry vermouth for red wine in step 3.

2. Add 1 tablespoon curry powder (no salt or pepper added) during step 4.

CAL	F	P:S	SOD	CAR	CHO	PRO
Per cup:						
171.5	7	4.4:1	76.5	23	–	6.5
Per tablespoon:						
11	0.5	4.4:1	5	1.5	–	0.5

Variations 1 and 2: No appreciable difference

Smooth Tomato Curry Purée

2 *large fresh tomatoes, skinned and chopped*
¼ *teaspoon ground ginger*
½ *teaspoon each dried tarragon and sweet basil leaves, crushed*
1 *tablespoon Italian olive oil*
2 *tablespoons minced fresh parsley*
6 *dashes ground red (cayenne) pepper*
1 *teaspoon each apple cider vinegar and wine vinegar*
2 *shallots, minced*
1 *large clove garlic, minced*
1 *tablespoon minced celery*
1 *teaspoon curry powder (no salt or pepper added)*

1. Combine all ingredients in small saucepan. Bring to simmering point. Cover partially and simmer for 4 minutes. Uncover and let cool.

2. Pour sauce into blender and purée until smooth (about 1 minute). Chill.

Yield: About 1¼ cups

Serving suggestions:

1. Pour over mashed potatoes.

2. Pour over just-boiled pasta.

3. Pour over plain boiled, sautéed, or broiled fish.

4. Pour over egg white omelette (See "Luncheon Omelettes" in *The Dieter's Gourmet Cookbook.*)

5. Pour over steamed cauliflower, asparagus, boiled rice, or barley.

6. Pour over sautéed or cooked portions of turkey, chicken, or meat.

7. Pour over 1 cup cooked lentils.

8. Pour over steakburgers (see *The Dieter's Gourmet Cookbook*).

CAL	F	P:S	SOD	CAR	CHO	PRO
Per cup:						
148	11	1.2:1	43	11.5	–	2.5
Per tablespoon:						
9	0.5	1.2:1	2.5	0.5	–	–

CONDIMENTS

Condiments are to great food what wit is to wisdom: they add a sparkling delight. They can be used in the cooking process per se, like my Make-Your-Own-Herb Vinegars (page 99), or they can be served as piquant accompaniments. In the latter category, may I introduce two condiments you've never tasted before—my Cranberry/Apple Chutney (recipe follows) and my Pickled Tarragon Mushrooms (page 98). But you'll want to taste them again. And again. And again.

Cranberry/Apple Chutney

5 large crisp, sweet apples, such as
  Washington State, peeled, cored,
  and diced
¾ cup apple cider vinegar
2 tablespoons honey
6 whole cloves
1 teaspoon ground ginger
1 medium sweet red pepper, seeded
  and coarsely chopped
1 medium onion, coarsely chopped
1 large clove garlic, minced
1 tablespoon minced fresh parsley
1 large shallot, minced
½ lime, skin left on, pitted and cubed
¾ cup fresh cranberries
¾ cup dark raisins

    1. Combine all ingredients in waterless cooker or stainless-steel pot. Bring to simmering point. Cover and simmer for 2 hours, stirring often. Finished chutney should be very thick.
    2. Partially remove cover and let cool in pot. Refrigerate in tightly covered glass jar. Remove from refrigerator 1 hour before serving.

Yield: About 1 quart

Note: Chutney tastes sweeter after chilling for 1 day. For a tarter chutney, cut down on amount of honey. Chutney will keep for 10 days in refrigerator.

CAL	F	P:S	SOD	CAR	CHO	PRO
Per tablespoon:						
34.5	–	–	1.5	7.5	–	1.5

Pickled Tarragon Mushrooms

¾ pound small fresh mushrooms,
  washed, dried, and trimmed
½ cup tarragon vinegar (page 99)
¼ cup dry vermouth
2 tablespoons each corn oil and
  Italian olive oil
2 tablespoons fresh lemon juice
¼ teaspoon each dried thyme and
  chervil leaves, crushed
1 bay leaf
2 large cloves garlic, minced
1 large shallot, minced
8 dashes ground red (cayenne)
  pepper

    1. Choose firm, white, short-stemmed mushrooms. After drying, let stand, uncovered, in shallow dish for 15 minutes.
    2. Combine balance of ingredients in saucepan. Cover partially and simmer gently for 10 minutes.
    3. Pour contents of saucepan over mushrooms, turning until well coated. Let stand at room temperature, spooning liquid over mushrooms from time to time, until they give up some of their juices.
    4. Transfer to tightly covered jar. Refrigerate for 24 hours, turning jar upside down several times.

Yield: As an appetizer, serves 6 (about 5 mushrooms per serving)

Variation: Substitute the following for mushrooms: sliced Kirby cucumbers, broccoli flowerets, or cauliflower flowerets. Pickled mushrooms or vegetables will keep for 1 week in refrigerator.

CAL	F	P:S	SOD	CAR	CHO	PRO
104.5	9	4.5:1	14	4.5	–	1.5

Make-Your-Own Herb Vinegars

If you use fresh herbs:

1. Wash herbs (enough sprigs to make 1 cup minced, loosely packed). Dry with paper toweling. Tear off a fresh sheet of paper toweling and lay herbs on toweling for 1 hour to dry thoroughly. Tear leaves off sprigs and mince to make 1 loosely packed cup; reserve sprigs.

2. Pour 1 quart apple cider or white wine vinegar (try both) into clean jar. Add minced herbs and sprigs. Cover tightly and let stand at room temperature for 2 weeks (in a sunny spot, preferably) turning upside down and back once a day.

3. Strain into sterile bottle. Close tightly. Store in dark, cool place. After bottle is opened, shelf life is 6 months.

If you use dried herbs:

1. Bring 1 cup apple cider or white wine vinegar (try both) to simmering point.

2. Place 4 teaspoons dried herbs in clean jar. Pour boiling vinegar over herbs. Stir vigorously. Cover tightly and let stand at room temperature for 2 weeks (in a sunny spot, preferably), turning upside down and back once a day.

3. Strain into sterile bottle. Close tightly. Store in dark, cool place. After bottle is opened, shelf life is 6 months.

Yield: 1 quart

CAL	F	P:S	SOD	CAR	CHO	PRO

With fresh herbs, apple cider vinegar (per tablespoon):

3	–	–	1	1	–	–

With fresh herbs, white wine vinegar (per tablespoon):

3	–	–	6	–	–	–

Wiith dried herbs, apple cider vinegar (per tablespoon):

3	–	–	2	1	–	–

With dried herbs, white wine vinegar (per tablespoon):

3	–	–	7	–	–	–

MARINADES

Marinades are magical liquids that transmute toughness to tenderness, and blandness to piquancy. My salt-free marinades will have you wondering what you ever saw in salt. And that's quite a trick, because traditional marinades don't exist without salt. (In fact, the word "marinade" is derived from the Latin *marinus*, which means "pertaining to the briny deep.") Most of my marinades are concocted for specific dishes, but here are four versatile versions for use with most any meat, fish, or fowl—and many vegetables, too. Let your taste buds be your guide.

Lime Marinade

1 teaspoon peeled and minced fresh ginger
2 large shallots, minced
4 large cloves garlic, minced
¼ cup fresh lime juice
2 tablespoons dry sherry
1 tablespoon honey
1 tablespoon corn oil
4 dashes ground red (cayenne) pepper
1 teaspoon chili con carne seasoning (no salt or pepper added)
1 teaspoon fennel seed, crushed

1. Combine all ingredients in jar. Shake well to blend.

Yield: About ½ cup (enough to marinate a 3-pound chicken or roast)

CAL	F	P:S	SOD	CAR	CHO	PRO

Per serving when dish serves 4:

61.5	3	4.5:1	9	8	–	–

Ginger Marinade

2 teaspoons ground ginger
6 dashes ground red (cayenne)
  pepper
2 large cloves garlic, minced
1 teaspoon dried rosemary leaves,
  crushed
¼ cup dry vermouth
½ cup Rich Chicken Stock (page 94)
1 tablespoon wine vinegar
1 tablespoon corn oil
1 tablespoon minced fresh parsley

1. Combine all ingredients in jar. Shake well to blend.

Yield: About ¾ cup (enough to marinate a 3-pound chicken or roast)

CAL	F	P:S	SOD	CAR	CHO	PRO
Per serving when dish serves 4:						
42	3	4.5:1	12.5	3	–	0.5

Light Curry Marinade

3 tablespoons each apple cider
  vinegar and wine vinegar
1 tablespoon corn oil
3 large cloves garlic, minced
1 teaspoon ground ginger
¼ teaspoon ground allspice
2 tablespoons curry powder (no salt
  or pepper added)
3 dashes ground red (cayenne)
  pepper
½ teaspoon dried rosemary leaves,
  crushed
¼ teaspoon dried thyme leaves,
  crushed

1. Combine all ingredients in jar. Shake well to blend.

Yield: About ½ cup (enough to marinade a 3-pound chicken or roast)

CAL	F	P:S	SOD	CAR	CHO	PRO
Per serving when dish serves 4:						
33.5	4.5	4.5:1	23.5	1	–	–

Buttermilk Marinade, Indian Style

¾ cup buttermilk (no salt added)
2 tablespoons finely minced celery
2 tablespoons peeled and grated
  carrot
2 tablespoons fresh lime juice
1 tablespoon corn oil
2 large cloves garlic, minced
2 large shallots, minced
1 teaspoon ground coriander or 2
  teaspoons coriander seeds,
  crushed
½ teaspoon each turmeric and
  cuminseed, crushed
¼ cup apple juice (no sugar added)
4 dashes ground red (cayenne)
  pepper

1. Combine all ingredients in jar. Shake well to blend.

Yield: About 1¼ cups (enough to marinate a 3-pound chicken and a 3-pound roast)

CAL	F	P:S	SOD	CAR	CHO	PRO
Per serving when dish serves 4:						
61	3	4.5:1	25	8	–	1.5

Breakfast and Luncheon Dishes, Hors d'oeuvres, and Salads

BREAKFAST DISHES

Breakfast dishes are to my mind the most important dishes of the day. They wake you up, get you into that oh-what-a-beautiful-morning/oh-what-a-beautiful-day mood, and keep your energy high until lunchtime. A good breakfast helps you fight off the temptation to binge at coffee-break time (the danger time for most dieters), and prevents excessive hunger pangs at noon.

I build our breakfasts around some simple carbohydrates (fresh and cooked fruits, unsweetened fruit juices, honey, and sugar-free preserves) to get us up and going; and on complex carbohydrates and proteins (mostly grains) to keep us going and "up" all morning long. An illustration of the former category is my Sweet Stewed Prunes (designed to give you new insight into the taste potential of these wrinkled delights). And in the latter category are my Splendiferous Griddle Cakes and my Stir-and-Bake Buckwheat Muffins (which are equally splendiferous). All three recipes follow.

Sweet Stewed Prunes

1 box (12 ounces) dried pitted prunes (no preservatives added)
1 cup unsweetened pineapple juice
1 thin lemon slice
3 whole cloves
⅛ teaspoon freshly grated or ground nutmeg

1. Place prunes in small heavy-bottomed saucepan. Add balance of ingredients. Bring to boil. Reduce heat, cover, and simmer for 15 minutes.
2. Turn off heat. Uncover. Let prunes cool completely in saucepan. Discard cloves.
3. Serve chilled or at room temperature.

Yield: 7 to 8 servings; allow 4 to 5 prunes per serving

Variations:
1. Pour ¼ cup skim milk over each serving. Sprinkle with 1 teaspoon toasted wheat germ (no sugar added) and serve.
2. Spoon 2 tablespoons evaporated skim milk (¼ percent milkfat) over each serving. Sprinkle with cinnamon and serve.

CAL	F	P:S	SOD	CAR	CHO	PRO
126	2	2:1	4.5	32.5	–	1
Variation 1:						
160	2.5	2.4:1	21	40	–	6
Variation 2:						
134	2	2:1	7	33	–	1.5

Splendiferous Griddle Cakes

¾ cup unbleached flour
3½ teaspoons low-sodium baking powder
½ teaspoon ground cinnamon
⅛ teaspoon each freshly grated or ground nutmeg and ground ginger
1 cup old-fashioned rolled oats
½ cup apple juice (no sugar added)
¾ cup nonfat liquid milk
⅓ cup evaporated skim milk (¼ percent milkfat)
½ egg yolk
1 tablespoon corn oil plus ½ teaspoon for skillet
2 egg whites, stiffly beaten

1. Sift flour, baking powder, and spices into bowl. Set aside.
2. Place oatmeal in large bowl. In saucepan, bring apple juice to boil. Pour over oatmeal, stirring until moistened. (Mixture will be very thick.)
3. Combine milks. Slowly stir into oatmeal mixture.
4. In small bowl, beat ½ egg yolk and 1 tablespoon oil until well blended. Pour into batter. Stir to blend.
5. Add dry ingredients from step 1. Stir until just moistened. No beating is necessary.
6. Fold in egg whites with wooden spoon. Do not overfold.
7. Heat large nonstick skillet until hot enough for a drop of water to bounce off. Brush lightly with oil. Cook 3 griddle cakes at a time. Turn when edges brown and top bubbles. Cook until golden brown and puffed up. Repeat for balance of griddle cakes.
8. Serve with your favorite honey.

Yield: 16 griddle cakes, 3 inches in diameter

Note: For light, fluffy, well-risen pancakes, cook immediately after batter is prepared.

CAL	F	P:S	SOD	CAR	CHO	PRO
Per griddle cake:						
62.5	7	3.9:1	13	17	16	3
Honey, per teaspoon:						
21	–	–	0.5	5	–	–

Stir-and-Bake Buckwheat Muffins

¼ cup raisins
4 dried dates, chopped
⅓ cup apple juice (no sugar added)
1½ cups unbleached flour
3 teaspoons low-sodium baking powder
½ teaspoon each ground ginger and cinnamon
½ cup kasha (whole buckwheat groats)
4½ teaspoons each corn oil and sweet (unsalted) 100 percent corn oil margarine, plus ½ teaspoon margarine for muffin cups
2 tablespoons honey
1 whole egg or ½ small egg yolk plus 2 egg whites
½ cup nonfat liquid milk
¼ cup evaporated skim milk (¼ percent milkfat)
1 teaspoon pure vanilla extract

1. Combine raisins, dates, and apple juice in saucepan. Bring to boil. Turn heat down to simmering. Cover and simmer for 5 minutes. All liquid will be absorbed. Uncover and let cool.
2. Sift flour, baking powder, and spices into bowl. Stir in buckwheat groats.
3. In another bowl, combine oil, margarine, and honey. Beat with fork

until blended. Add egg and beat until light.

4. Combine milks. Add to egg mixture alternately with dry ingredients, stirring with wooden spoon after each addition. Stir in vanilla.

5. Stir in cooled raisin/date mixture.

6. Half-fill margarine-greased 3-inch muffin cups with batter. Bake in preheated 400°F oven for 20 to 22 minutes. Finished muffins should be golden brown.

7. Place pans on rack and let cool for 5 minutes. With blunt knife, loosen around each muffin, then lift muffins out of pans. They'll come out easily. Serve warm.

Yield: 12 muffins

Note: If you prefer larger muffins, fill each cup almost to top for a yield of 9 muffins.

CAL	F	P:S	SOD	CAR	CHO	PRO
Per small muffin (with 1 egg):						
130	4	3.2:1	12	22	21	3.5
Per small muffin (with 1/2 egg yolk and 2 egg whites):						
129	4	3.3:1	15	22	11	3.5
Per large muffin (with 1 egg):						
173.5	5.5	3.2:1	16	28	28	4.5
Per large muffin (with 1/2 egg yolk and 2 egg whites):						
172.5	4	3.3:1	19	28	18	4.5

LUNCHEON DISHES AND HORS D'OEUVRES

Luncheon dishes and hors d'oeuvres in this section are the same dishes, differing only in the quantity served. In ample portions, these light but nutritious creations make satisfying noontime repasts that can keep you at peak energy until the dinner bell sounds. In morsels, these tantalizing delights can stimulate the appetite, as any hors d'oeuvre worthy of the name should do. Of the luncheon/hors d'oeuvres recipes offered here, I'd like to point with special pride to my Party Buckwheat Cakes (Blinis, page 104). They're pancakes with panache.

Crunchy Chicken Tidbits with Pineapple Dip

Everyone will love this parchment-crisp, bronze hors d'oeuvre dipped in pungent fruit sauce. Prepare it hours ahead of the final baking time and spend that much more time with your guests.

For the chicken tidbits:
1 whole chicken breast, boned and skinned (1 pound boned weight), flattened to uniform thickness
1 large clove garlic, minced
½ teaspoon ground ginger
⅛ teaspoon ground cloves
4 dashes ground red (cayenne) pepper
⅓ cup partially thawed frozen orange juice concentrate (no sugar added)
1 teaspoon apple cider vinegar
1 teaspoon finely minced fresh parsley
7 to 8 tablespoons Bread Crumbs (page 85; see also note)
¼ teaspoon corn oil, for baking dish

For the pineapple dip:
½ cup pineapple chunks packed in juice, drained
¼ cup fresh orange juice
½ teaspoon apple cider vinegar
¼ teaspoon dry mustard
¼ teaspoon ground ginger
½ teaspoon flavorful honey
2 dashes ground cloves
3 dashes ground red (cayenne) pepper

1. Prepare chicken tidbits. Rinse chicken and pat dry with paper toweling. Trim away any excess fat. Cut each breast into 6 or more pieces in a neat pattern.

2. Combine garlic, ginger, cloves, ground red pepper, orange juice concentrate, vinegar, and parsley in bowl. Add chicken pieces and turn to coat. Cover and marinate at room temperature for 1 hour.

3. Spread bread crumbs over flat plate. With fork, remove each piece of chicken from marinade and dip into crumbs, turning on all sides to coat. Transfer each piece of coated chicken to lightly oiled baking dish. Cover with plastic wrap and refrigerate for at least 30 minutes.

4. Bake chicken in preheated 425°F oven for 20 minutes, turning once carefully midway with spatula. Crust should be lightly browned.

5. While chicken tidbits are baking, prepare pineapple dip. Combine all ingredients in blender and blend for 30 seconds on low speed. Pour into small decorative serving bowl.

6. Remove chicken from oven. Serve immediately, pierced with colorful cocktail picks and accompanied by pineapple dip.

Yield: Serves 8 (about 3 pieces per serving; about ¾ cup of dip)

Note: The magic ingredient in this recipe is crumbs made from my Aromatic Rye (page 79) or Hearty French Bread (page 77).

CAL	F	P:S	SOD	CAR	CHO	PRO
Per tidbit:						
30	0.5	1.9:1	11	1.5	9.5	4.5
Dip (per teaspoon):						
2	–	–	0.5	–	–	–

Party Buckwheat Cakes (Blinis)

¼ cup apple juice (no sugar added)
½ cup water
1 tablespoon honey
1 tablespoon yeast or 1 premeasured package
½ cup buckwheat flour
1¼ cups unbleached flour
1 tablespoon corn oil plus ½ teaspoon for skillet
½ cup each liquid skim milk and evaporated skim milk (¼ percent milkfat)
¼ teaspoon ground cinnamon
½ teaspoon low-sodium baking powder
1 teaspoon freshly grated orange rind, preferably from navel orange

1. The night before cooking, combine in saucepan apple juice, water, and honey. Heat until warm (105° to 115°F).

2. Place yeast in large bowl. Pour warmed mixture over it. Beat with fork to blend. Stir in flours. Cover tightly with plastic wrap and let stand overnight.

3. Stir mixture down. Add 1 tablespoon oil, milks, cinnamon, baking powder, and orange rind, stirring after each addition.

4. Heat nonstick skillet over medium-high heat. Add a few drops of oil, spreading across skillet with spatula. Cook 3 small blinis at a time, turning to cook both sides uniformly, taking care not to scorch. Serve hot with your favorite honey for breakfast. (For lunch, see variations.)

Yield: About 26 blinis, 3 inches in diameter

Variations:
Prepare all blinis, and keep warm in baking dish in 250°F oven until ready

to serve. Place the following fillings and garnishes on the table in separate plates and bowls. Bring out the hot blinis arranged on a platter (do not stack), and let everyone help himself.

1. An 8-ounce cup of low-fat plain yogurt combined with 1 cup fresh blueberries, 1 tablespoon honey, and several dashes cinnamon. One dollop on a pancake is delicious.

2. Sliced white meat of chicken or turkey, arranged on platter.

3. Exotic Chicken Salad (page 110).

4. 1 cup dry-curd cottage cheese (no salt added; ½ percent milkfat) combined with 2 tablespoons minced scallion or onion, 6 dashes ground red (cayenne) pepper, ½ teaspoon curry powder (no salt or pepper added), 2 tablespoons low-fat plain yogurt, and 1 tablespoon minced fresh parsley.

5. Low-fat plain yogurt.

6. Lemon wedges.

7. Minced fresh parsley.

8. Egg/Cheese Salad (page 110).

9. Elegant Duxelles (page 56).

10. Honey.

11. Jellies made with honey (available in health food stores).

CAL	F	P:S	SOD	CAR	CHO	PRO
Per blini:						
47.5	1	3.9:1	3	8.5	15	1.5
Variation 1 (per tablespoon):						
9	–	–	4.5	2	0.5	0.5
Variation 2 (chicken, per 1-ounce slice):						
46.5	1	0.6:1	17.5	–	22.5	8.5
Variation 2 (turkey, per 1-ounce slice):						
50	1	0.7:1	23.5	–	22.5	9.5
Variation 3: See page 110						
Variation 4 (per tablespoon):						
12.5	–	–	9.5	1	0.5	2
Variation 5 (per tablespoon):						
31	1	0.04:1	31	3	4	2
Variation 6 (per wedge):						
2.5	–	–	0.5	–	–	–
Variation 7: No appreciable difference						
Variation 8: See page 110						
Variation 9: See page 56						
Variation 10 (per teaspoon):						
21	–	–	–	5	–	–
Variation 11 (per teaspoon):						
18	–	–	1	4	–	–

Baked Stuffed Mushrooms

¾ cup water or Rich Chicken Stock (page 94)
2 tablespoons kasha (whole buckwheat groats)
12 large firm mushrooms, washed, dried, and trimmed
2¼ teaspoons each corn oil and Italian olive oil, combined
2 cloves garlic, minced
1 large shallot, minced
1 tablespoon minced sweet red pepper
½ cup minced cooked chicken
4½ teaspoons minced fresh parsley
1 teaspoon tarragon vinegar (page 99) or wine vinegar
8 dashes ground red (cayenne) pepper
½ teaspoon each ground ginger, curry powder (no salt or pepper added), and crushed dried thyme leaves

1. In small saucepan, bring water or stock to rolling boil. Add kasha. Reduce heat to slow boil. Cook, uncovered, until all liquid is absorbed (about 8 minutes). Transfer to bowl and set aside.

2. Gently separate stems from mushroom caps. Mince stems. Set caps aside.

3. Heat 3 teaspoons combined oils in nonstick skillet until hot. Add minced mushroom stems, garlic, shallot, and sweet red pepper. Sauté until wilted.

4. Stir in minced chicken and 2¼ teaspoons parsley. Sprinkle with vinegar and stir. Transfer to bowl containing kasha. Add spices and thyme and blend. Wipe out skillet.

5. Heat balance of oil in skillet. Sauté mushroom caps on both sides for 1½ minutes.

6. Place mushroom caps, hollow

side up, in shallow baking dish. Fill mushroom caps with chicken mixture. Sprinkle with balance of parsley.

7. Bake in preheated 400°F oven for 10 minutes. Serve immediately.

Yield: Serves 4

Note: Stuffed mushroom caps may be prepared for baking (through step 6) ahead of time, covered, and refrigerated. Remove from refrigerator 30 minutes before baking.

CAL	F	P:S	SOD	CAR	CHO	PRO
With water:						
52.5	6	2.5:1	23	5	13.5	5.5
With chicken stock:						
62.5	6	2.5:1	27	6	13.5	8

Mushroom/Egg Spread

1 tablespoon corn oil
¼ pound fresh mushrooms, washed, dried, trimmed, and chopped
1 medium onion, minced
1 large clove garlic, minced
1 teaspoon peeled and minced fresh ginger
1 teaspoon curry powder (no salt or pepper added)
1 hard-boiled egg (use ½ yolk and all of white, and mash)
8 dashes ground red (cayenne) pepper
1 teaspoon fresh lemon juice
1 teaspoon each minced fresh parsley and dill
1 tablespoon Light Chicken Broth (page 95; optional)
2 teaspoons My Mayonnaise-Type Dressing (page 140)

1. Heat oil in skillet until hot. Over medium-high heat, sauté mushrooms, onion, garlic, and ginger until lightly browned. Sprinkle with curry powder and blend. Turn into bowl.

2. Add balance of ingredients in sequence. Mash to fine consistency. Chill.

Yield: See serving suggestions

Variation: Add to basic recipe ¼ cup chopped cooked chicken, 1 additional teaspoon mayonnaise, and 1 additional teaspoon lemon juice. Mash well.

Serving suggestion: To make sandwiches, spread over 4 thin slices of any of my breads (pages 68–85). Cover with watercress and add 4 more slices of bread. To make canapés, spread over 4 slices of any of my breads, cut each slice into quarters, and garnish with pimiento strips.

Yield: 4 sandwiches, 16 canapés

CAL	F	P:S	SOD	CAR	CHO	PRO
Basic recipe (per sandwich):						
141.5	7	3.6:1	61.5	13	31.5	6.5
Basic recipe (per canapé):						
30	1.5	3.6:1	14.5	3	8	1.5
Variation (per sandwich):						
160.5	7.5	2.9:1	78.5	14	36	10
Variation (per canapé):						
31.5	1.5	2.9:1	19.5	3	9	2.5

Basic recipe and variation with chicken broth: No appreciable difference

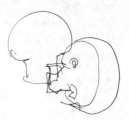

Chicken Spread

If you're thinking about what to do with some of the chicken left over from your stock, here's a recipe that will put your mind at ease—swiftly and deliciously.

⅓ cup Light Chicken Broth (page 95)
1½ teaspoons curry powder (no salt or pepper added)
¾ cup cubed cooked chicken, light and dark meat, at room temperature
2 teaspoons wine vinegar
2 teaspoons corn oil
2 teaspoons grated onion
6 dashes ground red (cayenne) pepper
2 tablespoons minced fresh coriander leaves or dill
  Minced fresh parsley

1. Combine broth and curry powder in saucepan. Heat until warm. Stir to dissolve curry powder.
2. Place chicken in bowl. Pour vinegar over and stir. Add warm broth and mash with fork.
3. Add oil and blend. Add balance of ingredients except parsley. Stir. Chill.

Yield: 16 hors d'oeuvres or 3 sandwiches

Serving suggestions: Spread on 4 thin slices of any of my breads (page 68–85; my rye breads are particularly delicious with this spread). Cut into quarters, sprinkle with parsley, and serve as hors d'oeuvres. Or spread on 3 slices of any of my breads, sprinkle with parsley, top with 3 additional slices of bread, and serve as sandwiches.

CAL	F	P:S	SOD	CAR	CHO	PRO
Per hors d'oeuvre:						
25	1	3:1	7.5	1	5	3
Per sandwich:						
149	5	3:1	39.5	6	26.5	16

Hot Cheese Hors d'Oeuvres

⅔ cup dry-curd cottage cheese (no salt added; ½ percent milkfat)
½ egg yolk
¼ cup tuna packed in water (no salt added), drained
1 teaspoon corn oil plus ¼ teaspoon for cookie sheet
1 tablespoon fresh lemon juice
1 shallot, minced
1 tablespoon minced onion or scallion
1 teaspoon minced fresh parsley
6 dashes ground red (cayenne) pepper
½ teaspoon curry powder (no salt or pepper added)
4½ teaspoons cornstarch

1. In bowl, combine cheese and ½ egg yolk and mash well.
2. In another bowl, combine tuna, 1 teaspoon oil, and lemon juice. Mash.
3. Stir tuna mixture into cheese mixture. Add balance of ingredients. Blend.
4. Drop by spoonfuls onto lightly oiled cookie sheet. Bake in preheated 350°F oven for 12 minutes. With spatula, carefully transfer to serving dish. Let cool for 1 minute. Pierce with cocktail picks and serve.

Yield: 12 hors d'oeuvres (3 per serving)

CAL	F	P:S	SOD	CAR	CHO	PRO
Per hors d'oeuvre:						
22.5	1.5	1.1:1	15	1	1.5	2

Sautéed Cracked-Wheat Patties

Duxelles and a touch of curry put these chewy patties in a taste-category of their own. A welcome change from potatoes, barley, kasha, or rice, they have all the stick-to-the-ribiness of those more familiar complex carbohydrates. Marvelous as a side dish accompanying almost anything, they also make a satisfying main dish at lunchtime.

1 cup cracked-wheat cereal
2 cups water (approximately)
1 tablespoon fresh lemon juice
2 large shallots, minced
2 medium scallions, all of white part, and half green part, minced
1 tablespoon minced fresh parsley
1 egg (use ½ yolk and all of white)
2 tablespoons peeled and finely grated carrot
2 fresh mushrooms, washed, dried, trimmed, and minced, or 2 tablespoons Elegant Duxelles (page 56)
4½ teaspoons Bread Crumbs (page 85)
2 teaspoons toasted wheat germ (no sugar added)
½ teaspoon curry powder (no salt and pepper added)
⅛ teaspoon ground red (cayenne) pepper
6 teaspoons corn oil
Parsley sprigs

1. Place cracked wheat in heavy-bottomed saucepan. Add about 2 cups water. Bring to boil. Reduce heat to slow boil. Cover partially and cook for 20 minutes. Drain, if necessary. Transfer to bowl. Let cool.
2. Add balance of ingredients except oil and parsley sprigs. Stir to blend. Chill until firm enough to shape into patties.

3. Shape into 8 patties. Heat 2 teaspoons oil in nonstick skillet until hot. Sauté 4 patties at a time, using 2 teaspoons oil for each batch and browning well on both sides. As each batch is sautéed, transfer to baking dish and keep warm in 250°F oven.
4. Arrange on serving platter (do not stack). Garnish with parsley.

Yield: Serves 4 as side dish, 2 as luncheon dish

Serving suggestion: Try an exciting contrast in texture. Serve patties with my Apple/Papaya Purée (page 114).

CAL	F	P:S	SOD	CAR	CHO	PRO
As side dish (with fresh mushrooms):						
145	7.5	4.3:1	22	13.5	–	4
As luncheon dish (with fresh mushrooms):						
290	15	4.3:1	44	27	–	8
As side dish (with duxelles):						
155	8.5	4.4:1	22.5	14.5	–	4
As luncheon dish (with duxelles):						
310	17	4.4:1	45	29	–	8

SALADS

Salads originated as greens dressed with salt ("salad" comes from the Latin sal, which means salt). And salt in virtually all salad dressings you can buy in a store or order in a restaurant is one of the hidden hazards of dieting. It makes no sense to restrict yourself to salads because of their low caloric content when their high salt content can fill you out with pounds of excess water weight. In my salads, you won't find a grain of salt. But you will find a bushelful of flavor.

Salads are no longer simple salted herbs and plants. Over the years they've evolved into sophisticated combinations of foods; and in the pages that follow you'll find some of the more complex ones (even though they're based on simple ingredients). Enjoy them as luncheon dishes, as accompaniments, or as hors d'oeuvres.

Red Kidney Bean Salad

1 cup dried red kidney beans
½ cup Smooth Tomato Curry Purée
   (page 97)
1 teaspoon wine vinegar
1 teaspoon fresh lemon juice
3 large scallions, sliced diagonally
   into ½-inch pieces
1 small sweet red pepper, seeded
   and cut into ⅜-inch slivers
1 medium zucchini, well scrubbed
   and cut into ¼-inch cubes
⅛ teaspoon ground red (cayenne)
   pepper
1 tablespoon minced fresh parsley
   Crisp lettuce cups

1. Wash beans. Soak overnight in water to cover. Drain.

2. Place beans in waterless cooker or stainless-steel pot. Add water to cover. Bring to rolling boil. Reduce heat to slow boil. Cover and cook until tender. Drain. Place in bowl. Cover and refrigerate until chilled.

3. Combine Smooth Tomato Curry Purée with vinegar and lemon juice. Pour over beans, stirring to coat.

4. Add scallions, sweet red pepper, and zucchini and stir. Sprinkle with ground red pepper and parsley. Blend. Chill.

5. Arrange lettuce cups on serving plate. Fill with salad.

Yield: Serves 6

CAL	F	P:S	SOD	CAR	CHO	PRO
129	1.5	2:1	7.6	22.5	–	1.5

Green Bean Salad

½ pound tender young green beans
4½ teaspoons each corn oil and
   Italian olive oil, combined
½-inch slice fresh ginger, peeled and
   shredded
1 small onion, thinly sliced,
   separated into rings
2 large cloves garlic, minced
2 shallots, minced
¼ pound fresh mushrooms, washed,
   dried, trimmed, and sliced
1 small sweet red pepper, seeded
   and cut into ⅜-inch slivers
½ teaspoon ground ginger
⅛ teaspoon ground red (cayenne)
   pepper
1 teaspoon wine vinegar
2 tablespoons tarragon vinegar
   (page 99)
1 teaspoon fresh lemon juice
2 tablespoons minced fresh basil
   (see note)

1. Trim ends of green beans. Leave whole. Wash well. Drop into pot of rapidly boiling water and cook until tender. Do not overcook. Pour into colander. Run cold water over beans until they are cool. Drain. Lay on paper toweling and blot until dry. Transfer to bowl.

2. Heat combined oils in nonstick skillet until hot. Add ginger, onion, garlic, shallots, and mushrooms. Sauté over high heat for 2 minutes, stirring constantly.

3. Add sweet red pepper. Sprinkle with spices. Sauté for 1 minute.

4. Add vinegars and lemon juice. Sauté for 30 seconds. Pour over cooked green beans.

5. Sprinkle with basil. Toss. Chill.

Yield: Serves 4

Note: Fresh herbs taste best in this recipe. If fresh basil is not available, substitute fresh dill or tarragon.

CAL	F	P:S	SOD	CAR	CHO	PRO
136.5	10	3:1	14	10	–	2.5

Exotic Chicken Salad

1 small sweet red pepper, seeded and cut into ¼-inch slices
6 large fresh mushrooms, washed, dried, trimmed, and thickly sliced
¼ pound fresh snow peas, washed, stem and string removed, and cut in half (see note 1)
3 cups cold cubed, cooked chicken (1-inch cubes) (see note 2)
1 large rib celery, diced
1 small carrot, peeled and grated
1 small onion, thinly sliced, separated into rings
1 small crisp, sweet apple, such as Washington State, unpeeled, cored and diced
2 tablespoons fresh lemon juice
1 tablespoon wine vinegar
1 tablespoon corn oil
2 large shallots, minced
6 dashes ground red (cayenne) pepper
2 teaspoons curry powder (no salt or pepper added)
½ cup thick buttermilk (no salt added)
2 tablespoons minced fresh parsley

1. Blanch sweet red pepper, mushrooms, and snow peas by dropping into rapidly boiling water, cooking for 30 seconds, and immediately draining in strainer. Set strainer under cold running water to cool vegetables completely. Drain on paper toweling and pat dry.
2. Place chicken in bowl. Add celery, carrot, onion, and apple. Toss gently.
3. Combine lemon juice, vinegar, oil, shallots, ground red pepper, and curry powder in cup. Beat with fork. Pour over salad.
4. Pour buttermilk over salad. Toss.

5. Turn onto serving dish. Sprinkle with parsley and serve.

Yield: Serves 6

Notes:
1. If fresh snow peas are not available, substitute green beans. (I shun frozen snow peas because salt is ordinarily added.) French-cut and cook green beans separately in rapidly boiling water for 7 minutes. Follow balance of instructions in step 1.
2. One convenient source of cooked chicken is the set-aside chicken from my recipe for Light Chicken Broth (page 95). Make the broth and get this mouth-watering chicken salad as a bonus.

CAL	F	P:S	SOD	CAR	CHO	PRO
188	6	2.2:1	83	10.5	53.5	23

Egg/Cheese Salad

4 large hard-boiled eggs
2 tablespoons dry-curd cottage cheese (no salt added, ½ percent milkfat)
5 teaspoons corn oil
1 teaspoon each wine vinegar and apple cider vinegar
1 large shallot, finely minced
1 teaspoon minced fresh tarragon leaves, or ½ teaspoon crushed dried tarragon leaves
2 tablespoons finely minced celery
½ teaspoon curry powder (no salt or pepper added)
8 dashes ground red (cayenne) pepper
1 tablespoon combined minced fresh parsley and dill

½ teaspoon tomato paste (no salt
  added)
Crisp lettuce leaves
Watercress and cherry tomatoes,
  or fresh fruit, for garnish

1. Cut eggs in half. Discard all egg yolks, except half of one. Mash whites and ½ yolk with fork.
2. Add cottage cheese, corn oil, and vinegars. Mash.
3. Add balance of ingredients, stirring to blend.
4. Serve on crisp lettuce leaves with garnish.

Yield: Serves 3

Variations:
1. Omitting lettuce and garnish, serve as a spread on 4 slices of any of my breads (pages 68–85). Cut each slice into quarters. Sprinkle with sesame or poppy seeds, plus a small amount of freshly grated orange rind.

Yield: 16 small canapés

2. Serve as a dip. Combine all ingredients except lettuce and garnish in food processor, with 1 tablespoon low-fat plain yogurt. Purée until smooth. Serve well chilled.

Yield: About 1 cup dip; allow 2 teaspoons per dip

CAL	F	P:S	SOD	CAR	CHO	PRO
127	8	4.4:1	110	3.5	–	7.6
Variation 1 (per canapé):						
29.5	1.5	4.4:1	21	2	–	2
Variation 2 (per dip):						
17	1	4.4:1	15	0.5	–	1

Colorful Onion and Pepper Salad

¼ cup each apple cider vinegar,
  wine vinegar, and apple juice (no
  sugar added)
1 tablespoon fresh lemon juice
2 large shallots, minced
4 dashes ground cloves
⅛ teaspoon ground red (cayenne)
  pepper
1 tablespoon each minced fresh dill
  and parsley
¼ teaspoon each dried rosemary
  and thyme leaves, crushed
1 tablespoon corn oil
1 sweet Spanish onion (about ¾
  pound), sliced ¼-inch thick
1 each sweet red pepper and green
  pepper, seeded and cut into ⅜-
  inch slivers

1. Combine first 8 ingredients in medium bowl, stirring to blend.
2. Add onion and peppers. Stir and turn until well coated. Let stand at room temperature for 1 hour, stirring and turning often, until vegetables give up some of their juices.
3. Salad may be eaten within 1 hour, or stored in glass jar and refrigerated. Turn jar upside down from time to time to distribute juices.

Yield: Serves 4

Note: Salad tastes best on first and second days.

CAL	F	P:S	SOD	CAR	CHO	PRO
97	3.5	4.5:1	27.5	16.5	–	1

Apple Mold with Yogurt Dressing

For the mold(s):
- 2 tablespoons each fresh lime juice and water
- 1 envelope plus 1 teaspoon unflavored gelatin
- 1½ cups apple juice (no sugar added)
- ½ cup unsweetened pineapple juice
- 1 tablespoon honey
- 4 dashes ground cloves
- ¼ teaspoon each ground cinnamon and ginger
- 1 teaspoon freshly grated orange rind, preferably from navel orange
- 1 small sweet green pepper, seeded and cut into ¼-inch slices, then cut into ½-inch pieces
- 1 cup peeled and cubed sweet, crisp apple, such as Washington State (¼-inch cubes)
- ½ cup pineapple tidbits packed in juice, drained
- 1 small rib celery, cut into ¼-inch cubes
- Lettuce leaves
- Crisp watercress sprigs

For the yogurt dressing:
- ⅓ cup low-fat plain yogurt
- ⅓ cup combined apple juice (no sugar added) and unsweetened pineapple juice
- ½ teaspoon fresh lemon juice
- 3 dashes ground cloves
- ½ teaspoon ground cinnamon
- ½ teaspoon freshly grated orange rind, preferably from navel orange

1. Prepare molds. Pour lime juice and water into bowl. Sprinkle in gelatin and let soften for 3 minutes.

2. In saucepan, heat apple and pineapple juice until hot. Stir in honey, spices, and orange rind. Pour over gelatin mixture, stirring until gelatin is dissolved. Chill until liquid thickens to a syrupy consistency. Stir to blend spices.

3. Chill again until mixture begins to thicken. Fold in balance of mold ingredients except for lettuce and watercress.

4. Pour into 4 decorative 1-cup molds (or into a 1-quart mold). Chill until set.

5. While salad is setting, combine all dressing ingredients in small bowl. Stir to blend. Pour into sauceboat.

6. Dip set mold(s) briefly into hot water. Unmold onto crisp lettuce leaves. Garnish with watercress sprigs and serve with dressing.

Yield: Serves 4; yogurt dressing makes about ¾ cup (2 tablespoons per serving)

CAL	F	P:S	SOD	CAR	CHO	PRO
Mold:						
137.5	–	–	29.5	29	–	3.5
Dressing:						
21	0.5	0.7:1	12	4	1.5	1

Eggplant Salad

- 1 tablespoon each Italian olive oil and corn oil, combined
- 1 medium eggplant, peeled and cut into ½-inch cubes (3 cups)
- 6 dashes ground red (cayenne) pepper
- 2 large cloves garlic, minced
- 1 large shallot, minced
- 1 medium onion, minced
- 2 tablespoons minced sweet red pepper
- 3 large fresh mushrooms, washed, dried, trimmed, and coarsely chopped
- 2 teaspoons wine vinegar
- ½ teaspoon each dried thyme and tarragon leaves, crushed

1 teaspoon chili con carne
  seasoning (no salt or pepper
  added)
1 tablespoon peeled and grated
  carrot
½ crisp, sweet apple, such as
  Washington State, peeled, cored,
  and coarsely chopped
1 tablespoon minced fresh parsley
  Crisp lettuce leaves

1. Heat 1 tablespoon combined oils in nonstick skillet until hot. Add eggplant. Sprinkle with ground red pepper. Sauté over medium-high heat for 4 minutes, turning continuously. Transfer to bowl.

2. Heat balance of oil in skillet until hot. Add garlic, shallot, onion, and sweet red pepper. Sauté for 3 minutes, turning continuously.

3. Add mushrooms, stirring to mix. Sauté for 1 minute. Add vinegar. Stir.

4. Pour contents of skillet into bowl with eggplant. Sprinkle with herbs and chili con carne seasoning. Stir to blend.

5. Add carrot, apple, and parsley. Stir gently until evenly distributed.

6. Serve on a bed of crisp lettuce, at room temperature or chilled.

Yield: Serves 6 as appetizer, 4 as main course

Serving suggestion: As a relish, turn into decorative bowl and serve along with any main course.

CAL	F	P:S	SOD	CAR	CHO	PRO
Main course:						
92.5	7	2.8:1	18	13	–	2
Appetizer:						
62	4.5	2.8:1	12	9	–	1

Desserts

Frozen Pineapple Cream

This exquisite dessert, which outshines ice cream, will keep in your freezer for 2 days. Transfer it to your refrigerator 2 hours before serving. If it's still firm, let it stand at room temperature until softened. It's then that you can savor its rich flavor.

1 can (20 ounces) pineapple chunks
  packed in unsweetened pineapple
  juice, including all but ¼ cup juice
  from can
2 teaspoons fresh lemon juice
¾ cup evaporated skim milk (¼
  percent milkfat)
4 dashes ground ginger
1 teaspoon sweet sherry

1. Combine all ingredients in blender. Blend on high speed for 1 minute.

2. Turn into freezer tray that has been rinsed in cold water. Place tray directly onto metal in freezer and freeze until almost firm (about 2 hours).

3. Beat with electric mixer in tray until light. Or turn into food processor and process on/off 3 times with metal blade. Pour back into freezer tray. Return tray to freezer. This time, do not place tray in direct contact with metal. Freeze for 1½ hours. Finished dessert should be creamy and semisoft.

Yield: Serves 6

Variation: Omit sherry from basic recipe. Spoon into dessert dishes and pour over dessert 1 tablespoon per serving of liqueur such as kirsch, Grand Marnier, or Cognac.

CAL	F	P:S	SOD	CAR	CHO	PRO
59	–	–	9	13	–	2

With liqueur topping instead of sherry: No appreciable difference

CAL	F	P:S	SOD	CAR	CHO	PRO
84.5	2.4	2:1	6	21.5	–	0.5

Apple/Papaya Purée

This musky, sweet-tart delight may be a health-conscious sweet-lover's dream come true. Vitamin C-packed papaya contains the digestive enzyme papain. And everybody knows an apple a day keeps the doctor away. Wonderful as a high-energy breakfast dish, too.

2 large crisp, sweet apples, such as Washington State, unpeeled, cored and thickly sliced
5 whole cloves
¼ teaspoon ground ginger
½ teaspoon ground cinnamon
1 teaspoon fresh lime juice
½ cup apple juice (no sugar added)
1 fresh ripe papaya, peeled and cut into 1-inch cubes (about 2 cups)
⅛ teaspoon ground allspice

1. Combine first 6 ingredients in heavy-bottomed saucepan. Bring to boil. Reduce heat to simmering and simmer, covered, for 5 minutes.
2. Add papaya. Bring to simmering point, re-cover, and simmer for 3 minutes. Uncover. Push fruit into liquid. Let cool in pot.
3. Pour into food mill and purée. Sprinkle with allspice and stir to blend. Serve warm or chilled.

Yield: Serves 4

Magic Apple/Papaya Cake

Why is it magic? Because—abracadabra!—and small-town applesauce cake turns into a Big Apple of a cake.

¾ cup apple juice (no sugar added)
¾ cup raisins
1 tablespoon Cognac
1 tablespoon honey (optional)
2 eggs (use ½ yolk and 2 whites)
2 tablespoons corn oil
2 tablespoons evaporated skim milk (¼ percent milkfat)
1 teaspoon pure vanilla extract
1 cup Apple/Papaya Purée (page 114)
1½ cups unbleached flour
2 teaspoons low-sodium baking powder (available in health food stores)
1 teaspoon ground cinnamon
⅛ teaspoon ground cloves
¼ teaspoon ground allspice
¼ teaspoon cream of tartar
½ teaspoon sweet (unsalted) 100 percent corn oil margarine, for pan and waxed paper

1. Combine apple juice, raisins, Cognac, and honey in saucepan. Bring to simmering point. Simmer, uncovered, for 10 minutes. Let cool in saucepan.
2. Combine egg yolk, oil, milk, and vanilla in bowl. Beat with whisk until light and well blended.
3. Pour in cooled raisin mixture. Stir in Apple/Papaya Purée.
4. Sift flour, baking powder, and spices into a bowl. Stir into batter, ¼

cup at a time, blending after each addition.

5. Beat egg whites with cream of tartar until stiff but not dry. Fold into batter. Do not overfold.

6. Lightly grease a 9- x 6- x 2½-inch loaf pan with margarine. Cut out a sheet of waxed paper to fit bottom of pan. Place on top of greased surface. Grease waxed paper lightly with margarine. Pour batter into pan.

7. Bake in preheated 325°F oven for 1 hour 10 minutes. Test for doneness: a toothpick inserted through center of cake should come out clean. Let pan cool on rack for 5 minutes. With blunt knife, loosen cake around sides and invert pan. Lift off pan and pull off waxed paper. Place cake right side up on rack. Let cool completely before slicing.

Yield: 10 slices

Note: Expect cake to shrink uniformly while cooling.

CAL	F	P:S	SOD	CAR	CHO	PRO
Per slice (without honey):						
150	4	4:1	17	28	13	5.5
With honey:						
156.5	4.5	4:1	17	32	13	5.5

Spiced Poached Pears

I have a confession to make: I have had a lifelong love affair with pears. They make so many kinds of exquisite desserts that I could write a whole cookbook about them. Here are simple—as in simply delicious—Spiced Poached Pears, which form the basis for the two imaginative recipes that follow: light-as-air Pear Fluff, and my Spiced Pear Ice, which is as refreshing as it is unusual. After that, enjoy my version of the classic French Poached Pears in Red Wine and the traditional Viennese Pear Cake. By and large, I prefer the d'Anjou pear because of its winy flavor; but the Bartlett is a close runner-up.

2 tablespoons fresh lemon juice
4 almost ripe d'Anjou pears, peeled, cut in half, and cored
¾ cup apple juice (no sugar added)
¼ cup unsweetened pineapple juice
½ teaspoon each ground ginger and cinnamon
2 whole cloves
1 tablespoon honey

1. Pour lemon juice into narrow waterless cooker or stainless-steel pot. As each pear is peeled, drop into lemon juice, turning to coat. (This will keep fruit from turning brown.)

2. Add balance of ingredients. Bring to simmering point. Cover and simmer for 10 minutes. With slotted spoon, transfer pears to bowl.

3. Turn heat up under pot to slow boil and reduce liquid to ½ cup. Discard cloves. Pour liquid over pears. Serve warm.

Yield: Serves 4

CAL	F	P:S	SOD	CAR	CHO	PRO
167.5	1	2:1	8	38	–	2

Pear Fluff

1 recipe Spiced Poached Pears
  (page 115), chilled
3 egg whites, stiffly beaten

1. Dice cooked pears. Pour with cooking liquid into blender. Purée until smooth. Pour into bowl.
2. Whisk one-third of egg whites into purée; fold in balance.
3. Spoon into 6 dessert dishes. Serve immediately.

Yield: Serves 6

CAL	F	P:S	SOD	CAR	CHO	PRO
119	5.5	2:1	26	26	–	1.5

Spiced Pear Ice

1 recipe Spiced Poached Pears
  (page 115), cooled
1 tablespoon kirsch liqueur
3 stiffly beaten egg whites

1. Dice cooked pears. Pour with poaching liquid and liqueur into blender (see note). Purée until smooth.
2. Pour purée into bowl. Whisk one-third of egg whites into purée. Fold in balance.
3. Turn into freezer tray that has been rinsed in cold water. Cover and place tray directly onto metal in freezer. Freeze for 1 hour. At this point, top has started to solidify and bottom has become slightly watery. Spoon liquid over solids. Stir to blend. Return to freezer.
4. Repeat freezing, stirring, and folding process twice more. Then beat with wire whisk or electric mixer in tray until smooth and light.
5. Return tray to freezer, but not in direct contact with metal. Ice will be fully ripened in about 4½ hours from starting time. Remove from freezer for 10 minutes if you prefer a softer consistency.
6. Spoon into 6 parfait or dessert dishes and serve.

Yield: Serves 6

Note: For a coarser-textured ice, purée pears in food mill instead of blender.

Serving suggestion:
  Serve with Strawberry Topping: ½ cup fresh sliced strawberries, ½ teaspoon fresh lemon juice, 2 tablespoons apple juice (no sugar added), and 1 teaspoon honey. Combine in small saucepan. Bring to boil. Reduce heat to simmering and simmer, covered, for 3 minutes. Cool. Pour into jar and chill. Serve in sauceboat along with ice.
Yield: About 1 cup

CAL	F	P:S	SOD	CAR	CHO	PRO
Ice:						
120.5	0.5	2:1	26	26	–	1
Topping:						
9	–	–	0.5	4	–	–

Poached Pears in Red Wine

4 medium, almost ripe d'Anjou
  pears
2 tablespoons fresh lemon juice
1 cup red wine
1 cup apple juice (no sugar added)
1 teaspoon ground cinnamon or ½
  teaspoon ground cinnamon plus 1
  small cinnamon stick
1 tablespoon honey

1. Pour lemon juice into small bowl. Peel pears, leaving stem on. Drop each pear into bowl as it is peeled, turning to coat. (This will keep fruit from turning brown.)

2. Combine balance of ingredients in narrow heavy-bottomed saucepan or waterless cooker. Bring to boil. Arrange pears in pot in standing position. Spoon with juices. Cover and simmer until tender (about 20 minutes, depending on size and ripeness of pears).

3. Transfer pears to bowl. Reduce cooking liquid by ⅓. Pour over pears.

4. Refrigerate and serve cold, with cooking juices poured over each portion.

Yield: Serves 4

Serving suggestion:
Serve with Pineapple Topping. Combine in blender 1 cup drained pineapple chunks packed in their own juice, ¼ cup evaporated skim milk (¼ percent milkfat), 2 tablespoons poaching liquid from pears, 4 dashes freshly grated nutmeg, and ¼ teaspoon pure vanilla extract. Purée for 1 minute. Serve to taste (watch the calories) over drained pears in individual dessert dishes. Yield: About 1 cup

CAL	F	P:S	SOD	CAR	CHO	PRO
Pears:						
194.5	1	2:1	18	50	–	1.5
Topping (per tablespoon):						
18.5	–	–	1	3.5	–	1

Viennese Pear Cake

For the cake:
1 *large egg (use ½ yolk and all of white)*
4½ *teaspoons corn oil*
1 *tablespoon honey*
4¾ *teaspoons sweet (unsalted) 100 percent corn oil margarine*
3 *tablespoons dry-curd cottage cheese (no salt added; ½ percent milkfat)*
3 *tablespoons unsweetened pineapple juice*
1 *teaspoon pure vanilla extract*
2 *ripe, firm Bartlett pears, unpeeled, washed, cored, and coarsely chopped*
½ *teaspoon cardamom seeds, crushed*
1½ *cups unbleached flour*
3 *teaspoons low-sodium baking powder (available in health food stores)*
⅓ *cup thick buttermilk (no salt added), at room temperature*

For the streusel:
2 *tablespoons unbleached flour*
1 *tablespoon date powder (also called date sugar) (available in health food stores)*
¼ *teaspoon ground ginger*
½ *teaspoon ground cinnamon*
1 *tablespoon coarsely chopped walnuts*
1½ *teaspoons sweet (unsalted) 100 percent corn oil margarine*

1. To prepare cake, combine egg, oil, honey, and 4½ teaspoons margarine in mixing bowl. Beat vigorously with wire whisk. Add cottage cheese and beat until well blended.

2. Stir in pineapple juice, vanilla, pears, and cardamom seeds.

3. Sift flour and baking powder into another bowl. Add flour mixture and milk to batter in small amounts al-

ternately, stirring with wooden spoon after each addition.

4. Grease a 9-inch square baking pan with remaining ¼ teaspoon margarine. Spoon batter into pan, spreading evenly.

5. To prepare streusel, combine flour, date powder, ginger, cinnamon, and nuts in bowl. Stir to blend. Add margarine and blend into dry ingredients with fork. Then use fingers to make a fine mixture. Sprinkle evenly over cake.

6. Bake in preheated 375°F oven for 45 to 50 minutes. When done, toothpick inserted in center of cake should emerge clean.

7. Let pan cool for 10 minutes on rack. Cut into 12 squares. Serve warm.

Yield: 12 squares

CAL	F	P:S	SOD	CAR	CHO	PRO
Per square:						
81	3.5	3.6:1	10	11.5	10.5	2.5

Pineapple-Prune Mousse

Prepare this delightful fluff of a dessert when you have my Stewed Sweet Prunes in your refrigerator. Combine with pineapple and stiffly beaten egg whites, and you'll get a new sensation with the traditional mousse texture. Tastes as rich as it is frothy.

1 recipe Stewed Sweet Prunes (page 101)
1 tablespoon fresh lemon juice
¼ teaspoon ground cinnamon
8 dashes ground ginger
⅓ cup unsweetened pineapple juice
1 envelope plain gelatin
¾ cup pineapple chunks packed in their own juice, drained

¼ cup evaporated skim milk (¼ percent milkfat)
1 teaspoon freshly grated orange rind, preferably from navel orange
2 large egg whites, stiffly beaten

1. Purée prunes in food mill (do not use blender). Measure out ½ cup purée (refrigerate remainder for a delightful breakfast treat). Turn into bowl. Add lemon juice, cinnamon, and ginger. Stir to blend.

2. Pour pineapple juice into saucepan. Sprinkle gelatin over juice, and let soften for 5 minutes. Heat and stir until gelatin is dissolved. Pour into prune mixture. Stir.

3. Combine pineapple chunks and evaporated milk in blender. Blend at high speed for 30 seconds. Pour into prune-gelatin mixture. Add orange rind. Stir well to blend. Refrigerate until mixture begins to thicken (30 minutes).

4. Fold in beaten egg whites.

5. Rinse a decorative quart mold in cold water. Spoon mixture into mold. Refrigerate until firm.

6. Unmold by dipping mold briefly into hot water. Invert onto serving plate. Serve.

Yield: Serves 4

Variation: Add 2 teaspoons Grand Marnier at the end of step 3.

CAL	F	P:S	SOD	CAR	CHO	PRO
56.5	–	–	28	9.5	1	5

With Grand Marnier: No appreciable difference

Orange Chiffon Cake with Iced Fruit Topping

Let's play a game. Answer yes or no to the following questions. Do you like honey-sweetened baked dough? Do you like the taste of almonds and vanilla? Do you like the flavor of orange rind? Do you like the smoothness of cheese and the tartness of yogurt? If you answered all questions yes—and the chances are you did—you'll love this cake.

For the cake:

1 egg yolk
2 tablespoons corn oil
½ cup fresh orange juice
2 teaspoons freshly grated orange rind, preferably from navel orange
3 tablespoons flavorful honey
1½ teaspoons pure vanilla extract
½ teaspoon almond extract
1¼ cups unbleached flour
2½ teaspoons low-sodium baking powder (available in health food stores)
4 egg whites, stiffly beaten with ¾ teaspoon cream of tartar

For the topping:

¾ cup pineapple chunks packed in unsweetened pineapple juice, drained
5 tablespoons dry-curd cottage cheese (no salt added; ½ percent milkfat)
1 teaspoon freshly grated orange rind, preferably from navel orange
2 tablespoons honey
¼ cup low-fat plain yogurt
1½ teaspoons pure vanilla extract

1. Prepare the cake first. In large bowl, combine egg yolk, oil, orange juice, orange rind, and honey. Using whisk, blend well. Add extracts, and blend again.

2. Sift flour three times into another bowl. Remeasure 1¼ cups. Sift again with baking powder. Add to egg yolk mixture in first bowl, beating with wooden spoon.

3. Carefully fold in egg whites. Do not overfold. Turn into ungreased 9-inch tube pan.

4. Bake in preheated 325°F oven for 50 minutes, or until toothpick inserted into cake comes out dry. Invert pan and let cool on rack. With spatula, loosen cake from sides and tube, then from bottom of pan. Place cake on rack.

5. To prepare the topping, place all topping ingredients in blender and purée for 30 seconds. Pour into freezer tray. Cover and freeze for 1 hour. Beat with whisk or electric mixer until smooth. Return, covered, to freezer for 1 hour. The topping is ready when it reaches a puddinglike consistency. Spoon over cake and serve.

Yield: Serves 8

Variation for the cake: Pineapple juice, no sugar added, may be substituted for orange juice, with the following changes:

1. Reduce honey to 2 tablespoons
2. Use 1 teaspoon grated orange rind instead of 2, and add ½ teaspoon freshly grated lemon rind

CAL	F	P:S	SOD	CAR	CHO	PRO
Cake:						
139.5	4.5	3.9:1	23	22	15.5	5
Topping:						
37.5	–	–	12.5	7.5	–	–
Variation:						
131.5	4.5	3.9:1	12.5	20	15.5	5

Sweet Buns

For breakfast or dessert. Charming.

For the buns:
2¼ to 2½ cups unbleached flour
  ¾ cup whole-wheat flour
  ¾ teaspoon low-sodium baking
      powder (available in health food
      stores)
  ½ teaspoon ground cinnamon
  ½ teaspoon aniseed, crushed
  1 tablespoon dry yeast or 1
      premeasured package
  ½ cup each apple juice (no sugar
      added) and evaporated skim milk
      (¼ percent milkfat)
  1 tablespoon honey
  3 tablespoons corn oil plus ¼
      teaspoon for bowl
  2 teaspoons freshly grated orange
      rind, preferably from navel orange
  1 whole egg or ½ egg yolk plus 2 egg
      whites
  ½ cup raisins
  ¼ teaspoon each almond extract
      and pure vanilla extract
  ½ teaspoon sweet (unsalted) 100
      percent corn oil margarine, for
      cookie sheets

For the milk wash and topping:
  1 tablespoon each evaporated skim
      milk (¼ percent milkfat) and
      honey, combined
  ¼ cup chopped walnuts
  2 tablespoons date powder (also
      called date sugar) (available in
      health food stores)

1. In bowl, combine flours, baking powder, cinnamon, and aniseed.

2. In large bowl, combine 1 cup of flour mixture with yeast. Heat apple juice, milk, honey, oil, and orange rind in saucepan until warm (110° to 115°F). Pour over yeast mixture and beat with wooden spoon for 30 seconds. Cover with plastic wrap, and let stand for 10 minutes.

3. Stir mixture down. Add egg. Beat until smooth. Stir in raisins and extracts.

4. Add all but ¼ cup of balance of flour mixture, ½ cup at a time, beating well with wooden spoon after each addition. When dough becomes too difficult to handle with spoon, turn onto lightly floured board and knead (or knead with doughhook; see note 1, page 71), using balance of flour, if necessary, to make a smooth and elastic dough.

5. Shape dough into ball. Drop into lightly oiled, fairly straight-sided bowl, turning to coat. Cover with plastic wrap and let rise at room temperature (70° to 80°F) until doubled in bulk (1 hour).

6. Punch dough down. Remove to board and knead briefly, squeezing out bubbles. Cover with plastic wrap and let rest for 5 minutes.

7. Roll out into an 8- x 12-inch rectangle. Cut lengthwise into 16½-inch strips. Roll each strip between palms of hands into a smooth cylinder. Roll each cylinder into a spiral, pinching ends to hold. Place on margarine-greased cookie sheets. Cover with plastic wrap and let rise until double in bulk (about 1 hour).

8. Brush top and sides of buns with milk-honey mixture, taking care that liquid doesn't drip onto cookie sheet. Sprinkle with combined nuts and date powder.

9. Bake in center section of preheated 350°F oven for 20 to 22 minutes. (If your oven is small, you may have to bake the buns in 2 batches.) Buns should be browned and sound hollow when tapped on bottom with knuckles.

10. Transfer to rack and let cool.

Yield: 16 buns

Note: These buns freeze very well. To reheat, wrap in aluminum foil and bake in 350°F oven for 12 minutes; then open aluminum foil and bake for an additional 3 minutes.

CAL	F	P:S	SOD	CAR	CHO	PRO

Per bun (with whole egg):

140	3.5	3.7:1	8.5	24.5	16	4.5

With ½ egg yolk and 2 egg whites:

131.5	2.5	3.8:1	11	24.5	8	4.5

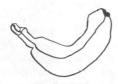

Teatime Bread

In the English countryside, teatime is a genteel ritual of buttered bread, cakes, scones, tiny sandwiches, and cups and cups of sweet tea. Dinner, which follows several hours later, is perforce a light meal, not to be regarded seriously. But in this country, where dinner is the climactic gastronomic event of the day, the sweet accompanying afternoon coffee break must not be destructive to the appetite. This teatime bread, as satisfying a snack as you can wish for, is not.

1 cup unbleached flour
½ cup whole-wheat flour
1 tablespoon low-sodium baking powder (available in health food stores)
2 tablespoons date powder (also called date sugar) (available in health food stores)
½ cup old-fashioned rolled oats
1 teaspoon ground cinnamon
1 teaspoon ground ginger
4½ teaspoons corn oil, at room temperature

4½ teaspoons sweet (unsalted) 100 percent corn oil margarine plus ¼ teaspoon for pan, at room temperature
2 tablespoons honey
1 whole egg or ½ yolk and 2 whites
½ cup evaporated skim milk (¼ percent milkfat)
¼ cup apple juice (no sugar added)
¼ cup raisins (optional)
1 teaspoon freshly grated orange rind, preferably from navel orange
1 teaspoon pure vanilla extract

1. Sift flours together with baking powder into bowl. Add date powder, rolled oats, cinnamon, and ginger. Stir to blend.
2. Combine oil, 4½ teaspoons margarine, and honey in mixing bowl. Beat with wire whisk or electric mixer until blended. Add egg. Beat until blended.
3. Combine milk with apple juice. Add alternately with flour to egg mixture, beating with wooden spoon or electric mixer only until flour is absorbed. Do not overbeat.
4. Stir in raisins, orange rind, and vanilla.
5. Lightly grease small (7⅜- x 3⅝- x 2¼-inch) loaf pan with ¼ teaspoon margarine. Pour mixture into pan. Bake in preheated 350°F oven for 50 minutes. Test for doneness: toothpick inserted in center should come out clean.
6. Remove from oven. Place pan on rack. Let cool for 5 minutes. With blunt knife, loosen cake around sides of pan. Invert onto rack and let cool for 15 minutes. Slice, and serve slightly warm.

Yield: 1 loaf, 14 slices (about ½-inch each)

Variation: For a special treat, spoon each slice with 1 tablespoon Cognac.

Note: This cake freezes very well. I slice it, wrap each slice in waxed paper, insert the slices in a paper bag, place the paper bag in a plastic bag, seal tightly, and slip into the freezer.

CAL	F	P:S	SOD	CAR	CHO	PRO
Per slice (with whole egg, without raisins):						
127.5	3.5	3.4:1	10	21	18.5	2
With ½ egg yolk, 2 egg whites:						
126.5	3.5	3.5:1	13	21	9.5	4
With raisins:						
136	3.5	3.4:1	11	27.5	28.5	4

Sweet and Tart Loaves

Ever feel the compelling urge for a sweet that's different? Here it is. It's a bread—redolent with cinnamon and anise, fruity and crunchy, and completely irresistible.

2   tablespoons dry yeast or 2 premeasured packages
½   cup nonfat dry milk
2   teaspoons aniseed, crushed
2   cups whole-wheat flour
4 to 4½   cups unbleached flour
¾   cup each apple juice (no sugar added) and water
4½   teaspoons corn oil, plus ½ teaspoon for pan and bowl
1   tablespoon honey (optional)
1½   teaspoons ground cinnamon
1   teaspoon freshly grated orange rind, preferably from navel orange
1   cup Half-and-Half Starter (page 70)
1   tablespoon white cornmeal

1. In large mixing bowl, combine yeast, milk, aniseed, all of whole-wheat flour, and 1 cup unbleached flour.

2. In saucepan, combine apple juice, water, 4½ teaspoons oil, honey, cinnamon, and orange rind. Heat until warm (105° to 115°F). Pour over dry ingredients and beat for 1 minute with wooden spoon.

3. Add starter. Beat on medium speed of electric mixer for 1 minute (or with wooden spoon for 2 minutes).

4. Add all but ½ cup of balance of flour, ½ cup at a time, beating with wooden spoon after each addition. When dough becomes too difficult to handle with spoon, turn onto lightly floured board and knead, using balance of flour if necessary, to make a smooth and elastic dough. (You'll find it a pleasure to handle. When fully kneaded, its texture is satin-smooth.)

5. Drop into fairly straight-sided bowl, oiled with ¼ teaspoon oil, turning to coat. Cover with plastic wrap. Let rise at room temperature (70° to 80°F) until doubled in bulk. Dough will rise rapidly within first 45 minutes, and less rapidly thereafter, doubling in bulk in about 1 hour 15 minutes.

6. Punch dough down. Transfer to board. If dough is sticky, sprinkle with 1 tablespoon flour and knead briefly. Cut into 2 equal parts. Shape into 2 smooth 10-inch-long loaves. Place on 11½- x 15½- x 1-inch jelly-roll pan that has been oiled with 1/4 teaspoon oil and sprinkled with cornmeal. Sprinkle loaves ever so lightly with unbleached flour (about 1 teaspoon), smoothing out on top with hands. Cover loosely with waxed paper and let rise until doubled in bulk (45 to 60 minutes).

7. Bake in center section of preheated 400°F oven for 15 minutes. Reduce heat to 375°F and continue baking for 30 minutes. Bread is done when you hear a hollow sound on tapping bottom with knuckles.

8. Remove from oven and let cool on rack before slicing.

Yield: 2 loaves, 25 slices (⅜-inch each) per loaf

CAL	F	P:S	SOD	CAR	CHO	PRO
Per slice:						
63.5	1	2.6:1	6.5	12	–	2.5
With honey: No appreciable difference						

Grand Finale

Simple, basic ingredients combine to make a spectacular no-bake-crust strawberry confection that deserves to be the grand finale of any meal. Enjoy this luscious sweet—guilt-free!

For the crust:
3½ shredded-wheat biscuits
 1 tablespoon date powder (also called date sugar) (available in health food stores)
⅓ cup toasted wheat germ (no sugar added)
¼ teaspoon each ground nutmeg and ground cinnamon
¼ cup old-fashioned rolled oats
¼ cup corn oil

For the filling:
 1 cup evaporated skim milk (¼ percent milkfat)
 3 cups sliced fresh strawberries
½ cup each apple juice (no sugar added) and unsweetened pineapple juice
 2 teaspoons fresh lemon juice
 2 tablespoons honey
 2 envelopes unflavored gelatin
 2 egg whites, stiffly beaten

1. Prepare pie crust first. Break up biscuits and place in blender or food processor fitted with metal blade. Blend to fine consistency.
2. Pour into bowl. Add date powder, wheat germ, and oatmeal. Stir to blend.
3. Dribble oil into dry mixture. Blend with fingers, then turn into 10-inch metal pie pan. Press to bottom and sides of pan. Refrigerate for 1 hour before filling.
4. Now prepare the filling. Combine milk and 2 cups sliced strawberries in blender or processor. Blend until smooth. Pour into large bowl.
5. Pour juices and honey into saucepan. Sprinkle with gelatin. Let gelatin soften for 3 minutes. Warm mixture on low heat, stirring until gelatin dissolves. Pour and stir into strawberry mixture. Chill until thickened but not set.
6. Whisk in one-third of egg whites. Fold in balance of egg whites and ½ cup strawberries.
7. Pile filling into pie shell. Garnish with balance of strawberries. Chill until set (about 2 hours).

Yield: Serves 10

Variation: The filling alone makes a rich-tasting dessert. Follow directions for variation #1 of Cranberry Chiffon Pie (page 141).

Yield: Serves 8

CAL	F	P:S	SOD	CAR	CHO	PRO
Crust:						
102.5	6	4.4:1	5	10	–	2.5
Filling:						
88	0.5	1:1	14.5	16.5	2	5

Part II
Quick/Easy Gourmet Cooking

My Quickest Recipes

Break the time barrier to gourmet cooking with these recipes, which take only 2 to 45 minutes to complete. They may be fast, but all make use of the meticulous attention to masterpiece-creating detail that you've come to expect from the haute cuisine of health.

Blueberry Muffins

1 large egg (use ½ yolk and all the white)
2 tablespoons corn oil
½ teaspoon freshly grated lemon rind
¼ cup apple juice (no sugar added)
½ cup nonfat liquid milk
¼ cup evaporated skim milk (½ percent milkfat)
1 tablespoon honey (optional)
½ cup whole-wheat flour
1¼ cups unbleached flour
4 teaspoons low-sodium baking powder, available in health food stores
¼ teaspoon ground cinnamon
1 cup fresh blueberries, picked over, washed, and patted dry with paper toweling

½ teaspoon pure vanilla extract
½ teaspoon cold sweet (unsalted) 100 percent corn oil margarine, for muffin pan

1. In bowl, combine egg, oil, and lemon rind. Beat with wooden spoon until blended. Stir in apple juice, milks, and honey.
2. Sift flours, baking powder, and cinnamon into liquid ingredients. Stir until flour is absorbed.
3. Fold in blueberries. Stir in vanilla.
4. Half-fill greased muffin cups with batter. Bake in preheated 400°F oven for 20 to 22 minutes, until well browned.
5. Remove pan from oven. Loosen muffins with blunt knife. Remove muffins from pan. Let cool on rack. Serve slightly warm.

Yield: 12 muffins

CAL	F	P:S	SOD	CAR	CHO	PRO
Per muffin:						
81.5	6.5	2.9:1	3	8.5	11	1.5
With honey:						
87	6.5	2.9:1	3	9.5	11	1.5

Spiced Mushroom Dip

½ cup dry-curd cottage cheese (no salt added; ½ percent milkfat)
2 teaspoons minced fresh dill
2 tablespoons coarsely chopped onion
¼ teaspoon chili con carne seasoning (no salt or pepper added)
¼ teaspoon dried chervil
1 teaspoon tomato paste (no salt added)
6 dashes ground red (cayenne) pepper
3 tablespoons cold Rich Chicken Stock (page 94)
2 tablespoons Elegant Duxelles (page 56)

1. Fit food processor with steel blade. Combine all ingredients except duxelles in work bowl. Process on/off 3 times. Scrape sides of bowl. Process for 5 seconds.
2. Transfer mixture to bowl. Add duxelles and stir until well blended.

Yield: ¾ cup

Variation: Serve as a canapé by spreading over 5 thinly sliced pieces of any of my breads (pages 68–85), then cutting each slice into thirds.

CAL	F	P:S	SOD	CAR	CHO	PRO
Per teaspoon:						
4.5	–	–	2.5	0.5	–	0.5
Per canapé:						
12	–	–	2.5	2	–	1

Curried Steak

1½ pounds lean boneless sirloin, 1 inch thick
¾ teaspoon combined rosemary and thyme leaves, crushed
2¼ teaspoons each corn oil and Italian olive oil, combined
2 large cloves garlic, minced
2 large shallots, minced
1 teaspoon peeled and minced fresh ginger
3 large fresh mushrooms, washed, dried, trimmed, and coarsely chopped
½ cup Rich Chicken Stock (page 94)
1 teaspoon fresh lime juice
1½ teaspoons curry powder (no salt or pepper added)
2 teaspoons minced fresh parsley
1 tablespoon medium-dry sherry

1. Wipe steak with paper toweling. Rub on both sides with dried herbs.
2. Heat 2¼ teaspoons combined oils in iron skillet until hot. Add steak and sauté for 4 minutes. Turn. Sauté for 4 minutes. Turn twice more, cooking for 2 to 3 minutes on each side. Steak should be browned on the outside, yet still pink on the inside. Transfer to carving board. Cover loosely with waxed paper.
3. Heat balance of oil in skillet. Add garlic, shallots, ginger, and mushrooms. Sauté over medium-high heat, stirring constantly until browned (about 3 minutes).
4. Combine stock, lime juice, and curry powder. Add to sautéed mixture, stirring and scraping skillet to remove browned particles. Sprinkle with parsley. Cook until liquid is reduced by one-third. Swirl in sherry.
5. Cut steak into serving portions. Place on warmed individual serving plates and spoon with thick, hot sauce.

Yield: Serves 4

CAL	F	P:S	SOD	CAR	CHO	PRO
288	14	1.1:1	100	3	125	36.5

Dante's Chicken (Particularly Hot)

1 whole chicken breast, skinned and boned (¾ pound boned weight)
2 small chicken legs with thighs (1¼ pounds), skinned, legs separated from thighs
½ teaspoon each ground ginger and curry powder (no salt or pepper added)
10 dashes ground red (cayenne) pepper
1 tablespoon corn oil
3 cloves garlic, minced
2 large shallots, minced
1 rib celery, minced
⅜-inch slice fresh ginger, peeled and shredded
½ medium sweet green pepper, peeled and cut into ¼-inch slivers
⅓ cup each Light Chicken Broth (page 95) or Rich Chicken Stock (page 94) and red wine, combined

1. Wash chicken and dry with paper toweling. Sprinkle ginger, curry powder, and ground red pepper on both sides. Rub into chicken.
2. Heat oil in nonstick skillet until hot. Add garlic, shallots, celery, ginger, and green pepper. Spread across skillet. Sauté for 1 minute.
3. Place chicken on top of sautéed mixture. Sauté on each side until slightly browned.
4. Pour broth and wine over chicken. Bring to simmering point. Spoon with liquid. Cover and simmer for 20 minutes, turning once midway.
5. Uncover. Reduce liquid by cooking over medium-high heat for 5 minutes, turning chicken every minute. Chicken will become brown and sauce will become syrupy.
6. Turn chicken into serving dish. Spoon with sauce and serve immediately.

Yield: Serves 4

CAL	F	P:S	SOD	CAR	CHO	PRO
257.5	8	2.3:1	151	4	107.5	39.5

Sautéed Chicken Breasts with White Wine

2 whole chicken breasts, skinned and boned (1½ pounds boned weight), flattened to ⅜-inch thickness
2 tablespoons fresh lemon juice
4½ teaspoons corn oil
3 cloves garlic, minced
2 shallots, minced
6 fresh mushrooms, washed, dried, trimmed, and thickly sliced
½ teaspoon dried rosemary leaves, crushed
1 teaspoon dried oregano leaves, crushed
1 tablespoon minced fresh parsley
6 dashes ground red (cayenne) pepper
1 teaspoon chili con carne seasoning (no salt or pepper added)
⅓ cup dry vermouth or white wine

1. Wash chicken and dry with paper toweling. Place in small bowl. Sprinkle with lemon juice. Turn to coat. Let marinate for 5 minutes. Drain on paper toweling.
2. Heat 2¼ teaspoons oil in nonstick skillet until hot. Add chicken and

brown lightly on both sides over medium-high heat. Transfer to plate. Wipe out skillet.

3. Heat balance of oil in skillet. Sauté garlic, shallots, and mushrooms over medium-high heat for 3 minutes, stirring constantly.

4. Return chicken to skillet. Sprinkle with herbs and spices. Stir to coat chicken evenly.

5. Pour vermouth over chicken. Bring to simmering point. Cover and simmer for 20 minutes, spooning with sauce and turning 3 times.

6. With slotted spoon, transfer chicken to covered serving bowl. Turn up heat under sauce and reduce by half. Spoon over chicken and serve.

Yield: Serves 4

Variation: In place of 2 whole chicken breasts, use 1 whole chicken breast (cutting it in half), and add 2 skinned legs with thighs, legs separated from thighs (1 pound). Cooking time is increased by only 5 minutes.

CAL	F	P:S	SOD	CAR	CHO	PRO
224	4	2.2:1	121	4	84	39.5
Variation:						
240	5	2.4:1	154	4	108	39.5

Sautéed Chicken Breasts with Red Wine

1 whole chicken breast, skinned and boned (¾ pound boned weight), flattened to ⅜-inch thickness
2 chicken legs with thighs (1 pound), skinned, legs separated from thighs
2 tablespoons fresh lime juice
1½ teaspoons each corn oil and Italian olive oil, combined

3 large cloves garlic, minced
2 shallots, minced
½ teaspoon dried sage leaves, crushed
1 teaspoon dried oregano leaves, crushed
6 dashes ground red (cayenne) pepper
⅓ cup dry red wine

1. Wash chicken and dry with paper toweling. Place in small bowl. Sprinkle with lime juice, turning to coat. Let marinate for 5 minutes. Drain on paper toweling.

2. Heat oil in nonstick skillet until hot. Sauté chicken over medium-high heat until lightly browned on one side. Turn. Add garlic and shallots and brown with chicken for 5 minutes.

3. Sprinkle with herbs and ground red pepper, turning and stirring to coat chicken evenly.

4. Add wine. Bring to simmering point. Cover and simmer gently for 25 minutes, turning every 5 minutes. (Cooking time may vary slightly, depending on thickness of dark meat.) Most of cooking liquid will be absorbed, producing a moist, delicious chicken. Serve immediately. It won't wait!

Yield: Serves 4

CAL	F	P:S	SOD	CAR	CHO	PRO
257	8	2.4:1	148.5	3	107.5	39.5

Note: If you're a chicken lover in a hurry, try also my Ten-Minute Chicken Stew (page 162).

Orange Veal Chops

4 loin veal chops (1½ pounds)
1 teaspoon ground ginger
8 dashes ground red (cayenne) pepper

1 teaspoon dried rosemary leaves,
   crushed
4½ teaspoons corn oil
1 medium onion, minced
3 large cloves garlic, minced
2 tablespoons finely minced sweet
   green pepper
4½ teaspoons apple cider vinegar
¼ cup each Rich Chicken Stock
   (page 94) and fresh orange juice
2 teaspoons minced fresh dill
1 small bay leaf
1 teaspoon freshly grated orange
   rind, preferably from navel orange
   Minced fresh parsley

1. Trim chops. Wipe with paper
toweling. Rub both sides with ginger,
ground red pepper, and rosemary. Set
aside.
2. Heat 2¼ teaspoons oil in large
iron skillet until hot. Add onion, garlic,
and green pepper. Sauté until lightly
browned. Push to side of skillet.
3. Add balance of oil to skillet.
Sauté chops until lightly browned on
both sides. Combine with sautéed
ingredients.
4. Add vinegar and cook for 1
minute.
5. Add balance of ingredients except parsley. Turn chops, and stir
minced mixture. Bring to simmering
point. Cover and simmer gently for 30
minutes, turning and spooning with
sauce twice.
6. Uncover. Continue cooking and
turning chops until most of liquid
is reduced and sauce is thickened.
Transfer to warmed individual serving
plates. Sprinkle with parsley and serve.

Yield: Serves 4

CAL	F	P:S	SOD	CAR	CHO	PRO
305.5	19	1.3:1	78.5	5	106	28

Sweet Meat Patties

½ pound each ground lean veal and
   beef
2 tablespoons toasted wheat germ
   (no sugar added)
½ cup cooked brown rice (see note
   page 65)
1 tablespoon peeled and finely
   grated carrot
½ crisp, sweet apple, such as
   Washington State, peeled, cored,
   and coarsely chopped
3 tablespoons unsweetened grape
   juice
1 tablespoon minced fresh parsley
4½ teaspoons corn oil
2 cloves garlic, minced
2 shallots, minced
3 fresh mushrooms, washed, dried,
   trimmed, and coarsely chopped
1 teaspoon ground ginger
8 dashes ground red (cayenne)
   pepper
¼ teaspoon ground allspice
½ teaspoon dried tarragon leaves,
   crushed
   Crisp watercress sprigs

1. Combine meat and next 6 ingredients in bowl. Blend well.
2. Heat 1½ teaspoons oil in nonstick skillet until hot. Add garlic, shallots, and mushrooms. Sauté over medium-high heat, stirring constantly, for
2 minutes. Pour into bowl with meat
mixture. Sprinkle with spices and tarragon. Blend. Shape into 8 patties.
3. Heat 1½ teaspoons oil in skillet
until hot. Sauté patties on one side until
brown. Add balance of oil to skillet.
Turn patties and sauté until brown. (If
meat browns too rapidly, and doesn't
cook through to medium-rare, flatten
patties with spatula.) Do not overcook.
4. Serve in warmed individual
serving plates garnished with crisp watercress sprigs.

Yield: Serves 4

Health hint: Do not cook well-done. Overcooking destroys about 50 percent of the nutritional value.

CAL	F	P:S	SOD	CAR	CHO	PRO
342.5	11	0.8:1	78	32.5	73	27

Soup Shangri-La

1 tablespoon corn oil
2 large shallots, minced
1 medium onion, minced
1 large clove garlic, minced
1 teaspoon wine vinegar
1½ cups Light Chicken Broth (page 95)
1 cup apple juice (no sugar added)
½ cup water
2 tart green apples, peeled, cored, and thickly sliced
1 tablespoon fresh lime juice
1 tablespoon coriander seeds, crushed and sifted through a medium-meshed strainer (discard shells)
6 dashes each ground nutmeg and ground ginger
⅓ cup evaporated skim milk (¼ percent milkfat)
1 tablespoon arrowroot flour dissolved in 1 tablespoon water
Minced fresh parsley

1. Heat oil in kettle until hot. Add shallots, onion, and garlic and sauté until wilted but not browned.
2. Add vinegar. Cook for 30 seconds.
3. Add all but last 3 ingredients. Bring to simmering point. Cover partially and simmer for 15 minutes. Uncover. Turn off heat and let stand for 5 minutes.
4. Pour into blender and purée for 30 seconds.
5. Add milk to blender, and purée for an additional 30 seconds. Pour back into kettle.

6. Add dissolved arrowroot flour. Slowly heat and stir until lightly thickened.
7. Pour into individual soup dishes. Sprinkle with parsley and serve.

Yield: Serves 4

CAL	F	P:S	SOD	CAR	CHO	PRO
155.5	4	4.1:1	50	21.5	1	4.5

Crisp Salad with Tomato Curry Dressing

For the dressing:
½ cup tomato juice (no salt added)
¼ cup Rich Chicken Stock (page 94)
¼ cup corn oil
1 tablespoon fresh lime juice
½ teaspoon ground ginger
1 teaspoon curry powder (no salt or pepper added)
6 dashes ground red (cayenne) pepper
1 tablespoon minced fresh parsley
2 shallots, minced

For the salad:
1 small head romaine lettuce (about 12 ounces)
1 large sweet Bermuda onion, thinly sliced, separated into rings
1 small carrot, peeled and cut into strips with swivel-bladed peeler
1 medium sweet red pepper, seeded and cut into ¼-inch slivers
5 large fresh mushrooms, washed, well dried, trimmed, and thinly sliced

1. Combine all dressing ingredients in jar, and shake well. Let stand for 15

minutes before using. Shake again before serving.

2. Separate lettuce leaves. Rinse under cold running water. Drain. Pat each leaf dry with paper toweling.

3. Tear leaves into bite-sized pieces. Place in bowl with balance of ingredients. Toss.

4. Pour 6 to 7 tablespoons dressing over salad. Toss gently. Serve in individual salad bowls.

Yield: Dressing, about 1⅛ cups; salad serves 4

CAL	F	P:S	SOD	CAR	CHO	PRO
Salad:						
66	0.5	2:1	22	7.5	–	2.5
Dressing:						
74	7	4.5:1	10	3	–	0.5

New Tunafish Salad

1 can (6½ ounces) albacore white tuna packed in water (no salt added)
1 tablespoon fresh lemon juice
6 dashes ground red (cayenne) pepper
½ teaspoon curry powder (no salt or pepper added)
1 tablespoon corn oil
1 medium onion, minced
1 rib celery, minced
½ sweet red pepper, seeded and coarsely chopped
1½ teaspoons each minced fresh parsley and dill, combined
2 tablespoons low-fat plain yogurt
Crisp lettuce leaves
Tomato slices and watercress sprigs

1. Drain tuna. Place in bowl. Add lemon juice. Mash.

2. Sprinkle with ground red pepper and curry powder. Add oil. Blend.

3. Stir in onion, celery, sweet red pepper, and fresh herbs. Add yogurt, stirring well.

4. Spoon onto crisp lettuce leaves. Garnish with tomato slices and watercress sprigs.

Yield: Serves 4

Variations:

1. Make the following ingredient changes:
   • Reduce lemon juice to 1 teaspoon
   • Replace corn oil and yogurt with 2 tablespoons My Mayonnaise-Type Dressing (page 140)

2. Tea sandwiches: Spread salad onto 5 slices of any of my breads (pages 68–85), thinly sliced. Cover with another slice of bread, pressing to hold. Cut each sandwich into 3 triangles. Secure with colorful cocktail picks. Yield: 15 tea sandwiches.

3. Add to salad ½ sweet apple, peeled, cored, and cut into ¼-inch cubes.

CAL	F	P:S	SOD	CAR	CHO	PRO
93	4	4.1:1	53	7	32	11.5
Variation 1:						
72	3.5	2.3:1	53.5	7	32	11.5
Variation 2:						
8	–	–	1.5	1.5	1	1
Variation 3:						
113	4	4.1:1	53	12	32	11.5

Tomatoes Grand Hotel

⅓ cup minced fresh basil
1 tablespoon minced fresh parsley
4 teaspoons Italian olive oil
½ teaspoon ground ginger
1 teaspoon each apple cider vinegar
　and wine vinegar
8 dashes ground red (cayenne)
　pepper
3 large fresh ripe tomatoes, skinned,
　cored, and chopped

1. Prepare salad just before serving. Combine in bowl all ingredients except tomatoes. Stir to blend.
2. Add tomatoes, turning and stirring to coat.
3. Spoon onto individual salad plates.

Yield: Serves 4

CAL	F	P:S	SOD	CAR	CHO	PRO
56	4.5	1.2:1	8.5	3.5	–	0.5

Broiled Lemon Sole with Orange Sauce

1 shallot, minced
1 clove garlic, minced
¼ cup fresh orange juice
2 tablespoons fresh lemon juice
1 tablespoon dry vermouth
½ teaspoon freshly grated orange
　rind, preferably from navel orange
6 dashes ground red (cayenne)
　pepper
½ teaspoon ground ginger
1½ pounds fresh lemon sole fillets, cut
　into serving pieces
1¼ teaspoons sweet (unsalted) 100
　percent corn oil margarine (melt 1
　teaspoon)
1 teaspoon corn oil

1. Combine first 8 ingredients in bowl to make marinade.
2. Wash fish and pat dry with paper toweling. Add to marinade, turning to coat. Let stand at room temperature for 15 minutes.
3. Heat broiler. Lightly grease metal baking pan with ¼ teaspoon margarine. Remove fish from marinade and place in pan. Pour 2 tablespoons marinade over fish. Pour balance into saucepan, and slow-boil for 5 minutes.
4. Combine 1 teaspoon melted margarine and corn oil. Drizzle half of mixture over fish. Broil fish close to heat for 6 minutes. Turn. Pour balance of oil-margarine mixture and balance of marinade over fish. Broil for 3 minutes. Transfer to warmed serving platter.
5. Pour broiling liquid into saucepan and reduce for 3 minutes over medium-high heat.
6. Pour into blender and blend for 30 seconds. Spoon frothy sauce over fish. Serve.

Yield: Serves 4

Variation: For a creamier sauce, add 2 tablespoons evaporated skim milk (¼ percent milkfat) to blender in step 6.

Note: For greater expediency, step 6 may be omitted. Sauce will be thin but flavorful.

CAL	F	P:S	SOD	CAR	CHO	PRO
160	2.5	2.7:1	137	3.5	94.5	28.5

Poached Asparagus—New Style

1½ pounds fresh asparagus, well
　washed, tough ends removed
½ cup Rich Chicken Stock (page 94)

2 shallots, minced
½ teaspoon ground ginger
8 dashes ground red (cayenne) pepper
½ teaspoon dried rosemary leaves, crushed
1 tablespoon minced fresh parsley
1 teaspoon tomato paste (no salt added)
2 tablespoons evaporated skim milk (¼ percent milkfat)

1. Place asparagus in wide-bottomed saucepan. Combine stock, shallots, ginger, ground red pepper, rosemary, and parsley. Pour over asparagus. Bring to boil. Reduce heat. Cover and poach for 7 to 8 minutes, spooning with poaching liquid twice. (Cooking time will vary with thickness of asparagus.) With slotted spatula, transfer to serving plate. Cover with waxed paper to keep warm.

2. Add tomato paste to poaching liquid. Stir over heat until blended. Add milk. Bring to simmering point.

3. Pour sauce over asparagus. Serve immediately.

Yield: Serves 4

CAL	F	P:S	SOD	CAR	CHO	PRO
36.5	–	–	11.5	7.5	–	4.5

Fresh Corn with Peppers

3 whole, fresh ears of corn (medium size, with small kernels)
1 teaspoon tarragon vinegar (page 99)
1½ teaspoons each corn oil and Italian olive oil, combined
1 large clove garlic, minced
2 large shallots, minced

¼-inch slice fresh ginger, peeled and shredded
1 small sweet red pepper, seeded and cut into ¼-inch slivers
6 dashes ground red (cayenne) pepper
¼ teaspoon smoked yeast (optional) (available in health food stores)
1 tablespoon minced fresh basil

1. Boil corn in water to cover for 10 to 12 minutes. Drain. Stand cobs upright on cutting board. Cut kernels from cob with sharp knife, taking care not to cut too closely to cob. Transfer to bowl. Sprinkle with vinegar.

2. Heat combined oils in nonstick skillet until hot. Add garlic, shallots, and ginger and sauté for 2 minutes, stirring constantly.

3. Add slivered pepper and sauté for 1 minute.

4. Add corn. Sprinkle with ground red pepper and smoked yeast and sauté briefly until hot.

5. Add fresh basil, tossing to blend. Serve immediately.

Yield: Serves 4

Note: Fresh basil adds a wonderful flavor to this dish. Don't settle for the dry. If the fresh herb is not available, substitute fresh tarragon or dill.

CAL	F	P:S	SOD	CAR	CHO	PRO
124	7	3.1	6	15	–	2

With smoked yeast: No appreciable difference

Tomatoes and Okra over Rice

1   box (10 ounces) frozen sliced okra
1   cup water
¼   cup white vinegar
1   tablespoon corn oil
½   rib celery, minced
1   small onion, minced
2   large cloves garlic, minced
½-inch slice fresh ginger, peeled and
    minced
1   cup canned tomatoes (no salt
    added), chopped
8   dashes ground red (cayenne)
    pepper
1   tablespoon minced fresh basil or 1
    teaspoon dried sweet basil leaves,
    crushed
¼   teaspoon dried thyme leaves,
    crushed
¼   cup red wine
2   cups just-boiled rice (see note
    page 65)

1. Place okra, water, and vinegar in small saucepan. Bring to boil. Reduce heat to slow boil. Cook, uncovered, for 3 minutes. Drain.

2. Heat oil in nonstick skillet until hot. Add celery, onion, garlic, and ginger and sauté for 3 minutes. Do not brown.

3. Add drained okra. Sauté and stir for 1 minute.

4. Add tomatoes and balance of ingredients. Bring to simmering point. Cover and simmer gently for 10 minutes.

5. Serve equal portions of rice on warmed individual serving plates. Spoon tomatoes and okra over rice and serve piping hot.

Yield: Serves 4 as main dish, 6 as side dish

Variation: Serve grated no-fat Sap Sago cheese on side to sprinkle over dish. Use sparingly.

CAL	F	P:S	SOD	CAR	CHO	PRO
191	3.5	4.3:1	25	25	–	3.5

Variation: Sap Sago, per teaspoon

CAL	F	P:S	SOD	CAR	CHO	PRO
2.5	–	–	2.5	–	–	1

Curried Kasha

1   tablespoon corn oil
1   clove garlic, minced
2   large shallots, minced
1   small onion, minced
1   teaspoon peeled and minced fresh
    ginger
1   teaspoon peeled and grated carrot
1   teaspoon wine vinegar
2   cups Light Chicken Broth (page
    95) or Rich Chicken Stock (page
    94)
1   cup water
1   cup kasha (whole buckwheat
    groats)
2   teaspoons minced fresh dill
4   dashes ground red (cayenne)
    pepper
1   teaspoon curry powder (no salt
    or pepper added)
1   tablespoon minced fresh parsley

1. Heat oil in nonstick skillet until hot. Add garlic, shallots, onion, and ginger and sauté over medium-high heat until wilted but not browned.

2. Add carrot and vinegar. Cook for 30 seconds.

3. Add broth, water, and balance of ingredients. Bring to boil. Reduce heat to slow boil and continue cooking, uncovered, for exactly 8 minutes, stirring often. All liquid should be absorbed. Add a small amount of water if necessary to complete cooking time.

4. Cover and let stand for 5 minutes.

5. Turn into serving dish. Sprinkle with parsley and serve.

Yield: Serves 4

CAL	F	P:S	SOD	CAR	CHO	PRO
102	3.5	4.4:1	16.5	4.5	–	4

Sautéed Yams

1¼ pounds yams, peeled and cut into
    1-inch cubes
1 tablespoon fresh lemon juice
1 teaspoon tarragon vinegar (page
    99)
2¼ teaspoons each corn oil and
    Italian olive oil, combined
2 cloves garlic, minced
2 large shallots, minced
¼ teaspoon ground ginger
10 dashes ground red (cayenne)
    pepper
¼ teaspoon chili con carne
    seasoning (no salt or pepper
    added)
2 teaspoons minced fresh tarragon
    or 1 teaspoon dried tarragon
    leaves, crushed
2 teaspoons minced fresh parsley

1. Boil yams in water to cover for 12 minutes. Drain. Let cool.

2. Turn yams into bowl. Sprinkle with lemon juice and vinegar, turning to coat.

3. Heat combined oils in nonstick skillet until hot. Sauté garlic and shallots for 30 seconds. Add yams and sauté for 1 minute.

4. Sprinkle with spices. Stir and sauté until well heated. Sprinkle with herbs. Shake skillet to distribute herbs evenly. Transfer to warmed serving plate. Serve immediately.

Yield: Serves 4

CAL	F	P:S	SOD	CAR	CHO	PRO
175.5	5	3.5:1	17.5	5	–	2.5

Baked French-Fried Potatoes

4 medium Idaho potatoes, peeled,
    cut into French-fry strips about ½-
    inch thick
2 tablespoons corn oil
2 large shallots, minced
2 large cloves garlic, minced
8 dashes ground red (cayenne)
    pepper
¾ teaspoon combined dried thyme
    and marjoram leaves, crushed

1. Lay strips of potatoes on paper toweling. Pat dry.

2. Combine oil, shallots, and garlic in dish. Spread over 11½- x 15½- x 1-inch jelly-roll pan. Heat in 450°F oven for 3 minutes.

3. Add potatoes in one layer. Sprinkle with ground red pepper and herbs, turning with spatula to coat evenly.

4. Bake about 15 minutes, turning often, until potatoes are brown and tender. Transfer to open serving dish.

Yield: Serves 4

CAL	F	P:S	SOD	CAR	CHO	PRO
152	7.5	4.4:1	9	21	–	2.5

Jiffy Pineapple Rice

2¼ teaspoons corn oil
2 scallions, minced
1 large clove garlic, minced
2 shallots, minced
2 cups cooked rice, cooled (see note page 65)
2 teaspoons tarragon vinegar (page 99)
8 dashes ground red (cayenne) pepper
¾ teaspoon chili con carne seasoning (no salt or pepper added)
¾ cup pineapple tidbits packed in unsweetened pineapple juice, drained but ⅓ cup juice reserved
1 tablespoon minced fresh parsley

1. Heat oil in nonstick skillet until hot. Add scallions, garlic, and shallots. Sauté for 2 minutes.
2. Add rice. Cook for 1 minute, stirring to cool. Add vinegar. Cook for 1 minute.
3. Sprinkle with spices. Stir to blend. Add pineapple tidbits and juice. Cook until pineapple heats through.
4. Sprinkle with parsley. Cook and stir for 1 minute. Serve.

Yield: Serves 4

CAL	F	P:S	SOD	CAR	CHO	PRO
104.5	2	4.4:1	7	24	–	2.5

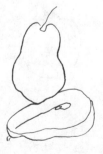

Herb Sauce

1 tablespoon corn oil
2 teaspoons sweet (unsalted) 100 percent corn oil margarine
2 large shallots, minced
4½ teaspoons unbleached flour
2 teaspoons medium-dry sherry
1 teaspoon fresh lime juice
⅔ cup Light Chicken Broth (page 95)
1 tablespoon minced fresh basil, dill, or tarragon
6 dashes ground red (cayenne) pepper
1 teaspoon tomato paste (no salt added)
⅓ cup nonfat liquid milk
¼ cup evaporated skim milk (¼ percent milkfat)

1. Heat oil and margarine in heavy-bottomed saucepan until hot. Add shallots and cook for 1 minute, taking care they don't brown. Reduce heat.
2. Add flour. Stir and cook for 1½ minutes. Rapidly whisk in sherry and lime juice.
3. Add broth, basil, ground red pepper, and tomato paste. Cook and whisk over medium heat until sauce thickens. Remove from heat.
4. Combine milks. Whisk into hot sauce. Place over low heat and heat only to simmering point. *Do not boil.* Serve immediately.

Yield: About 1⅓ cups

Serving suggestions: See serving suggestions for Smooth Tomato Curry Purée (page 97)

CAL	F	P:S	SOD	CAR	CHO	PRO
Per tablespoon:						
16.5	1	3.7:1	3	1	–	0.5

Any-Time-of-Day Milk Shake

½ cup nonfat liquid milk
4 pineapple chunks packed in
  unsweetened pineapple juice,
  drained
¼ cup fresh orange juice
2 tablespoons evaporated skim milk
  (¼ percent milkfat)
1 teaspoon honey (optional)
⅛ teaspoon ground cinnamon
3 dashes ground nutmeg
3 ice cubes, crushed

1. Combine all ingredients in blender and blend on high speed for 1 minute.
2. Pour into tall glass, and serve.

Yield: Serves 1

CAL	F	P:S	SOD	CAR	CHO	PRO
112.5	1.5	1.5:1	59	20.5	2	7.5
With honey:						
133.5	1.5	1.5:1	59.5	26	2.5	7.5

Those Amazing Cooking Machines

THE FOOD PROCESSOR

This amazing machine is indisputably the greatest aid to speed-cooking ever invented. It will, in breathtakingly brief whirs of its multifarious attachments, chop, grind, mince, purée, grate, shred, slice, julienne, blend, and combine. It will even knead dough for bread and pastry. Laborious chores that once deterred even the devoted cook can now be accomplished with the push of a button and faithful adherence to the manufacturer's how-to-do-it manual.

But the processor per se is no robotic way to great cooking. The machine has intrinsic drawbacks that must be compensated for with old-fashioned handwrought love and care.

To illustrate: Mincing garlic, shallots, and onions makes their flavors available when these herbs are placed in a skillet. The blending of these flavors with other ingredients to be sautéed is a technique I invented to give food the snap (but not the taste) of salt on a salt-free diet. But the processor (or at least mine) does not mince these soft ingredients, but rather mashes them—which releases the flavoring essences prematurely. On the way to the skillet part of them are destroyed by air; and in the skillet, the remainder are volatilized at the first touch of heat. So for me, it's back to the cutting board.

Another illustration: One of the technological wonders of the food processor is its ability to knead dough in seconds. But the processing produces a dough heavier than that produced by hand. So I elect to start kneading in the processor (to save time) and to finish it by hand (to save lightness). The result is a lighter dough than could be obtained by using the processor alone.

What I've done in preparing the recipes in this section is taken advantage of the processor's virtues for some parts of the recipes, and fallen back on my own resources for other parts when I knew the processor couldn't do what I wanted it to do. Here then are my original haute cuisine of health processor recipes for you to use whenever you're budgeting your time and effort.

Chicken-Veal Patties

1½ plain matzohs (no salt, shortening, or egg added), broken into small pieces
2 tablespoons toasted wheat germ (no sugar added)
1 teaspoon grated no-fat Sap Sago cheese
½ carrot, peeled and cut into small pieces
½-inch slice peeled fresh ginger, cut in half
4 fresh mushrooms, washed, dried, trimmed, and quartered
1 whole chicken breast, skinned and boned (¾ pound boned weight), washed, dried, trimmed, and cut into 1-inch pieces
½ pound lean veal, ground or boned and cut into 1-inch cubes
2 tablespoons corn oil
1 small onion, minced
2 large shallots, minced
2 cloves garlic, minced
2 teaspoons medium-dry sherry
1 tablespoon fresh lime juice
1 tablespoon minced fresh basil
1 egg (use ½ yolk and all of white), beaten with fork
Curly parsley sprigs and lemon wedges

1. Fit processor with steel blade. Combine matzoh, wheat germ, and Sap Sago cheese in work bowl of food processor. Turn on/off 10 times or more until matzoh is reduced to crumbs. Pour into bowl. Wipe out work bowl.
2. Combine carrot and ginger in work bowl. Turn on/off 8 times. Both should be finely chopped but not puréed. Scrape into dish.
3. Add mushrooms to work bowl. Process on/off 5 times. Turn into dish.
4. Place chicken in work bowl. Turn on/off rapidly 3 times. Chicken should be coarsely chopped. Pour into bowl with matzoh crumbs. Add ground veal and blend. (If using cubed veal, process together with chicken.)
5. Heat 1 tablespoon corn oil in nonstick skillet until hot. Sauté onion, shallots, garlic, ginger, carrot, and mushrooms over medium-high heat for 3 minutes, turning continuously. Add sherry and lime juice. Cook for 1 minute. Pour into meat mixture. Add basil and egg. Blend. Shape into 8 patties ½-inch thick.
6. Heat balance of oil in skillet. Sauté patties on both sides until golden brown. Total cooking time should be about 8 minutes.
7. Arrange on warmed serving platter, garnished with curly parsley sprigs and lemon wedges.

Yield: Serves 4

Serving suggestions:
1. Serve with quickly made Tomatoes Grand Hotel (page 132).
2. Serve with Herb Sauce (page 136) poured over patties.

Note: Fresh basil tastes best. If not available, you may substitute 1 teaspoon dried basil leaves, crushed.

CAL	F	P:S	SOD	CAR	CHO	PRO
302.5	13	2.5:1	105	9.5	108.5	32.5

Stick-to-the-Ribs Rye Bread

1 tablespoon dry yeast or 1 premeasured package
¼ cup warm water (105° to 115°F)
½ teaspoon honey
¾ cup rye flour
1½ cups unbleached flour
⅓ cup gluten flour
2 tablespoons toasted wheat germ (no sugar added)

½ teaspoon ground cinnamon
1½ teaspoons caraway seeds, lightly
  crushed
½ teaspoon poppy seeds
¼ cup apple juice (no sugar added)
½ cup thick buttermilk (no salt
  added)
2¼ teaspoons corn oil
1 teaspoon freshly grated orange
  rind, preferably from navel orange
½ teaspoon sweet (unsalted) 100
  percent corn oil margarine, for
  pan and waxed paper

1. Combine yeast, water, and honey in small bowl. Beat with fork to blend. Let stand for 10 minutes.
2. Fit processor with steel blade. In work bowl, combine flours, wheat germ, cinnamon, and seeds. Turn processor on/off 3 times.
3. Pour yeast mixture over flour. Process on/off 3 times.
4. Heat apple juice, buttermilk, 2 teaspoons oil, and orange rind until lukewarm (105° to 115°F). Turn processor on. Slowly pour liquid through feed tube. Dough will form into a ball as soon as all liquid is absorbed. Process for 15 seconds after ball forms. Turn ball onto board and knead for one minute.
5. Form dough into ball. Place in fairly straight-sided bowl greased with ½ teaspoon oil, turning to coat. Cover tightly with plastic wrap and let rise at room temperature (70° to 80°F) until doubled in bulk (about 1 hour 15 minutes).
6. Punch dough down. Transfer to board and knead for 1 minute. Shape into loaf. Place in small (7⅜- x 3⅝- x 2¼-inch) loaf pan greased with ¼ teaspoon margarine. Lightly grease a sheet of waxed paper with balance of margarine. Place over loaf, greased side down. Let rise until doubled.
7. Bake in preheated 375°F oven for 45 to 50 minutes. Bread is completely baked when you tap with knuckles and hear a hollow sound.

8. Remove from pan and let cool thoroughly before slicing.

Yield: 1 loaf, 20 slices (⅜-inch each)

CAL	F	P:S	SOD	CAR	CHO	PRO
Per slice:						
62.5	0.5	3.7:1	2.5	11.5	–	3

Spiced Whole-Wheat Loaf

¼ cup warm water (105° to 115°F)
1 tablespoon dry yeast or 1
  premeasured package
¼ teaspoon honey
1¼ cups whole-wheat flour
1 cup unbleached flour
¼ cup date powder (also called date
  sugar) (available in health food
  stores)
½ teaspoon each ground ginger and
  cinnamon
¾ cup thick buttermilk (no salt
  added), room temperature
1 teaspoon freshly grated orange
  rind, preferably from navel orange
½ teaspoon aniseed, crushed
1 tablespoon corn oil plus ¼
  teaspoon for bowl
¼ teaspoon sweet (unsalted) 100
  percent corn oil margarine, for
  pan
2 teaspoons nonfat liquid milk

1. In cup, combine water, yeast, and honey. Beat with fork until yeast is dissolved. Let stand for 10 minutes.
2. Fit processor with steel blade. In work bowl, combine 1 cup whole-wheat flour, all of unbleached flour, date powder, and spices. Turn on/off twice. Turn on again and pour dissolved yeast mixture through feed tube. Process for 15 seconds.
3. In bowl, combine buttermilk, or-

ange rind, aniseed, and 1 tablespoon oil. Turn on processor and pour liquid slowly through feed tube. Process on/off for 15 seconds. Remove dough to board and knead for 1 minute.

4. Shape dough into ball. Drop into large, lightly oiled bowl, turning to coat. Cover tightly with plastic wrap and let rise at room temperature (70° to 80°F) until doubled in bulk (about 1½ hours).

5. Punch dough down. Transfer to board and knead for 15 seconds. Shape into loaf. Place in small (7⅜- x 3⅝- x 2¼-inch) loaf pan lightly greased with margarine. With sharp knife, make two diagonal slashes ¼ inch deep across loaf. Cover loosely with waxed paper. Let rise until doubled in bulk (about 1 hour).

6. Brush loaf lightly with milk. Bake in preheated 375°F oven for 40 minutes. Remove bread from pan. Replace bread in oven directly on rack. Bake for 3 to 5 minutes. Loaf should be browned, and bottom should be crisp to the touch.

7. Let cool on rack. Serve slightly warm, at room temperature, or toasted —it's delicious all three ways.

Yield: 1 loaf, 20 slices (⅜-inch each)

Variation: For a sweet, almost cakelike loaf, add 1½ teaspoons honey and ¼ cup raisins to saucepan during step 3.

CAL	F	P:S	SOD	CAR	CHO	PRO
Per slice:						
71	1	3.9:1	4	14	–	2
Variation:						
78.5	1	3.9:1	4.5	16	–	2

My Mayonnaise-Type Dressing

½ cup Light Chicken Broth (page 95)
¼ cup water
½ teaspoon dried sweet basil or tarragon leaves, crushed
1 large clove garlic, minced (optional)
¼ teaspoon ground ginger
4 dashes ground red (cayenne) pepper
2 teaspoons arrowroot flour
1 teaspoon tarragon vinegar (page 99)
1 tablespoon fresh lemon juice
1 egg yolk
½ teaspoon prepared Dijon mustard (no salt added)
¼ cup corn oil
1 tablespoon minced fresh parsley

1. Combine broth and next 5 ingredients in saucepan. Bring to simmering point. Whisk in arrowroot flour. Continue simmering and whisking for 1 minute. Add vinegar and lemon juice. Whisk and simmer for 1 minute more. Let cool.

2. Fit processor with steel blade. Combine egg yolk and mustard in work bowl. Turn on processor for 15 seconds. Turn off.

3. Process for 15 seconds while dribbling oil through feed tube. Mixture will be thick. Turn on processor and slowly pour broth mixture through feed tube.

4. Turn off processor. Pour mixture into jar. Chill for 2 hours before serving.

Yield: ¾ cup

Note: Mayonnaise thins down after addition of stock mixture. It will thicken after chilling.

CAL	F	P:S	SOD	CAR	CHO	PRO
Per tablespoon:						
50	5	4.2:1	3	1	–	0.5

Cranberry Chiffon Pie

For the crust:
- ⅞ cup buckwheat flour
- 1 cup unbleached flour
- ½ cup whole-wheat flour
- 2 tablespoons date powder (also called date sugar) (available in health food stores)
- 3 tablespoons sweet (unsalted) 100 percent corn oil margarine
- 1 tablespoon corn oil
- 4 to 5 tablespoons ice water

For the filling:
- 2 cups fresh cranberries, washed
- ⅔ cup unsweetened pineapple juice
- 3 tablespoons honey
- 1 navel orange slice, peeled
- ¾ cup pineapple chunks packed in unsweetened pineapple juice, drained
- 2 envelopes plain gelatin
- ¼ cup fresh orange juice
- 2 tablespoons dry-curd cottage cheese (no salt added; ½ percent milkfat)
- ½ cup evaporated skim milk (¼ percent milkfat)
- 1 teaspoon pure vanilla extract
- 2 egg whites, stiffly beaten
- 2 tablespoons coarsely chopped walnuts

1. Prepare crust first. Fit processor with steel blade. Combine and process in work bowl all crust ingredients except water, turning machine on/off 4 times.

2. Turn machine on and dribble water through feed tube. Shape processed mixture into ball. Wrap in waxed paper. Refrigerate for 30 minutes.

3. With rolling pin, roll pastry out between 2 fresh sheets of waxed paper to a circle with a diameter of 11½ inches. Peel off top sheet. Lay 10-inch aluminum pie pan on top of pastry. Invert. Gently peel off bottom sheet of paper. Ease pastry into bottom and sides of pan. Patch where necessary. Flute edges.

4. Bake in preheated 375°F oven for 35 minutes. Let pan cool on rack completely before filling.

5. Now prepare filling. Combine cranberries, pineapple juice, honey, and orange slice in small saucepan. Bring to simmering point. Cover partially and simmer for 10 minutes. Add pineapple. Stir. Let cool. Pour into work bowl of processor fitted with steel blade. Set aside.

6. Pour orange juice into saucepan. Sprinkle with gelatin. Let soften for 3 minutes. Heat and stir until gelatin dissolves. Add to processor bowl. Turn processor on/off once.

7. Drop cheese through feed tube. Add milk. Process on/off 3 times. Add vanilla. Process on/off once. Pour into bowl and chill until mixture begins to thicken (about 25 minutes). Do not let mixture set.

8. Whisk one-third of beaten egg whites into thickened mixture. Fold in balance.

9. Pour filling into pie shell. Sprinkle with nuts. Refrigerate until set (about 2 hours).

Yield: Serves 10

Variations: The filling alone makes a delicious and eye-appealing dessert. Try serving it in these two ways:

1. Pour mixture (step 8) into 8 parfait glasses. Sprinkle with nuts. Refrigerate until set.

2. Sprinkle nuts on bottom of decorative 2-quart mold. Fill mold with

mixture (step 8). Chill until set. Remove from refrigerator 15 minutes before unmolding.

Yield: Serves 8

CAL	F	P:S	SOD	CAR	CHO	PRO
Pie (per serving):						
218	6.5	3.3:1	14	33	0.5	6.5
Filling (per serving):						
110	1.5	6.7:1	14	17.5	0.5	4

Banana Raisin Bars

1½ cups unbleached flour
½ cup whole-wheat flour
½ teaspoon each ground ginger and cinnamon
2½ teaspoons low-sodium baking powder
2 small ripe bananas, thinly sliced (1⅓ cups)
1 tablespoon fresh lemon juice
2 tablespoons sweet (unsalted) 100 percent corn oil margarine plus ½ teaspoon for baking pan
2 tablespoons corn oil
1 egg (use ½ yolk and all of white)
2 tablespoons honey
½ cup evaporated skim milk (¼ percent milkfat)
1 teaspoon pure vanilla extract
¼ cup raisins
3 tablespoons coarsely chopped walnuts

1. Sift flours, spices, and baking powder into bowl. Set aside.

2. Fit processor with steel blade. Combine bananas and lemon juice in work bowl. Turn on/off 5 times.

3. Add 2 tablespoons margarine, oil, egg, and honey. Process for 15 seconds.

4. Add half of sifted mixture and ¼ cup milk. Process on/off 5 times.

5. Add balance of sifted mixture and vanilla. Process on/off 4 times.

6. Pour balance of milk through feed tube. Process on/off twice.

7. Drop raisins through feed tube. Process on/off once.

8. Spread batter into margarine-greased 9-inch square baking pan. Sprinkle with nuts, pressing them lightly into batter. Bake in preheated 375°F oven for 35 minutes. Top of cake should be golden brown.

9. Place pan on rack to cool for 10 minutes. Cut into 16 squares. Serve warm or cooled.

Yield: 16 bars

CAL	F	P:S	SOD	CAR	CHO	PRO
Per bar:						
100	4.5	4.3:1	10	11.5	9	2

Apple-Cranberry Cake

¼ cup raisins
¼ cup unsweetened pineapple juice
2 tablespoons honey
1 cup fresh whole cranberries
⅓ cup broken walnuts
2-inch slice orange peel, preferably from navel orange
1 crisp, sweet apple, such as Washington State, peeled, cored, and cubed
2¼ cups unbleached flour
¼ cup toasted wheat germ (no sugar added)
3 teaspoons low-sodium baking powder (available in health food stores)
2 tablespoons sweet (unsalted) 100 percent corn oil margarine plus ¼ teaspoon for pan
1 egg (use ½ yolk and all of white)
2 tablespoons corn oil
¼ cup evaporated skim milk (¼ percent milkfat)

1. In small heavy-bottomed sauce-pan, combine raisins, pineapple juice, and honey. Bring to simmering point. Cover partially and simmer for 5 minutes. Uncover and let cool. Set aside.

2. Fit processor with steel blade. Place cranberries, nuts, orange rind, and apple in work bowl. Process on/off 10 times.

3. Add flour, wheat germ, baking powder, and 2 tablespoons margarine. Process on/off 5 times.

4. Combine egg, oil, milk, and cooked raisin mixture. Add to bowl. Process on/off 5 times.

5. Spoon into small (7⅜- x 3⅝- x 2¼-inch) loaf pan lightly greased with margarine. Bake in preheated 350°F oven for 1 hour, or until toothpick inserted through center of cake comes out clean.

6. Remove from oven and let pan cool on rack for 10 minutes. Remove cake from pan and let cool completely on rack before serving.

Yield: 14 slices

CAL	F	P:S	SOD	CAR	CHO	PRO
Per slice:						
165	6	4.8:1	6	22.9	–	4

Noodle Doodles

2 cups unbleached flour plus flour for sprinkling board
½ cup whole-wheat flour
¼ cup toasted wheat germ (no sugar added)
¼ teaspoon ground ginger
6 dashes ground red (cayenne) pepper
¼ cup corn oil
¾ cup plus 2 tablespoons cold water

1. Fit processor with steel blade. Combine first 5 ingredients in work bowl. Turn on/off twice.

2. Add oil. Turn on/off 5 times.

3. With processor on, pour water slowly through feed tube until dough forms ball and rotates around bowl for 20 seconds. Remove from bowl. Shape into smooth ball. Lay on board. Cover with waxed paper and let rest for 5 minutes.

4. Cut dough into 4 equal pieces. Sprinkle board lightly with flour. Roll each piece of dough into a 10- x 12-inch rectangle. Cut into ½-inch lengthwise strips, then cut each strip in half. Lay on lightly floured surface and let dry for 1½ to 2 hours.

5. Transfer to ungreased cookie sheet. Bake in preheated 375°F oven for 40 minutes, turning every 10 minutes until lightly browned and crisp. Remove from oven. Let cool on cookie sheet. Store in tightly closed glass jar.

Yield: About 150 Noodle Doodles

Note: Dough may be put through pasta maker in step 4.

CAL	F	P:S	SOD	CAR	CHO	PRO
Per noodle doodle:						
8	0.5	4.3:1	–	0.5	–	0.5

Dilled Chicken Mousse

1 cup Rich Chicken Stock (page 94), at room temperature
1 package unflavored gelatin
2 cups cut-up cooked chicken (1-inch pieces)
¼ cup just-snipped dill
2 tablespoons fresh lime juice
1 tablespoon corn oil
2 teaspoons prepared Dijon mustard (no salt added)
3 large shallots, coarsely chopped
½ teaspoon curry powder (no salt or pepper added)
8 dashes ground red (cayenne) pepper
¾ cup evaporated skim milk (¼ percent milkfat)
½ cup tomato juice (no salt added)
1 sweet red pepper, seeded and half minced, half slivered
1 large egg white, stiffly beaten
Fresh dill sprigs and lettuce leaves

1. Pour stock into saucepan. Sprinkle with gelatin and let soften for 3 minutes. Heat slowly, stirring to dissolve. Cool.

2. Fit processor with steel blade. Combine next 8 ingredients in work bowl. Turn on/off 5 times.

3. Combine milk with tomato juice. Turn on processor. Pour liquid through feed tube and process for 5 seconds.

4. Pour cooled stock mixture through feed tube. Process on/off once.

5. Turn mixture into bowl. Stir in minced sweet red pepper. Refrigerate until mixture starts to thicken (about 30 minutes).

6. Fold in beaten egg white. Spoon into 1½-quart decorative mold or 8½- x 4½- x 2½-inch loaf pan that has been rinsed in cold water. Refrigerate until set (about 2 hours).

7. To unmold, place mold or loaf pan briefly in hot water. Invert. Garnish with lettuce leaves, slivered pepper, and dill sprigs.

Yield: Serves 6 as luncheon dish, 12 as first course

CAL	F	P:S	SOD	CAR	CHO	PRO
Luncheon dish:						
152	4.5	2.4:1	58	7.5	37.5	19
First course:						
76	2	2.4:1	29	4	19	9.5

Cucumber Sauce

2 medium cucumbers, peeled and cut into 1-inch chunks
1 tablespoon each fresh lemon juice and lime juice
2 shallots, quartered
1 small onion, cut into 1-inch chunks
⅓ cup dry-curd cottage cheese (no salt added; ½ percent milkfat)
1 tablespoon low-fat plain yogurt
¼ teaspoon ground ginger
1 teaspoon minced fresh tarragon or ½ teaspoon dried tarragon leaves, crushed
6 dashes ground red (cayenne) pepper
Flowerets from 1 large curly parsley sprig

1. Fit processor with steel blade. Combine all ingredients in work bowl. Process on/off 3 times. Then process for 10 seconds.

2. Turn into bowl. Chill.

Yield: About 1½ cups

Serving suggestion: Delicious with poached fish or salads.

Variation: In place of tarragon, substitute 1 tablespoon minced fresh basil leaves or ¾ teaspoon dried sweet basil leaves, crushed.

CAL	F	P:S	SOD	CAR	CHO	PRO
Per tablespoon:						
8.5	–	–	4.5	2	–	0.5
Variation: No appreciable difference						

Fish Wurst

1¼ pounds fresh lemon sole fillets
 3 large egg whites
 3 tablespoons fresh lemon juice
 ½ teaspoon prepared Dijon mustard
     (no salt added)
 6 dashes ground red (cayenne)
     pepper
 ½ teaspoon ground ginger
 2 teaspoons minced fresh tarragon
     or 1 teaspoon dried tarragon
     leaves, crushed
 1 tablespoon minced fresh parsley
 2 shallots, minced
 1 clove garlic, minced
 2 tablespoons Matzoh Crumbs (page
     85)
 ¼ cup evaporated skim milk (¼
     percent milkfat), very cold
 ½ teaspoon sweet (unsalted) 100
     percent corn oil margarine, for
     loaf pan
 5 whole jarred pimientos (no salt
     added)
     Lettuce leaves, parsley sprigs, and
     lemon wedges

1. Cut away bones running down center of each fillet. Cut fish into 1-inch pieces.
2. Fit processor with steel blade. Place fish and egg whites in work bowl. Process on/off 3 times. Then process for 15 seconds. Add lemon juice. Process on/off twice.
3. Add mustard, spices, herbs, shallots, garlic, and matzoh crumbs. Process for 15 seconds. Turn mixture into bowl. Cover and refrigerate for 2 hours.
4. Using portable mixing machine or hand beater, gradually beat milk into mixture until light and fluffy. Spoon half of mixture into small (7⅜- x 3⅝- x

2¼-inch) loaf pan greased with margarine, spreading out evenly.
5. Drain pimientos on paper toweling. Arrange 4 pimientos over fish in one layer. Spoon balance of fish over pimientos. Cover loosely with aluminum foil. Bake in preheated 350°F oven for 45 minutes.
6. Let cool in pan on rack at room temperature. Refrigerate until well chilled.
7. Loosen mold around sides with blunt knife. Invert onto lettuce-lined platter. Garnish with balance of pimiento cut into slivers, parsley sprigs, and lemon wedges.

Yield: Serves 4

CAL	F	P:S	SOD	CAR	CHO	PRO
162	1.5	1.4:1	167.5	9	80	26

Artichoke Soup

1 large artichoke (1½ pounds)
3 large cloves garlic, coarsely
    chopped
1 large shallot, coarsely chopped
1 teaspoon dried thyme leaves,
    crushed
2 tablespoons fresh lemon juice
1 tablespoon each corn oil and
    Italian olive oil, combined
1 leek, white part only, well washed
    and coarsely chopped
2 cups Rich Chicken Stock (page 94)
8 dashes ground red (cayenne)
    pepper
¼ cup each nonfat liquid milk, and
    evaporated skim milk (¼ percent
    milkfat)
    Minced fresh parsley

1. Choose an all-green artichoke with no brown outer leaves. Wash under cold running water. Drain. Fill narrow waterless cooker or stainless steel pot with 2 inches water. Add one-third of garlic, all of shallot, ½ teaspoon

thyme, and lemon juice. Bring to boil. Dip leaf side of artichoke into mixture. Then stand, stem side down, in pot. Cover and simmer for 45 minutes, spooning with liquid from time to time. Drain artichoke. Discard cooking liquid.

2. Fit processor with steel blade. Remove all petals from artichoke. Scrape off pulp. Place pulp in measuring cup. Coarsely shop heart. Add to measuring cup. There should be about 1¼ cups. Transfer to work bowl of processor.

3. Heat combined oils in nonstick skillet until hot. Add balance of garlic and leek. Sauté for 2 minutes. Do not brown.

4. Add stock, balance of thyme, and ground red pepper. Bring to simmering point. Cover and simmer for 10 minutes.

5. With slotted spoon, transfer solids from skillet to work bowl. Add 1 tablespoon stock. Turn processor on/off 3 times. Then process for 1 minute. Pour balance of stock through feed tube. Process on/off for 15 seconds.

6. Slowly reheat soup in heavy-bottomed saucepan to simmering point. Gradually stir in milks, heating only to simmering point. *Do not boil.* Serve immediately, sprinkled with fresh parsley.

Yield: Serves 4

CAL	F	P:S	SOD	CAR	CHO	PRO
147	7	4.4:1	39.5	47.5	1	8

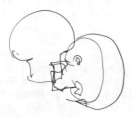

Brown Cabbage Soup

1 *head green cabbage (2 pounds)*
1 *leek, white part only, well washed*
4 *large cloves garlic*
1 *crisp, sweet apple, such as Washington State, peeled, cored, and cut into quarters*
1 *tablespoon each corn oil and sweet (unsalted) 100 percent corn oil margarine*
¼ *teaspoon ground red (cayenne) pepper*
½ *teaspoon ground cinnamon*
1 *tablespoon honey (optional)*
½ *teaspoon dried thyme leaves, crushed*
1 *teaspoon apple cider vinegar*
4 *cups Rich Chicken Stock (page 94) or Light Chicken Broth (page 95)*
½ *cup water*
3 *whole cloves*

1. Fit processor with shredding or slicing disc. Cut cabbage into quarters. Cut away tough center section. Cut each quarter into pieces to fit feed tube. Shred or slice cabbage, taking care not to overfill work bowl. Yield is about 4 cups of cut cabbage.

2. Push leek through tube. Turn mixture into bowl and combine.

3. Fit processor with steel blade. Add garlic and apple. Turn on/off until coarsely chopped. Add to cabbage mixture.

4. In large iron skillet, heat combined oil and margarine until hot. Add all of processed mixture. Add spices, honey, and thyme. Stir and sauté, uncovered, until reduced and browned (about 40 to 45 minutes).

5. Add vinegar. Cook and stir for 2 minutes.

6. Add 1 cup stock, stirring and loosening crusty particles from skillet.

7. Pour into waterless cooker or stainless-steel pot. Add balance of

stock, water, and cloves. Bring to simmering point. Cover and simmer for 1½ hours, and serve.

Yield: Serves 6

Variations:

1. To prepare as vegetable, follow steps 1 through 5. Add ¼ cup stock only. Stir and cook for 10 minutes. Yield: Serves 8.

2. To prepare with steak as main course, follow steps 1 through 5. Cut 1 pound lean boned sirloin steak into slivers. Heat 1 teaspoon corn oil in nonstick skillet until hot. Add steak and cook until browned. Add steak and ¼ cup stock to cabbage. Stir and cook for 1 minute. Yield: Serves 4.

3. To prepare with meatballs, as main course, follow steps 1 through 5. Combine ½ pound each ground lean beef and pork with 2 tablespoons Bread Crumbs (page 85), 2 tablespoons dry red wine, and 2 minced shallots. Shape into 16 meatballs. Heat 1 teaspoon corn oil in nonstick skillet until hot. Add meatballs and brown on all sides. Add meatballs and ½ cup stock to cabbage. Stir and cook over medium-high heat for 5 minutes. Yield: Serves 6.

Note: Cabbage is a superbly nutritious and economical vegetable, often overlooked in gourmet cooking. When prepared my style, in these and other ways, it adds a delicious versatility to your menus. And, delicate eaters, take heart—no cabbage recipe of mine is anything but highly digestible!

CAL	F	P:S	SOD	CAR	CHO	PRO
135	4.5	3:1	52.5	17.5	–	7
Variation 1:						
101	3.5	3:1	39.5	13	–	5.5
Variation 2:						
265.5	11.5	1.5:1	90.5	17.5	50	22.5
Variation 3:						
202.5	11	1.7:1	85	18	40.5	20
With honey, add to basic dish and variations, per serving:						
10.5	–	–	–	2.5	–	–

THE OPEN INDOOR ROTISSERIE / BROILER

Rotissing *inside* your home much as you would on an open hearth outside your home is an exciting departure from sautéing, oven roasting, and broiling. It's a recommended way of preparing meat, fish, and fowl because the freely circulating air seals in the natural juices while allowing the fat to drip off. Slow-cooking from heating elements *below* the food (in enclosed rotisseries the heating elements are above the food) produces uniform browning, and a roast done literally to a turn.

It's a comfortable way to rotiss: there's no smoke, very little spattering, and no excessive heat. It's time and effort saving because it's self-basting. And it's simple. Just balance your food on the skewer, insert it, turn on, and relax while the rotisserie goes to work for you.

But the secret of superb rotissing is not the machine itself, as extraordinary as it is, but the way the food is prepared before it goes into the machine. That secret is revealed in the recipes in this section. You'll also discover how to create masterpieces when you use the machine to broil chicken, halibut, sirloin, and lamb-eggplant kebabs.

Roast Stuffed Flank Steak

For the meat and marinade:
1 flank steak (about 1½ pounds), well trimmed
1 tablespoon fresh lime juice
1 tablespoon corn oil
1 tablespoon apple juice (no sugar added)
¼ cup medium-dry sherry
1 tablespoon Rich Chicken Stock (page 94)
½ teaspoon ground ginger
½ teaspoon dried thyme leaves, crushed

For the stuffing:
1 cup lightly toasted dark bread cubes (about 3 slices) (see note)
1 tablespoon corn oil
1 small onion, minced
½ small sweet red pepper, seeded and minced
2 large cloves garlic, minced
2 tablespoons minced celery
2 large fresh mushrooms, washed, dried, trimmed, and coarsely chopped
6 dashes ground red (cayenne) pepper
½ teaspoon curry powder (no salt or pepper added)
¼ teaspoon dried thyme leaves, crushed
1 tablespoon combined minced fresh parsley and dill
¼ cup peeled and coarsely chopped sweet, crisp apple, such as Washington State
¼ cup Rich Chicken Stock (page 94)

1. Prepare the meat and marinade first. Wipe meat with damp paper toweling. Make two pockets in the meat as follows: Insert knife into one of the small ends of the steak and cut almost to the center, then toward each side, stopping within 1 inch from edges. Repeat for other small end. Do not cut through center of steak. Place in bowl.

2. Combine balance of ingredients in jar for marinade. Shake well to blend. Pour over meat and into pockets, turning well to coat. Cover, and marinate for 1 to 2 hours at room temperature.

3. Prepare stuffing as meat is marinating. Place cubed bread in bowl. Heat oil in nonstick skillet until hot. Sauté onion, sweet red pepper, garlic, celery, and mushrooms for 3 minutes, stirring constantly.

4. Sprinkle with spices and herbs, blending well. Stir in apple.

5. Pour into bowl with bread. Sprinkle with stock and mix until bread is well moistened.

6. Drain meat, reserving marinade. Pat with paper toweling. Spoon stuffing equally into pockets, pressing with hands. Roll up, starting from small end. Secure temporarily with toothpicks. Tie with string, pulling tightly where necessary, to form meat into a cylindrical shape. Remove toothpicks.

7. Preheat rotisserie. Insert spit so that meat is evenly balanced. Place spit as close as possible to heat, without meat actually touching it. For medium-rare roast, rotiss for 40 minutes, brushing several times with marinade.

8. Remove string. With very sharp knife, slice meat 1/2 inch thick, taking care not to press down on meat. Allow 2 slices per serving.

Yield: Serves 4

Note: The tartness of Sourdough Whole Wheat Bread (page 70), which I use in this recipe, is a perfect foil for the slight sweetness of the other ingredients.

	CAL	F	P:S	SOD	CAR	CHO	PRO
Meat and marinade:	208.5	7	1.6:1	73.5	3.5	112.5	26.5
Stuffing:	89	4	4.4:1	14.5	5	–	2.5

Gingered Roast Chicken

1 broiling chicken (3 pounds),
  skinned, wing tips removed
1 recipe Ginger Marinade (page 100)
2 tart green apples, peeled, cored,
  and thickly sliced
2 tablespoons minced fresh parsley
1 bay leaf
  Parsley sprigs

1. The night before roasting, rinse skinned chicken inside and out with cold running water. Dry thoroughly with paper toweling. Place in large bowl.

2. Pour marinade over bird, spooning a tablespoon into cavity. Turn to coat. Cover tightly with plastic wrap and place in refrigerator overnight.

3. Remove chicken from refrigerator 1 hour before roasting. Drain, reserving marinade. Pat lightly with paper toweling so that bird will be easy to handle. Stuff cavity with apples, minced parsley, and bay leaf. Sew up cavity or secure with small skewers. (Be sure the skewers do not interfere with the revolving spit.) Truss bird securely.

4. Preheat rotisserie. Insert spit through center of bird so that it is evenly balanced. Adjust spit so that chicken rotates close to, but not touching, heating element.

5. Roast chicken for 1 hour, spooning 4 to 5 times with reserved marinade. Turn off rotisserie. Let chicken stand for 5 minutes on spit.

6. Transfer to carving board. Remove trussing and skewers. Spoon apple stuffing into serving dish. Discard bay leaf. Cut bird into serving pieces. Arrange on warmed serving platter. Garnish with parsley sprigs. Serve apple stuffing along with chicken.

Yield: Serves 4

CAL	F	P:S	SOD	CAR	CHO	PRO
288.5	10	1.9:1	91.6	13	94.5	46.5

Indian-Style Roast Leg of Lamb

½ leg of lamb, preferably shank end
  (3½ pounds), well trimmed, boned
⅓ cup dry vermouth
⅓ cup unsweetened pineapple juice
2 large cloves garlic, minced
4 whole cloves
2 teaspoons curry powder (no salt
  or pepper added)
2 teaspoons coriander seeds,
  crushed
½ teaspoon ground ginger
1 thin lime slice
1 bay leaf
3 teaspoons corn oil

1. The day before roasting, wipe meat with damp paper toweling. Place in bowl.

2. In saucepan, combine balance of ingredients except for oil. Simmer for 3 minutes. Pour over meat, turning to coat. Roll up meat. Cover and refrigerate overnight.

3. Preheat broiler. Adjust rack so that it is in high position. Brush rack with 1/2 teaspoon oil. Unroll and drain meat, reserving marinade. Brush broiling side with 1/4 teaspoon oil. Lay meat flat on rack. Brush with balance of oil. Broil for 12 minutes. Spoon with some marinade. Turn, and broil for 10 minutes. Spoon again. Cover loosely with aluminum foil. Broil for 5 minutes for medium-rare. (Cooking time will vary with thickness of meat.)

4. Transfer to carving board. Slice thin at an angle. Serve immediately.

Yield: Serves 6

CAL	F	P:S	SOD	CAR	CHO	PRO
317	13	0.8:1	117	3	153.5	44

Crisp and Moist Leg of Lamb

½ leg of lamb (3½ pounds), preferably shank end, well trimmed
¾ teaspoon combined dried sage, rosemary, and thyme leaves, crushed
2 tablespoons corn oil
1 teaspoon lime juice
1 tablespoon wine vinegar
¾ teaspoon ground ginger
4 large cloves garlic, minced
2 tablespoons medium-dry sherry

1. Wipe meat with damp paper toweling.

2. In small bowl, combine and blend balance of ingredients except for sherry. Place meat on dish, and spread with marinade mixture (it will be thick), turning to coat. Cover tightly with aluminum foil and let marinate in refrigerator for 4 to 6 hours. Remove from refrigerator 1 hour before cooking.

3. Preheat rotisserie. Insert spit through lamb so that meat is evenly balanced. Adjust spit so that meat is close to heat but not touching heating element. Rotiss for 25 minutes, brushing with sherry while spit is rotating.

4. Continue roasting, and brushing with sherry from time to time, for a total of 1½ hours (rare, which is the way we like it) or for an additional 15 minutes (medium-rare).

5. Turn off rotisserie and let meat stand on spit for 5 minutes. Remove, slice thin, and serve.

Yield: Serves 6

CAL	F	P:S	SOD	CAR	CHO	PRO
332.5	15	1.4:1	112.5	1	153.5	44

Festive Roast Turkey

All of us like to fuss at holiday time. So why not fuss to make this superb bird, with its sumptuous flavors and very low-calorie gravy? To simplify your stint in the kitchen, my bread for the stuffing (you'll never use store-bought stuffing again) can be prepared weeks in advance, and the simple gravy can be started the day before. My subtle use of herbs and spices will make this a memorable holiday dish; it's like no turkey you ever tasted before. The compliments from your family will make you glow like the ornaments on your Christmas tree. Worth the fuss, isn't it?

For the gravy:
   Neck and gizzard from turkey, washed and trimmed
1 teaspoon juniper berries, crushed
½ teaspoon dried thyme leaves, crushed
1 teaspoon curry powder (no salt or pepper added)
2 whole cloves
½ rib celery, sliced
2 cloves garlic, minced
1 small leek, well washed, white part plus 1 inch green part, sliced
½ carrot, peeled and sliced
1 small white turnip, peeled and diced
6 dashes ground red (cayenne) pepper
   Bouquet garni (1 sprig parsley, 1 bay leaf, tied together with white thread)
   Water to cover (about 2½ cups)
1 tablespoon minced fresh parsley

For the stuffing:
⅓ cup brown rice, well washed and drained
5 cups toasted Potato Braid cubes (page 74; and see note below)

1 each small green apple and sweet
   apple, peeled, cored, and diced
3 tablespoons combined minced
   fresh parsley and dill
4½ teaspoons each corn oil and sweet
   (unsalted) 100 percent corn oil
   margarine
5 large cloves garlic, minced
1 rib celery, minced
3 large shallots, minced
½ pound fresh mushrooms, washed,
   dried, trimmed, and sliced ¼ inch
   thick
½ pound ground lean veal
⅛ teaspoon ground red (cayenne)
   pepper
1 teaspoon each dried thyme and
   rosemary leaves, crushed
1 teaspoon curry powder (no salt or
   pepper added)
1½ teaspoons ground ginger
2 tablespoons apple cider vinegar
1½ cups Rich Chicken Stock (page 94)
   or Light Chicken Broth (page 95)

For the turkey:
1 fresh turkey (6 pounds)
1 tablespoon corn oil
1 tablespoon dry vermouth
½ teaspoon each dried thyme and
   rosemary leaves, crushed
1 teaspoon curry powder (no salt or
   pepper added)
½ teaspoon ground ginger
8 dashes ground red (cayenne)
   pepper

1. Start the gravy a day ahead.
Combine all gravy ingredients except minced parsley in small heavy-
bottomed saucepan. Bring to boil. Boil,
uncovered, for 3 minutes, removing
scum that rises to top.

2. Lower heat, cover partially, and
simmer for 1½ hours. Let cool in pot.

3. Remove neck, gizzard, and bouquet garni. Discard. Pour balance of
ingredients in pot into heatproof bowl.
Cover and refrigerate overnight.

4. To prepare stuffing, cook rice
in rapidly boiling water to cover for

15 minutes, stirring from time to time.
Drain. Rice will be slightly undercooked.

5. Place rice, bread cubes, apples,
and fresh herbs in bowl. Toss to blend.

6. Heat 1½ teaspoons each oil and
margarine in nonstick skillet until hot.
Sauté garlic, celery, and shallots for 2
minutes, stirring constantly. Push to
side of skillet.

7. Add 1½ teaspoons each oil and
margarine to skillet. Sauté mushrooms
over medium-high heat for 2 minutes.
Combine all ingredients in skillet and
sauté for 1 minute. Pour into bread mixture.

8. Heat balance of oil and margarine in skillet until hot. Add veal, breaking into pieces with spoon. Sauté until
meat just starts to lose its pinkness
(about 4 minutes).

9. Sprinkle with dried herbs and
spices, stirring to blend.

10. Add vinegar and cook for 1 minute. Add to rice mix in bowl, tossing to
blend.

11. Gradually add stock to bowl
while tossing, so that bread cubes are
evenly moistened. Set stuffing aside.

12. Trim any fat from turkey. Wash
inside and out. Wipe dry with paper
toweling.

13. Fill body and neck cavities with
stuffing. Sew up openings. Truss turkey, making certain that wings are tied
to body of bird. Push spit through center of turkey, securing with prongs.

14. Prick skin of turkey every inch
with sharp-pronged fork. Combine oil,
vermouth, herbs, and spices. Spread
over turkey.

15. Preheat rotisserie. Insert spit so
that turkey is well balanced. Place spit
on supports. Roast for about 1½ hours.
Test for doneness by pricking turkey
near bottom of thigh. Juices should not
run pink. If they do, roast an additional
10 to 15 minutes, then test again. When
turkey is done, let rest on spit for 5
minutes. Remove from spit and place
on carving board. Cover loosely with

waxed paper and let stand for 10 minutes.

16. Now complete gravy. Discard any fat from cold prepared gravy-and-vegetable mixture. Place in heavy-bottomed saucepan. Bring to simmering point and simmer, uncovered, for 5 minutes.

17. Pour into blender and purée for 1 minute. Pour back into saucepan. Add minced parsley and reheat briefly, adding more ground red pepper if necessary. Serve in sauceboat along with turkey and stuffing.

Yield: Turkey and stuffing serve 8; gravy yields about 1¾ cups (allow 3 tablespoons per serving)

Note: Potato Braids can be prepared well ahead of time and kept frozen until ready to use. Half the recipe can be made into a plain high round loaf for stuffing, and the other half braided into a crusty, beautiful loaf for sandwiches, toast, or eating au naturel. This bread helps make one of the most extraordinary stuffings you'll ever taste.

CAL	F	P:S	SOD	CAR	CHO	PRO
Turkey:						
271	6.5	0.7:1	163	–	53	49.5
Stuffing:						
234.5	7	2.1:1	47	32	23	13
Gravy (per tablespoon):						
36.5	–	–	51	8	–	1.5

Chicken with Sweet and Pungent Sauce

For the chicken and marinade:
½ cup Light Chicken Broth (page 95)
1 tablespoon corn oil plus ½ teaspoon for rack

1 teaspoon honey
1 teaspoon peeled and minced fresh ginger
1 tablespoon medium-dry sherry
1 large clove garlic, minced
1 teaspoon grated onion
1 tablespoon apple cider vinegar
4 dashes ground red (cayenne) pepper
1 broiling chicken (3 pounds), skinned, cut into serving pieces

For the sauce:
⅓ cup fresh orange juice
½ cup unsweetened pineapple juice
1 teaspoon apple cider vinegar
2 teaspoons fresh lemon juice
2 dashes ground ginger
½ teaspoon freshly grated orange rind, preferably from navel orange
2 teaspoons honey
1 teaspoon minced fresh parsley
1 tablespoon cornstarch dissolved in 1 tablespoon water

1. Prepare marinade by combining broth, 1 tablespoon oil, and next 7 ingredients in jar and shaking well.

2. Wash chicken and dry with paper toweling. Place in bowl. Pour all but ¼ cup marinade over chicken. (Reserve remainder of marinade, strained, for sauce.) Cover chicken and refrigerate for 3 to 4 hours. Remove from refrigerator 1 hour before broiling.

3. Preheat broiler. Adjust rack to high position (about 2 to 2½ inches from heating element). Brush rack with oil.

4. Place chicken on rack and broil for 7 minutes. Spoon with marinade. Turn and broil for 7 minutes. Turn once more, and continue broiling, spooning with marinade and turning every 7 minutes until chicken is done (total broiling time is 35 minutes). Should smaller pieces be done first, lay them on larger pieces to keep warm.

5. Start preparing sauce 10 minutes before chicken is done. In saucepan, combine ¼ cup strained marinade and balance of sauce ingredients except for

cornstarch mixture. Bring to simmering point and simmer for 2 minutes.

6. Dribble in only enough cornstarch mixture to thicken sauce lightly.

7. Transfer chicken to warmed serving platter. Spoon with sauce and serve immediately.

Yield: Serves 4

	CAL	F	P:S	SOD	CAR	CHO	PRO
Chicken:	269	6	4.1:1	81.5	2.5	94.5	37
Sauce:	32.5	–	–	2.5	7.5	–	0.5

Barbecued Halibut Steaks

2 halibut steaks (1¾ pounds total), each steak cut in half
1 tablespoon corn oil plus ½ teaspoon for rack
2 teaspoons prepared Dijon mustard (no salt added)
1½ teaspoons chili con carne seasoning (no salt or pepper added)
1 large clove garlic, minced
2 tablespoons fresh lemon juice
½ cup pineapple chunks packed in juice, drained
Minced fresh parsley

1. Wash fish and dry with paper toweling.

2. In blender, combine 1 tablespoon oil with balance of ingredients except for parsley. Purée for 1 minute. Mixture should be smooth.

3. Place fish in shallow dish. Spread puréed mixture over both sides of fish. Cover with plastic wrap and let stand for 30 minutes at room temperature.

4. Preheat broiler. Set rack in high position. Brush with oil. Broil fish 7 to 8 minutes on each side. Transfer to warmed individual serving plates. Sprinkle with parsley and serve.

Yield: Serves 4

CAL	F	P:S	SOD	CAR	CHO	PRO
250.5	6	3.2:1	113.5	5	96	42

Broiled Lamb-Eggplant Kebabs

1 pound lean boneless lamb, cut from leg, cut into 1-inch cubes
1 eggplant (about ¾ pound), peeled and cut into 1-inch cubes
¼ cup each wine vinegar and apple cider vinegar
2 teaspoons each corn oil and Italian olive oil, combined
1 tablespoon fresh lime juice
2 tablespoons unsweetened pineapple juice
2 tablespoons Rich Chicken Stock (page 94)
½ teaspoon each ground ginger, curry powder (no salt or pepper added), and coriander seeds, crushed
½ teaspoon dried sweet basil leaves, crushed
6 dashes ground red (cayenne) pepper
1 tablespoon minced fresh parsley
1 medium sweet red pepper, seeded and cut into 1-inch pieces

1. Place cubed lamb and eggplant in bowl.

2. In jar, combine balance of ingredients except for sweet red pepper, shaking well. Pour over meat and eggplant, turning to coat evenly. Cover with plastic wrap and let marinate for 1 hour at room temperature.

3. Drain meat and eggplant, reserving marinade. On each of 4 long skewers, alternate meat, eggplant, and sweet red pepper.

4. Preheat broiler. Set rack close to heating element. Place skewers across rack and broil for 5 minutes. Turn, spoon a small amount of reserved marinade over kebabs, and broil for an additional 5 minutes. Turn, spoon with balance of marinade, and broil for 3 minutes. Turn, and broil for another 3 minutes. Turn once again and broil for still another 3 minutes. Meat is now deliciously rare (total cooking time is about 19 minutes).

Yield: Serves 4

Variations:

1. Marinate 8 mushroom caps for 30 minutes with meat and eggplant, and include on each skewer.

2. Add 2 pineapple chunks packed in unsweetened pineapple juice to each skewer.

Note: A colorful buffet dish, these kebabs will serve 8 when accompanied by other food.

CAL	F	P:S	SOD	CAR	CHO	PRO
Basic Recipe (serves 4):						
208	9	1.4:1	71.5	10.5	66	20.5
With 8 mushrooms:						
214	9	1.4:1	74.5	11.5	66	21
With 2 pineapple chunks:						
216	9	1.4:1	71.5	12.5	66	20.5
Basic recipe (serves 8):						
104	4.5	1.4:1	36	5	33	10
With 8 mushrooms:						
107	4.5	1.4:1	37.5	5.5	33	10
With 2 pineapple chunks:						
108	4.5	1.4:1	36	6	33	10

Hibachi-Style Steak I

⅓ cup low-fat plain yogurt
1 tablespoon fresh lime juice
1 scallion, minced
2 teaspoons toasted coriander seeds, well crushed (see note 1, page 77)
2 teaspoons minced fresh parsley
¼ cup fresh orange juice
1 teaspoon corn oil
1½ pounds lean boneless sirloin steak, cut into 3- x 1-inch strips

1. Combine first 6 ingredients and ½ teaspoon corn oil in bowl. Add steak, turning to coat. Cover tightly with plastic wrap and marinate for 1 hour (see note).

2. Drain meat, reserving marinade. Place rack close to heating element. Brush with balance of oil. Preheat broiler. Add meat and broil for 5 minutes on each side, basting with reserved marinade before turning. Meat will be rare. For medium-rare, spoon meat again with marinade and broil an additional 3 minutes. Serve immediately.

Yield: Serves 4

Note: If time permits, marinate meat for 6 hours before broiling.

CAL	F	P:S	SOD	CAR	CHO	PRO
238.5	10	1.6:1	76.5	7	114	27

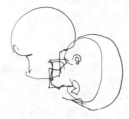

Hibachi-Style Steak II

1 tablespoon corn oil plus ½ teaspoon for rack
2 tablespoons fresh lemon juice
1 teaspoon wine vinegar
1 tablespoon minced fresh parsley
2 large cloves garlic, minced
1 large shallot, minced
¼ cup apple juice (no sugar added)
¼ teaspoon each ground ginger and curry powder (no salt or pepper added)
6 dashes ground red (cayenne) pepper
½ teaspoon chili con carne seasoning (no salt or pepper added)
1½ pounds lean boneless sirloin steak, cut into 3- x 1-inch strips
1 medium sweet green pepper, seeded and cut into 2-inch pieces
1 large carrot, peeled and cut diagonally into ¼-inch slices

1. Combine 1 tablespoon oil with next 9 ingredients in bowl. Blend. Add steak, pepper, and carrot. Cover tightly with plastic wrap and marinate for 1 hour.

2. Drain meat, reserving marinade. Place rack close to heating element. Brush with oil. Preheat broiler. Add meat and vegetables and broil for 5 minutes on each side, basting with reserved marinade before turning. Meat will be rare. For medium-rare, spoon meat again with marinade and broil an additional 3 minutes, pushing vegetables to side of broiler where heat is less intense.

Yield: Serves 4

CAL	F	P:S	SOD	CAR	CHO	PRO
234	11	1.9:1	79.5	4.6	113	26.5

Chicken Kebabs Hors d'Oeuvres

1 pound boneless, skinned chicken breasts, flattened to uniform thickness
½ teaspoon each ground ginger and curry powder (no salt or pepper added)
¼ teaspoon each ground turmeric and crushed cardamom seeds
¼ teaspoon chili con carne seasoning (no salt or pepper added)
1 teaspoon each fresh lime juice and wine vinegar
4 dashes ground red (cayenne) pepper
1 tablespoon minced fresh parsley
2 tablespoons thick buttermilk (no salt added)
1 sweet red pepper, seeded and cut into 1½-inch pieces
6 slices (⅜-inch each) sweet Bermuda onion
½ teaspoon corn oil, for rack
Lemon wedges

1. Wash chicken and wipe dry with paper toweling. Cut into 1½-inch pieces.

2. In small bowl, combine next 7 ingredients. Blend with fork. Add chicken and turn to coat. Cover and let stand at room temperature for 1 hour.

3. On each of 6 small skewers, alternate pieces of chicken, red pepper, and onion.

4. Preheat broiler. Set rack close to heat. Brush with oil. Broil kebabs for 15 to 20 minutes, turning 4 times. Arrange on serving plate garnished with lemon wedges. Serve.

Yield: Serves 6

CAL	F	P:S	SOD	CAR	CHO	PRO
105.5	2	2.1	69.5	3.5	38	18

Broiled Lime Chicken

1 broiling chicken (3 pounds), skinned, wing tips removed, and cut into serving pieces
1 recipe Lime Marinade (page 99)
½ teaspoon corn oil, for rack
1½ teaspoons each minced fresh parsley and dill, combined

1. Wash chicken and pat dry with paper toweling.

2. Place chicken in bowl. Pour marinade over bird, turning to coat. Cover tightly with plastic wrap and refrigerate for 6 hours or overnight. Remove from refrigerator 1 hour before broiling.

3. Drain chicken, reserving marinade. Preheat broiler. Set rack in high position. Brush with oil. Lay chicken on rack and broil for 7 minutes. Turn. Brush with marinade and broil for 7 minutes. Turn and brush again, then continue to broil, turning and brushing twice more at 7-minute intervals, until done (total cooking time is 35 minutes). Should smaller parts be done before rest of bird, lay them on larger pieces to keep warm.

4. Serve immediately, sprinkled with parsley and dill.

Yield: Serves 4

CAL	F	P:S	SOD	CAR	CHO	PRO
221.5	7.5	1.2:1	80	2	94.5	38

THE WOK

This thousands-of-years old, all-purpose cooking utensil is a frying pan in the shape of a sphere cut in half. Excitingly novel to Americans, it is a staple in the kitchens of China, India, Vietnam, Malaysia, Java—indeed throughout the Far East.

Extraordinarily versatile, it can be used for stir-frying, deep-frying, parboiling, poaching, simmering, braising, barbecuing, and steaming. (It becomes a steamer just by setting a wire rack on the bottom and boiling water under the rack. You can even steam-bake cakes this way.) But it is stir-frying that has sustained the perennial popularity of the wok, and deservedly so.

Stir-frying means just what it says: you stir while you fry. The geometry of the wok speeds up cooking time astonishingly. This means the pure tastes and textures of the ingredients are retained; and vegetable hues deepen into the dramatic brilliance of TV colors. In this wizard's alembic of a vessel, hot oil sears in the ingredients' juices while extracting their flavors, which quickly commingle to create exquisite sauces. No loss here, as there is in standard Western cooking, of precious nutrients as cooking waters are poured down the drain.

Because the wok is unfamiliar to many Americans, I've prepared the following detailed instructions for its use. Don't let the length of these guidelines deter you from an unforgettable adventure into an entirely new cuisine. Truly, stir-fry cooking is simple, and simply enthralling.

Choosing your wok and accessories: I find that the most inexpensive kind, a 14-inch wok made from cold-pressed steel (mine is imported from Taiwan) gives the best results for my recipes. Be sure that you also buy a cover, and a metal ring to hold the wok upright on your stove and to remove it from the source of heat (although both accessories usually come with the wok, one or the other may not).

No other unusual accessories are needed. If you have a slotted spatula or spoon and a long-handled spoon (preferably with a shovel-shaped mouth), you're ready to begin. Chances are you have both in your kitchen right now.

Preparing your wok: Before you can use your wok, it must be "seasoned," that is to say, treated in such a way as to close up the pores of the metal, thus preventing anything from sticking to it. Here's how to do it:

1. Using steel wool, gently remove the coating of machine oil in which the wok has been packed. (Never again use steel wool on the wok.) Rinse and dry.

2. Rub the interior of the wok with paper toweling soaked in corn oil.

3. Place wok on metal ring and heat for 1 minute.

4. Remove wok to sink and rinse with hot water. Repeat the heating and rinsing process twice. The inside of the wok has now turned mostly black, and it's ready to use.

5. As you use your wok, you'll find from time to time that ingredients will begin to stick. That's the time to season your wok again.

Caution: Some woks come with specific instructions for seasoning. Follow them.

Cleaning your wok: As soon as you've finished cooking, remove wok to sink, fill vessel with sudsy water, and let soak. Scrub with bamboo brush to remove cooked food. Rinse in hot water and *immediately* remove to ring and dry over high heat. (This prevents rusting.) Let cool. Brush lightly with corn oil and wipe off excess with paper toweling.

Preparing stir-fry dishes: Stir-frying is the cooking process used in all my recipes in this section. It's fun when you follow these guidelines:

1. Read the recipe before you begin to cook. Stir-fry cooking demands forethought and organization, so it will be helpful to get a general idea of what has to be done before you do it.

2. Prepare ingredients and place them in transparent containers. Have rice cooked and steaming. Be sure your parboiled vegetables are ready.

To parboil, bring pot of water to rolling boil. Drop prepared vegetables in water. Boil for 30 seconds to 1 minute. Pour into colander. Place under cold running water until vegetables are cool. Let drain until ready to use. Then dry with paper toweling.

Hard vegetables should be cut diagonally; soft vegetables, vertically or horizontally. Meat, fish, and poultry should be sliced into bite-sized bits. The object is to expose to heat as much of the surface of the food as possible in order to hasten cooking.

3. Arrange ingredients near stove in the order in which they will be used. The ingredients will be added to the wok in sequence on a rigid, fast-paced schedule. If you're not ready with an ingredient at the right moment, your dish could be ruined.

4. Invite your family or guests to be seated at the dining table. You'll be finished cooking in a few minutes; and stir-fried food, to be fully enjoyed, must be eaten as soon as it is served.

5. Heat empty wok over high heat for 1½ minutes. Pour oil around rim of wok. The oil will slide down the flared sides, coating them uniformly and forming a pool at the bottom.

6. Add ingredients in the order in which you have arranged them, following the time schedule in the recipe. Solid ingredients are added directly to the pool; liquid ingredients are poured around the rim of the wok. Never add wet ingredients to the pool; the sudden contact of water with oil will flare into mini-explosions. Solid ingredients are seared instantly by the hot oil.

7. Toss ingredients, then stir with long-handled spoon. The wok's flared sides will cause the morsels to slide back into the pool almost at once,

quickening the searing process. Since the sides of the wok are as hot or hotter than the bottom, the food is flash-sizzled when it hits them.

8. Don't hesitate to add cornstarch in the final seconds, as the Chinese do, to thicken the sauce. One tablespoon adds only about 7 calories and 0 milligrams of sodium per serving.

9. Have serving plates warm and ready. Turn off heat (the wok cools down rapidly, forestalling in-pot over-cooking), and serve immediately. Do not cover serving platter (covered dishes continue the cooking process).

Traditional stir-fry cooking is lighter than most American cooking, but the calorie counts are about the same as for haute cuisine of health cooking, and the sodium counts are phenomenally higher. I use the wok because of the interesting textures and tastes I achieve, and because the swift pace of stir-fry cooking gives me exhilarating minutes in the kitchen. The stir-fry recipes that follow are not Chinese, but rather original healthful American recipes influenced by the cuisines of the Orient and Chinatown, U.S.A.

Light and Spicy Chicken and Shrimps

½ pound boneless, skinned chicken breasts cut lengthwise into ¼-inch strips
⅔ cup Light Chicken Broth (page 95)
6 dashes ground red (cayenne) pepper

½ teaspoon chili con carne seasoning (no salt or pepper added)
½ teaspoon ground ginger
1 teaspoon tomato paste (no salt added)
½ pound fresh shrimp, shelled and deveined
6 teaspoons corn oil
3 large cloves garlic, minced
1 small wedge Chinese cabbage, cut lengthwise into ½-inch strips
⅓ cup bamboo shoots, rinsed, dried, and sliced
10 fresh snow peas, washed, dried, and stems and strings removed (see note 1, page 110)
7 water chestnuts, rinsed, dried, and sliced
1 tablespoon cornstarch dissolved in 1 tablespoon cold water
1 tablespoon medium-dry sherry

1. Rinse chicken and shrimp under cold running water and dry with paper toweling.
2. In a bowl, combine broth, ground red pepper, chili con carne seasoning, ginger, and tomato paste. Set aside.
3. Heat wok over high heat for 1½ minutes. Pour 2¼ teaspoons oil around rim of wok. When oil drips down, add one-third of garlic. Stir-fry for 30 seconds. Add chicken. Cook on each side for 1 minute. Transfer to plate. Set aside.
4. Pour 2¼ teaspoons oil around rim of wok. Add second third of garlic. Stir-fry for 30 seconds. Add shrimp and cook for 1 minute on each side. Transfer to plate. Set aside.
5. Pour balance of oil around rim of wok. Add balance of garlic and stir-fry for 30 seconds. Add cabbage, bamboo shoots, snow peas, and water chestnuts. Stir-fry for 2 minutes, turning constantly. Return chicken and shrimp to wok. Stir.
6. Pour reserved broth mixture

slowly around rim of wok. Stir and cook for 1 minute.

7. Pour cornstarch mixture around rim of wok. Cook for 30 seconds.

8. Stir in sherry rapidly. Serve immediately.

Yield: Serves 4

CAL	F	P:S	SOD	CAR	CHO	PRO
213	10.5	2.9:1	110	11	74.5	22

Broccoli and Tomatoes over Pasta

½ pound pasta (fettuccelle no. 14; see note)

1 tablespoon each corn oil and Italian olive oil, combined

1 leek, white part only, well washed and coarsely chopped

3 large cloves garlic, minced

½-inch slice fresh ginger, peeled and shredded

1 small sweet red pepper, seeded and cut into ½-inch slivers Flowerets plus ½ inch of stem from 2 large stalks broccoli

8 dashes ground red (cayenne) pepper

½ teaspoon dried thyme leaves, crushed

1 teaspoon curry powder (no salt or pepper added)

2 ripe fresh tomatoes, skinned, cored, and coarsely chopped

2 teaspoons tomato paste (no salt added)

¼ cup dry vermouth

¾ cup Rich Chicken Stock (page 94) or Light Chicken Broth (page 95)

1 tablespoon cornstarch dissolved in 1 tablespoon cold water

1 tablespoon minced fresh parsley

1. Bring large pot of water to rolling boil. Add fettuccelle and cook for 10 to 12 minutes. Drain. Cover.

2. While pasta is cooking, start the sauce. Heat wok over high heat for 1½ minutes. Pour combined oils around rim. When oil drips down, add leek, garlic, and ginger. Stir-fry for 1 minute. Add slivered pepper and stir-fry for 20 seconds.

3. Add broccoli flowerets to wok. Sprinkle with ground red pepper, thyme, and curry powder. Stir-fry for 1½ minutes.

4. Add tomatoes and tomato paste to wok. Cook for 1 minute.

5. Pour vermouth around rim of wok. Stir and cook for 30 seconds.

6. Slowly pour stock around rim of wok. Cover and cook over medium heat for 2 minutes.

7. Uncover and pour cornstarch mixture around rim of wok. Cook briefly until thickened.

8. Transfer pasta to serving dish. Pour sauce over center of pasta, spreading out to within 1 inch from edge of pasta. Sprinkle with parsley. Serve.

Yield: Serves 4

Note: Fettuccelle no. 14 is a delicious commercial flat pasta. If fettuccelle is not available, substitute spaghetti, vermicelli, elbow macaroni, or any pasta made without eggs and salt.

CAL	F	P:S	SOD	CAR	CHO	PRO
334	7	4.4:1	24	54.5	–	10

With other spaghettis: No appreciable difference

Flash-Cooked Flounder with Leek

3 tablespoons distilled white
    vinegar
1 whole clove, crushed
1½ pounds flounder fillets, washed,
    dried, and cut into 1½-inch pieces
2 tablespoons plus 1½ teaspoons
    corn oil
2 large cloves garlic, minced
½-inch slice fresh ginger, peeled and
    shredded
½ small sweet red pepper, seeded
    and cut into ¼-inch slivers
1 large leek, white part only, well
    washed, dried, and cut into ¼-inch
    slices
16 fresh snow peas, washed, dried,
    and stems and strings removed
    (see note 1, page 110)
6 water chestnuts, rinsed in cold
    water, patted dry, and sliced
    (optional)
⅓ cup Rich Chicken Stock (page 94)
6 dashes ground red (cayenne)
    pepper
1 tablespoon cornstarch dissolved
    in 1 tablespoon cold water
1 tablespoon medium-dry sherry

1. In bowl, combine vinegar and clove. Add fish. Let stand at room temperature for 15 minutes, turning once. Drain on paper toweling.

2. Heat wok over high heat for 1½ minutes. Pour 1 tablespoon oil around rim of wok. Add one-third each garlic and ginger. Stir-fry for 30 seconds.

3. Add half of fish. Cook on one side for 1½ minutes without moving fish. Turn carefully and cook for another 1½ minutes, taking care that fish pieces do not touch each other (to prevent juices from oozing out of fish). Transfer to warm plate. Cover loosely with waxed paper.

4. Pour 1 tablespoon oil around rim of wok. Add second third each of garlic and ginger. Stir-fry for 30 seconds. Add balance of fish and repeat step 3.

5. Pour balance of oil around rim of wok. Add balance of garlic and ginger. Stir-fry for 30 seconds. Add slivered pepper and leek. Stir-fry for 2 minutes.

6. Add snow peas and water chestnuts. Stir-fry for 30 seconds.

7. Pour stock around rim of wok. Add ground red pepper. Cover and cook over medium heat for 30 seconds.

8. Uncover and pour cornstarch mixture around rim of wok, stirring to blend.

9. Stir in sherry. Pour over fish and serve.

Yield: Serves 4

CAL	F	P:S	SOD	CAR	CHO	PRO
243	8	4:1	145.5	8.5	94.5	30
With water chestnuts:						
264.5	8	4:1	150	13	94.5	31

Colorful Stir-Fried Chicken

5 teaspoons cornstarch
1 teaspoon each ground ginger and
    curry powder (no salt or pepper
    added)
8 dashes ground red (cayenne)
    pepper
¼ teaspoon dried thyme leaves,
    crushed
1 teaspoon fresh lemon juice
1 tablespoon medium-dry sherry
1 egg white
2 small whole chicken breasts,
    boned and skinned (1¼ pounds
    boned weight)
2 tablespoons corn oil
3 large cloves garlic, minced

½-inch slice fresh ginger, peeled and
    shredded
1 small sweet red pepper, seeded
    and cut into ¼-inch slivers
¼ pound fresh snow peas, washed,
    dried, and stems and strings
    removed (see note 1 page 110)
¼ pound fresh mushrooms, washed,
    dried, trimmed, and thickly sliced
½ cup Rich Chicken Stock (page 94)
1 tablespoon minced Chinese
    parsley (see note page 165)

1. Combine first 7 ingredients in
bowl. Beat with fork to blend.
2. Wash chicken and wipe dry with
paper toweling. Cut into 1-inch cubes.
Add to bowl, turning until well coated.
Let stand for 10 minutes.
3. Heat wok over high heat for 1½
minutes. Pour 1 tablespoon oil around
rim of wok. When oil drops down, add
half each of garlic and ginger. Stir-fry
for 30 seconds. Add chicken. Spread
across wok in 1 layer. Cook for 2 minutes on each side. Transfer to plate.
4. Pour balance of oil around rim of
wok. Add pepper slivers, snow peas,
and mushrooms. Stir-fry for 2 minutes.
Return chicken to wok. Stir quickly to
combine.
5. Pour stock around rim of wok.
Stir. Cover and cook over medium heat
for 2 minutes. Pour into serving bowl.
Sprinkle with Chinese parsley and
serve.

Yield: Serves 4

CAL	F	P:S	SOD	CAR	CHO	PRO
271.5	8.5	3.7:1	121.5	9	84	38

Rice in a Wok

2 tablespoons corn oil
3 large cloves garlic, minced
½-inch slice fresh ginger, peeled and
    shredded

1 large onion, thinly sliced
1 medium sweet red pepper, seeded
    and cut into ⅜-inch slices
½ pound fresh mushrooms, washed,
    dried, trimmed, and sliced ¼-inch
    thick
¾ teaspoon combined dried thyme
    and basil leaves, crushed
½ teaspoon ground turmeric
1 teaspoon curry powder (no salt or
    pepper added)
6 dashes ground red (cayenne)
    pepper
¾ cup rice
½ cup warm Rich Chicken Stock
    (page 94)
¾ cup warm water
1 green apple, peeled, cored,
    quartered, and thinly sliced

1. Heat wok over high heat for 1½
minutes. Pour 1 tablespoon oil around
rim of wok. Add garlic, ginger, and onion. Stir-fry for 1 minute. Push mixture
up sides of wok.
2. Add balance of oil to rim of wok.
Add sliced sweet red pepper and mushrooms. Stir-fry for 2 minutes. Combine
mushrooms with mixture already in
wok.
3. Sprinkle with herbs and spices.
Add rice and stir-fry for 1 minute.
4. Pour warm stock and water over
mixture. Add apple and bring to boil.
Lower heat, cover, and cook for 12 minutes, uncovering and stirring once midway. Uncover and stir again at the end
of 12 minutes.
5. Re-cover, remove from heat, and
let stand for 2 minutes before serving.

Yield: Serves 6 as side dish, 4 as
luncheon dish

CAL	F	P:S	SOD	CAR	CHO	PRO
Side dish:						
168	5	4.3:1	18	29	–	4.5
Luncheon dish:						
252	7	4.3:1	26.5	43.5	–	6.5

Lucky Thirteen Chicken

This dish originally had thirteen ingredients, hence the title. Then I got even luckier, added two more ingredients, and came up with an extraordinary dish. But I just couldn't bear to change the title.

2 small whole chicken breasts, boned and skinned (1¼ pounds boned weight)
2 tablespoons fresh lemon juice
3 tablespoons cornstarch
2 tablespoons corn oil
½-inch slice fresh ginger, peeled and shredded
2 large cloves garlic, minced
1 medium onion, thinly sliced
1 rib celery, cut diagonally into ¼-inch slices
½ each medium sweet green pepper and red pepper, cut into ¼-inch slivers
4 large fresh mushrooms, washed, dried, trimmed, and thickly sliced
8 dashes ground red (cayenne) pepper
2 teaspoons coriander seeds, crushed
½ cup Rich Chicken Stock (page 94)
1 tablespoon medium-dry sherry
⅓ cup pineapple tidbits packed in unsweetened pineapple juice, drained

1. Wash chicken and wipe dry with paper toweling. Place in bowl. Pour lemon juice over chicken, turning to coat. Let stand at room temperature for 15 minutes. Drain on paper toweling.
2. Dip each piece of chicken into cornstarch, shaking off excess. Set aside.
3. Heat wok over high heat for 1½ minutes. Pour 1 tablespoon oil around rim of wok. When oil drips down, add half each of ginger and garlic. Stir-fry for 30 seconds.
4. Add chicken to wok and stir-fry until lightly browned (about 3 minutes). Transfer to plate.
5. Add balance of oil to rim of wok. Add balance of ginger and garlic. Stir-fry for 30 seconds.
6. Add onion, celery, pepper slivers, and mushrooms. Stir-fry for 2 minutes. Return chicken to wok. Sprinkle with ground red pepper and coriander seeds. Stir.
7. Add stock, sherry, and pineapple chunks. Cover and cook over medium heat for 1 minute. Serve.

Yield: Serves 4

CAL	F	P:S	SOD	CAR	CHO	PRO
278	8.5	3.7:1	115	12	84	34.5

Ten-Minute Chicken Stew

1 pound boneless, skinned chicken breast
2 tablespoons fresh lime juice
2 teaspoons tomato paste (no salt added)
⅓ cup Rich Chicken Stock (page 94)
¼ cup dry vermouth
½ teaspoon chili con carne seasoning (no salt or pepper added)
2 tablespoons corn oil
1 small leek, white part only, well washed, dried, and sliced ½-inch thick
2 cloves garlic, minced
1 small rib celery, cut diagonally into ½-inch pieces
½-inch slice fresh ginger, peeled and shredded

8 dashes ground red (cayenne)
  pepper
1 small sweet green pepper, seeded
  and cut into ¼-inch slivers
2 small ripe tomatoes, cored and cut
  into 1-inch chunks
1 teaspoon dried tarragon leaves,
  crushed
1 large Idaho potato, peeled, cut
  into 1-inch cubes, and boiled
  (slightly undercooked)
1 tablespoon cornstarch dissolved
  in 1 tablespoon cold water

1. Wash chicken and dry with paper toweling. Cut into 1-inch cubes. Place in bowl. Pour lime juice over chicken, turning to coat. Let stand at room temperature for 15 to 20 minutes. Drain on paper toweling.

2. In separate bowl, combine tomato paste, stock, vermouth, and chili con carne seasoning. Set aside.

3. Heat wok over high heat for 1½ minutes. Pour 1 tablespoon oil around rim of wok. Add half each of leek, garlic, celery, and ginger. Stir-fry for 1 minute. Add chicken, placing across wok in one layer. Sprinkle with 4 dashes ground red pepper. Cook on each side for 2 minutes. Transfer all ingredients to plate.

4. Pour balance of oil around rim of wok. Add balance of leek, garlic, celery, and ginger. Stir-fry for 1 minute. Add pepper slivers, tomatoes, balance of ground red pepper, and tarragon. Stir-fry for 2 minutes. Return chicken mixture to wok. Stir all ingredients together.

5. Pour reserved tomato paste mixture around rim of wok. Stir. Cover and simmer over medium-high heat for 2 minutes.

6. Add potatoes. Re-cover and simmer for 1 minute.

7. Add cornstarch mixture. Cook briefly, uncovered, until thickened. Serve immediately.

Yield: Serves 4

CAL	F	P:S	SOD	CAR	CHO	PRO
283.5	8.5	3.7:1	103.5	21	56	29

Stir-Fried Cabbage with Meat

½ green cabbage (about ½ pound),
  tough center removed, cut into
  wedges, then cut into ½-inch strips
1 small carrot, peeled and sliced
  diagonally ¼-inch thick
2 tablespoons corn oil
2 large cloves garlic, minced
1-inch slice fresh ginger, peeled and
  shredded
½ pound fresh mushrooms, washed,
  dried, trimmed, and sliced ¼-inch
  thick
3 large scallions, cut diagonally into
  1-inch pieces
½ sweet green pepper, cut into ¼-
  inch slivers (optional)
1 cup cooked beef, lamb, or veal, cut
  into ½-inch cubes
⅛ teaspoon ground red (cayenne)
  pepper
¼ teaspoon aniseed, crushed
2 teaspoons wine vinegar
½ cup Light Chicken Broth (page 95)
1 tablespoon cornstarch dissolved
  in 2 tablespoons cold water
1 tablespoon medium-dry sherry

1. Parboil cabbage and carrot by dropping into rapidly boiling water and boiling for 1 minute. Drain. Place on paper toweling and set aside.

2. Heat wok over high heat for 1½ minutes. Pour 1 tablespoon oil around rim. When oil drips down, add half each of garlic and ginger. Stir-fry for 30 seconds. Add mushrooms and scallions. Stir-fry for 2 minutes. Remove to bowl. Do not cover.

3. Pour balance of oil around rim of wok. Add balance of garlic and ginger. Stir-fry for 30 seconds. Add cabbage, carrot, and green pepper. Stir-fry for 2 minutes.

4. Add meat. Sprinkle with ground red pepper and aniseed. Stir-fry for 30 seconds.

5. Pour vinegar around rim of wok. Cook for 30 seconds.

6. Pour stock around rim of wok. Cover and cook over medium heat for 1 minute.

7. Uncover and return mushroom-scallion mixture to wok. Pour cornstarch mixture around rim of wok. Stir rapidly while small amount of liquid thickens.

8. Stir in sherry. Serve immediately.

Yield: Serves 4

CAL	F	P:S	SOD	CAR	CHO	PRO
With beef:						
159	10.5	3.8:1	52.5	11	19	8.5
With lamb:						
143.5	9	3.8:1	50	11	16.5	5
With veal:						
153	10	3.8:1	48	11	17.5	6.5
With green pepper, add:						
2	–	–	1	2	–	–

Chinese-Style Meatballs

½ pound each ground lean beef and pork
2 tablespoons Bread Crumbs (page 85)
2 cloves garlic, minced
6 dashes ground red (cayenne) pepper
¼ teaspoon each dried thyme leaves and aniseed, crushed
3 tablespoons unsweetened pineapple juice
2 tablespoons corn oil
3 cloves garlic, minced
½-inch slice peeled and minced fresh ginger
1 medium onion, cut into ½-inch slices
1 rib celery, cut diagonally into ⅜-inch slices
½ small sweet green pepper, seeded and cut into ⅜-inch slivers
¼ pound mushrooms, washed, dried, trimmed, and thickly sliced
⅓ cup water chestnuts, rinsed in cold water and dried
1 teaspoon white vinegar
¼ cup Rich Chicken Stock (page 94)
¼ cup unsweetened pineapple juice
1 teaspoon chili con carne seasoning (no salt or pepper added)
1 tablespoon cornstarch dissolved in 1 tablespoon cold water

1. Combine first 6 ingredients in sequence in small bowl. Blend with fingers. Shape into 16 balls.

2. Heat wok over high heat for 1½ minutes. Pour 1 tablespoon oil around rim. When oil drips down, add half each of garlic and ginger. Stir-fry for 15 seconds. Add meatballs. Brown on all sides, pushing meatballs to circumference of wok so that fat will drip down. With slotted spoon, transfer browned meat to bowl. Pour out drippings.

3. Pour balance of oil around rim of wok. Add balance of garlic and ginger. Stir-fry for 5 seconds. Add onion, celery, and green pepper. Stir-fry for 1½ minutes. Add mushrooms. Stir-fry for 1 minute. Add water chestnuts and stir.

4. Return meatballs to wok. Pour vinegar around rim of wok. Stir to blend.

5. Pour stock and pineapple juice around rim of wok. Sprinkle with chili con carne seasoning. Stir. Cover and cook over medium heat for 2 minutes.

6. Uncover and pour cornstarch mixture around rim of wok. Stir until liquid thickens. Serve immediately.

Yield: Serves 4

CAL	F	P:S	SOD	CAR	CHO	PRO
300	15.5	2:1	85	17	61	22

Hot Beef with Peppers

1 egg white
2 teaspoons cornstarch
8 dashes ground red (cayenne) pepper
2½ teaspoons medium-dry sherry
1 pound lean, tender boneless sirloin or flank steak, cut into 2½- x ½-inch strips
1 teaspoon cold water
1 teaspoon dry mustard
1½ teaspoons curry powder (no salt or pepper added)
2 teaspoons tomato paste (no salt added)
2 tablespoons corn oil
3 cloves garlic, minced
1-inch slice fresh ginger, peeled and shredded
1 large sweet green pepper, cut into ⅜-inch slivers
⅔ cup Light Chicken Broth (page 95) or Rich Chicken Stock (page 94)

½ cup bamboo shoots, rinsed under cold running water and drained on paper toweling
Minced fresh Chinese parsley (see note)

1. Combine egg white, 1 teaspoon cornstarch, ground red pepper, and sherry in bowl. Beat with fork to blend. Add meat. Stir until well coated. Cover and let stand for 15 minutes.

2. In small bowl, dissolve 1 teaspoon cornstarch in 1 teaspoon water. Add mustard, curry powder, and tomato paste. Stir to combine. Set aside.

3. Heat wok over high heat for 1½ minutes. Pour 1 tablespoon oil around rim of wok. Add half each of garlic and ginger. Stir-fry for 30 seconds. Add meat. Stir-fry until meat gives up some of its pinkness (about 2 minutes). Transfer contents of wok to plate. Do not cover.

4. Pour balance of oil around rim of wok. Add balance of garlic and ginger. Stir-fry for 30 seconds. Add pepper slivers. Stir-fry for 1 minute.

5. Return meat to wok. Add broth and bamboo shoots. Stir in reserved cornstarch-mustard mixture. Cover and cook over medium heat for 1 minute.

6. Turn onto serving plate. Sprinkle with Chinese parsley and serve.

Yield: Serves 4

Note: Minced flat-leaf (Italian) parsley may be substituted for Chinese parsley.

CAL	F	P:S	SOD	CAR	CHO	PRO
203.5	11	2.8:1	66	5.5	75	19

Bean Curd with Broccoli

2 tablespoons corn oil
2 large cloves garlic, minced
¼ pound fresh mushrooms, washed, dried, trimmed, and thickly sliced
1 3-inch cake bean curd, dried and cut into ½-inch cubes
6 dashes smoked yeast (optional) (available in health food stores)
1 leek, white part only, well washed and sliced diagonally into ½-inch pieces
1 medium onion, thinly sliced
1 small wedge Chinese cabbage, cut lengthwise into ¼-inch strips Flowerets from 2 stalks fresh broccoli
6 dashes ground red (cayenne) pepper
½ cup Light Chicken Broth (page 95)
2 tablespoons medium-dry sherry
½ teaspoon ground ginger
1 tablespoon cornstarch dissolved in 1 tablespoon cold water

1. Heat wok for 1½ minutes over high heat. Pour 1 tablespoon oil around rim of wok. Add garlic. Stir-fry for 15 seconds.

2. Add mushrooms. Stir-fry for 2 minutes. Push garlic and mushrooms up side of wok. Add bean curd. Sprinkle with smoked yeast and stir-fry for 2 minutes. Transfer contents of wok to plate.

3. Pour balance of oil around rim of wok. Add leek and onion. Stir-fry for 2 minutes.

4. Add cabbage. Stir-fry for 2 minutes.

5. Add broccoli. Sprinkle with ground red pepper. Stir-fry for 1 minute. Return bean-curd mixture to wok. Gently stir.

6. Combine broth, sherry, and ginger. Pour around rim of wok. Cover and cook over medium heat for 1½ minutes.

7. Uncover and pour cornstarch mixture around rim of wok. Cook briefly until thickened. Serve immediately.

Yield: Serves 4

CAL	F	P:S	SOD	CAR	CHO	PRO
131	8	4.3:1	21	9.5	–	4

With smoked yeast: No appreciable difference

THE CLAY POT

Long before the dawn of history, one of mankind's great culinary geniuses invented a magnificent way of cooking. He—women had no lib in the days of the caveman—wrapped wild game in wet clay and placed it in the glowing coals of a campfire. An hour or so later, the clay was shattered, and a moist, flavorsome bird was greedily devoured.

Now, millennia later, wet-clay cooking is enjoying a renaissance without the economic waste of the clay-shattering ceremony. Long-lived clay pots are now on sale at department stores and specialty shops everywhere; and a whole new cuisine—clay-pot cookery—has burgeoned in the last several years, with results that range from the so-so to the sublime.

The clay pot is actually a covered casserole made from porous clay. It's the porosity that sets it apart from other cooking vessels. Before each use, the pot and its cover are soaked in water for some time; and the water is absorbed, spongelike, by the pores. As the wet clay dries in the heat of the oven, the pores release their moisture ever so slowly, bathing the food in a gentle cloud of steam.

In this steamy atmosphere, food does not stick to the pot, so you can be stingy with fats and oils. That's a health-promoting advantage alone worth the price of the utensil. Here's another. The steam minimizes the use of water, so there's no cooking liquid to be discarded with its rich cargo of nutrients. All that's wholesome in the food remains in the pot ready to serve—and that includes flavor.

During oven time, the steam cloud captures the essences of the seasoning and permeates the food with them, producing a richness of flavor. The taste is like nothing you have ever sampled; for the food, steamed and baked simultaneously, seems to the palate to be a potted/roasted hybrid. Meats and fowl, which cook superbly in the ambiance of the clay pot, emerge so meltingly tender that I've come to look on this vessel as *the* tenderizer without peer.

Add one more laudable characteristic: it's an effort saver. Just place it in the oven and forget about it; it's self-basting. At the most, one basting is required when you're reaching for the impeccable dish.

Here are some hints on using a clay pot:

1. Before every use, immerse entire pot in tepid water for 20 to 30 minutes.

2. Place pot in *cold* oven. Then set the thermostat. The pot must heat up slowly, because a sudden temperature change will shatter it (and then you will have made no gain since prehistoric times).

3. Place pot in the center of the oven. If you don't want it to crack, keep it away from the sides.

4. Be wary about time and temperature instructions in the manufacturers' brochures. Cooking heats are often set too high, and cooking times too long. The correct time/temperature data are specified in my recipes, but alter them to fit the idiosyncrasies of your own oven. When in doubt, remember that less is best.

5. To brown food and reduce liquid, remove cover 10 to 15 minutes before the end of cooking time, and return to oven, uncovered, until done.

6. Never subject pot to top-of-stove heat, or any other direct heat.

7. Use heavy potholders when removing pot from oven (the pot is very hot, somewhat unwieldy, and not feather-light).

8. Place hot pot on a wooden board, trivet, or dish towel—never on a cold surface (which will shatter it).

9. Move your head away from the pot as you remove cover to avoid direct contact with heat and steam.

10. After each use, soak pot with warm water containing a drop of detergent. Scrub with stiff brush, using baking soda if necessary. Never use soap, which clogs the pores, or steel wool, which smooths out the pores. With use, the pot will "season," mottling at first, then taking on a uniform patina.

11. And finally, be guided by the manufacturer's instructions concerning safeguards.

In the recipes in this section, two new cuisines—my haute cuisine of health and clay-pot cooking—blend to bring new elegance to your favorite roasts and stews, and to create innovative dishes that will become your favorites, too.

Elegant Chicken-Veal Stew

1 pound boneless light and dark
    meat of broiling chicken (see
    note), cut into 1-inch pieces
½ pound lean stewing veal
3 tablespoons fresh lime juice
4 large cloves garlic, minced
1½ teaspoons each corn oil and
    Italian olive oil, combined
2 tablespoons each minced sweet
    red pepper and green pepper
3 scallions, washed, cut into 1-inch
    pieces
4 large fresh firm mushrooms,
    washed, dried, trimmed, and
    sliced
¼ cup medium-dry sherry
½ cup Rich Chicken Stock (page 94)
¼ cup apple juice (no sugar added)
½ teaspoon dried rosemary leaves,
    crushed
1 teaspoon ground ginger
1 crisp, sweet apple, such as
    Washington State, peeled, cored,
    and sliced ½-inch thick
    Bouquet garni (1 sprig fresh
    parsley, 1 bay leaf, tied together
    with white thread)
½ cup evaporated skim milk (¼
    percent milkfat)

1. Wash chicken and pat dry with paper toweling. Wipe veal with paper toweling. Place veal and chicken in bowl. Add lime juice and garlic, turning to coat. Let stand for 1½ to 2 hours before cooking.

2. Soak clay pot in tepid water for 20 minutes.

3. Heat combined oils in nonstick skillet. Add red and green pepper, scallions, and mushrooms. Sauté until wilted (about 3 minutes).

4. Add sherry, stock, apple juice, rosemary, ginger, apple, and bouquet garni. Bring to simmering point.

5. Transfer contents of bowl con-taining meats into clay pot, spreading to cover bottom. Pour over hot mixture from skillet. Cover clay pot. Place in center position of cold oven. Set oven at 400°F. Bake for 1 hour 15 minutes.

6. With slotted spoon, transfer chicken and veal to warmed serving bowl. Cover to keep warm. Discard bouquet garni. Pour cooking juices into heavy-bottomed saucepan. Cook over medium-high heat until reduced by half.

7. Reduce heat. Slowly stir in milk. Heat sauce to just under simmering point. Do not boil. Pour over chicken-veal mélange and serve.

Yield: Serves 4

Note: Bone and skin a 3-pound chicken. Use meat from breast, legs, and thighs, net weight of which is about 1 pound. Reserve wings and bones for your stock pot.

CAL	F	P:S	SOD	CAR	CHO	PRO
239	13	1.5:1	61	5.5	65.5	23

Creamy Veal Stew

1 teaspoon corn oil
½ cup fresh orange juice
¼ cup dry vermouth or white wine
¼ teaspoon ground ginger
⅛ teaspoon ground cloves
6 dashes ground red (cayenne)
    pepper
1 teaspoon juniper berries, crushed
½ teaspoon dried sage leaves,
    crushed
2½ pounds lean boneless stewing
    veal, cut into 1-inch cubes

1 medium onion, minced
3 large cloves garlic, minced
2 large shallots, minced
2 tablespoons minced sweet green
   pepper
2 tablespoons minced fresh parsley
2 teaspoons arrowroot flour
   dissolved in 1 tablespoon water
¼ cup evaporated skim milk (¼
   percent milkfat)

1. Combine first 8 ingredients in bowl. Blend. Wipe meat with paper toweling. Add to bowl, turning to coat. Marinate for 1 hour at room temperature.

2. Soak clay pot in tepid water for 20 minutes.

3. Combine onion, garlic, shallots, and green pepper. Sprinkle half of mixture over bottom of clay pot. Cover with meat and marinade. Sprinkle balance of mixture over meat and marinade. Sprinkle with parsley.

4. Cover pot. Place in center section of cold oven. Set oven at 375°F. Bake for 1½ hours. Remove from oven, remove cover, and stir. Return to oven and bake for 30 minutes.

5. With slotted spoon, transfer meat to warmed serving bowl. Cover to keep warm.

6. Place strainer over heavy-bottomed saucepan. Pour contents of clay pot into strainer, pressing out juices. Reduce strained gravy over high heat for 2 minutes.

7. Slowly add arrowroot mixture, stirring constantly until lightly thickened.

8. Gradually add milk, stirring constantly. Heat to simmering point. *Do not boil.* Pour over meat and serve.

Yield: Serves 6

CAL	F	P:S	SOD	CAR	CHO	PRO
329	25	1.5:1	31.5	7	118.5	37

Tender Roast Veal

½ cup Rich Chicken Stock (page 94)
¼ cup medium-dry sherry
¼ cup tomato juice (no salt added)
2 teaspoons fresh lemon juice
2 large cloves garlic, minced
½ teaspoon dried rosemary leaves,
   crushed
½ teaspoon ground ginger
⅛ teaspoon ground red (cayenne)
   pepper
   Large bouquet garni (2 sprigs fresh
   parsley, 1 bay leaf, tied together
   with white thread)
1 piece (3 pounds) boned leg of veal,
   rolled
2 tablespoons corn oil
1 large onion, thinly sliced

1. Prepare marinade by combining first 9 ingredients in heavy-bottomed saucepan. Bring to simmering point. Cover partially and simmer for 2 minutes. Let cool.

2. Wipe meat with paper toweling. Place in bowl. Pour cooled marinade over meat. Cover tightly with plastic wrap and let stand at room temperature for 2 hours, turning once.

3. Soak clay pot in tepid water for 20 minutes.

4. Drain meat. Roll on paper toweling. Heat oil in nonstick skillet until hot. Lightly brown meat on all sides over medium-high heat. While meat is browning, heat marinade to simmering point.

5. Place onion slices across bottom of clay pot. Place browned meat over onions. Pour heated marinade over meat. Cover tightly. Place in center section of cold oven. Set oven at 400°F. Bake for 2 hours.

6. Transfer meat to carving board. Cover with waxed paper and let stand for 5 minutes before carving.

7. Strain cooking juices into saucepan. Reheat to simmering point. Add any exuded juices from carving board

to saucepan. Cut meat into ⅜-inch slices. Arrange on warmed serving platter. Serve hot cooking juices in sauceboat along with meat.

Yield: Serves 6

Variation: After cooking juices have been brought to simmering point in step 7, add ¼ cup evaporated skim milk. Heat just to simmering point. *Do not boil.* Pour into sauceboat and serve along with sliced meat.

CAL	F	P:S	SOD	CAR	CHO	PRO
398.5	21	1.7:1	113	4.5	141	44.5

With evaporated skim milk:

CAL	F	P:S	SOD	CAR	CHO	PRO
407	21.5	1.6:1	115.5	6	142	45.5

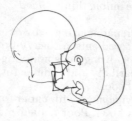

Stuffed Herbed Chicken

For the stuffing:
½ cup Rich Chicken Stock (page 94)
1½ cups water
¾ cup cracked-wheat cereal (whole or coarse)
1 tablespoon corn oil
2 large cloves garlic, minced
1 large shallot, minced
2 large fresh mushrooms, washed, dried, trimmed, and coarsely chopped
1 tablespoon minced sweet green pepper

1 tablespoon dry vermouth
4 water chestnuts, rinsed in cold water, dried, and coarsely chopped
1 tablespoon peeled and grated carrot
2 tablespoons fresh parsley, minced
1 teaspoon ground ginger
4 dashes ground red (cayenne) pepper

For the chicken:
1 broiling chicken (3½ pounds), skinned, wing tips removed
1 teaspoon Italian olive oil
1½ teaspoons each dried rosemary and thyme leaves, crushed
4 dashes ground red (cayenne) pepper
2 large cloves garlic, minced
1 tablespoon peeled and minced fresh ginger
1 medium onion, thinly sliced
2 large fresh mushrooms, washed, dried, trimmed, and sliced
½ carrot, peeled and sliced
1 large fresh tomato, cored and coarsely chopped
¼ cup Rich Chicken Stock (page 94)
1 tablespoon medium-dry sherry

1. Soak clay pot in tepid water for 20 minutes.
2. Prepare the stuffing first. Combine stock and water in small saucepan. Bring to boil. Add cracked wheat in a steady stream. Reduce heat to simmering and cook, uncovered, until all liquid is absorbed (18 to 20 minutes). Let cool. (Cracked wheat may be prepared well ahead of time and refrigerated until ready to use.)
3. Heat oil in nonstick skillet until hot. Sauté garlic, shallots, mushrooms, and green pepper over medium-high heat until lightly browned. Add vermouth and cook 1 minute.
4. Pour into cooled cracked wheat. Add balance of stuffing ingredients. Toss to blend.
5. Now prepare chicken. Wash

chicken inside and out and wipe dry with paper toweling. Fill cavity with stuffing. Truss.

6. Rub bird with oil. Sprinkle with dried herbs and ground red pepper, pressing into flesh.

7. Strew half of garlic, ginger, onion, mushrooms, carrot, and tomato over bottom of clay pot. Place chicken on top of mixture. Strew balance of same ingredients over chicken. Add stock. Cover pot. Place in center section of cold oven. Set oven at 400°F and bake for 1½ hours.

8. Transfer chicken to carving board. Cut into serving pieces. Arrange on warmed platter.

9. Add sherry to clay pot. Stir. Pour cooking juices and vegetables over chicken and serve.

Yield: Serves 4

CAL	F	P:S	SOD	CAR	CHO	PRO
Chicken:						
273.5	8	0.6:1	108.5	115	110	43
Stuffing:						
89.5	3.5	4.4:1	14	9	–	2

All-American Pot Roast

1 slice (2 pounds) top round beef, well trimmed, or very lean center-cut shoulder steak, cut 1 inch thick
8 dashes ground red (cayenne) pepper
½ teaspoon each dried thyme and rosemary leaves, crushed
1 tablespoon each corn oil and Italian olive oil, combined
2 tablespoons fresh lemon juice
3 large cloves garlic, minced
1 large onion, coarsely chopped
2 large fresh mushrooms, washed, dried, trimmed, and coarsely chopped

½ cup peeled and cubed yellow turnip (½-inch cubes)
1 carrot, peeled and diced
½ cup dry red wine
¾ cup Rich Chicken Stock (page 94)
½ cup tomato purée (no salt added) (available in health food stores)
1½ tablespoons tomato paste (no salt added)
2 teaspoons caraway seeds, crushed
Bouquet garni (1 sprig each fresh parsley and dill, and large bay leaf, tied together with white thread)

1. Soak clay pot in tepid water for 20 minutes.

2. Wipe meat with paper toweling. Rub on both sides with ground red pepper and dried herbs, pressing herbs into meat.

3. Heat 1 tablespoon combined oils in iron skillet until hot. Add meat and brown lightly on both sides. Transfer to plate. Sprinkle on both sides with lemon juice.

4. Heat balance of oil in skillet. Sauté garlic, onion, and mushrooms until lightly browned, stirring continuously. Add turnip and carrot. Sauté for 1 minute.

5. Combine wine with stock, tomato purée, and tomato paste. Stir into sautéed mixture.

6. Add caraway seeds and bouquet garni. Bring to simmering point and simmer for 1 minute.

7. Pour half of mixture in skillet across bottom of clay pot. Place meat on top of mixture. Pour balance of skillet mixture over meat. Cover tightly. Place in center section of cold oven. Set oven at 400°F. Bake for 1 hour 15 minutes.

8. Uncover and turn meat. Baste. Re-cover and let stand at room temperature for 10 minutes. Discard bouquet garni. Transfer meat to carving board. Cover with waxed paper.

9. Pour cooking juices into heavy-bottomed saucepan. Slowly reheat.

Slice meat ⅜-inch thick, and arrange on warmed serving platter. Spoon with cooking juices and serve.

Yield: Serves 6

Note: Should sauce be too thick to your liking, thin down with ¼ cup chicken stock.

CAL	F	P:S	SOD	CAR	CHO	PRO
343.5	17	0.8:1	108.5	12	100	32.4

Tender Curried Beef

1 slice (2 pounds) top round beef, well trimmed, or very lean center-cut shoulder steak, cut 1¼ inches thick
1 tablespoon coriander seeds, crushed
2 tablespoons fresh lime juice
1 tablespoon each corn oil and sweet (unsalted) 100 percent corn oil margarine
1 large onion, coarsely chopped
4 large cloves garlic, minced
1 medium sweet green pepper, seeded and cut into ¼-inch slivers
1 sweet, crisp apple, such as Washington State, peeled, cored, and cut into 1-inch cubes
1 cup canned tomatoes (no salt added), chopped
½ teaspoon each cuminseed and dried crushed thyme leaves
4½ teaspoons curry powder (no salt or pepper added)
6 dashes ground red (cayenne) pepper
1 tablespoon minced fresh parsley
1 tablespoon raisins

1. Soak clay pot in tepid water for 20 minutes.
2. Wipe meat with paper toweling. Make 5 diagonal ¼-inch gashes across meat on both sides. Sprinkle with crushed coriander. With heel of hand, press into meat. Place on rack. Sprinkle with lime juice on both sides. Let stand on rack at room temperature, uncovered, for 3 hours. Meat should be dry to the touch when ready to cook.
3. Heat 1½ teaspoons each oil and margarine in iron skillet until very hot. Add meat and cook about 3 minutes on each side, until lightly browned. Transfer to plate.
4. Reduce heat under skillet. Add balance of oil and margarine. Sauté onion, garlic, and green pepper until lightly browned. Add apple and sauté for 1 minute.
5. Add balance of ingredients. Simmer for 2 minutes.
6. Pour half of mixture in skillet into clay pot. Place meat on top of mixture. Pour balance of skillet mixture over meat. Cover tightly. Place in center section of cold oven. Set oven at 400°F. Bake for 1 hour 25 minutes.
7. Uncover and turn meat. Baste. Re-cover and let stand at room temperature for 10 minutes. Transfer meat to carving board. Cover with waxed paper.
8. Pour thick sauce into heavy-bottomed saucepan. Slowly reheat. Slice meat ⅜-inch thick and arrange on warmed serving platter. Spoon with sauce and serve.

Yield: Serves 5

CAL	F	P:S	SOD	CAR	CHO	PRO
376.5	3.5	0.9:1	17	1.5	20	8

Bracciole with Wild Rice

For the stuffing:

¼ cup wild rice
1 tablespoon corn oil
3 large cloves garlic, minced
2 large shallots, minced
¼ pound each ground lean pork and veal
8 dashes ground red (cayenne) pepper
½ teaspoon dried thyme leaves, crushed
2 tablespoons toasted wheat germ (no sugar added)
2 tablespoons Bread Crumbs (page 85)
1 tablespoon minced fresh parsley
3 tablespoons Rich Chicken Stock (page 94)
3 tablespoons rinsed and chopped water chestnuts

For the meat:

4 slices (2 pounds) brasciole (center of top round, cut ¼ inch thick and flattened with mallet to thickness of ⅛ inch)
1½ teaspoons each corn oil and Italian olive oil, combined
2 large cloves garlic, minced
2 large shallots, minced
4 large fresh mushrooms, washed, dried, trimmed, and minced
⅔ cup red wine
3 tablespoons tomato paste (no salt added)
1 cup Rich Chicken Stock (page 94)
½ teaspoon dry mustard dissolved in 1 teaspoon water
1 teaspoon chili con carne seasoning (no salt or pepper added)
Bouquet garni (1 sprig fresh parsley, 1 bay leaf, tied together with white thread)
Minced fresh parsley

1. Prepare stuffing first. Pour rice into strainer. Wash under cold running water. Drain. Transfer to heavy-bottomed saucepan. Add 1¼ cups water. Bring to boil. Reduce heat, and simmer gently for 40 minutes uncovered. Drain. Turn into bowl.

2. Heat oil in nonstick skillet until hot. Sauté garlic and shallots for 1 minute.

3. Add meats. Sauté for 3 minutes, breaking up pieces with spoon. Sprinkle with ground red pepper and thyme. Stir to blend. Turn into bowl with rice.

4. Add to bowl balance of stuffing ingredients except for water chestnuts.

5. Work water chestnuts into mixture with fork.

6. Soak clay pot in tepid water for 20 minutes.

7. To prepare bracciole, cut each slice in half. Place a tablespoon of stuffing on top of each half, pressing to hold. Roll up carefully, tucking in ends where possible. Secure with small skewers or string.

8. Heat 1½ teaspoons combined oils in nonstick skillet until hot. Sauté bracciole briefly on each side until lightly browned. Transfer to clay pot.

9. Heat balance of oil in skillet until hot. Sauté garlic, shallots, and mushrooms until lightly browned.

10. Combine wine, tomato paste, stock, mustard, and chili con carne seasoning. Add to skillet. Bring to simmering point. Pour over meat.

11. Push bouquet garni into liquid in clay pot. Place in center section of cold oven. Set oven at 425°F. Bake for 1½ hours.

12. Remove pot from oven. Baste. Re-cover pot. Let stand at room temperature for 10 minutes. Remove skewers or string and bouquet garni.

13. Arrange bracciole on serving dish. (Finished bracciole are coated with thick sauce; there is little pourable sauce.) Sprinkle with parsley, and serve.

Yield: Serves 8

Note: These bracciole freeze extremely well. I freeze my leftovers in thick plastic freezeproof bags, which I heat-seal. When ready to use, I drop the bags in boiling water and boil for 15 minutes. Tastes just-cooked!

CAL	F	P:S	SOD	CAR	CHO	PRO
301	15.5	1.8:1	83.5	10	90	30.5

Braised Lamb with Okra

½ pound fresh okra, washed and
   ends trimmed
2 tablespoons distilled white
   vinegar
3 pounds lean boneless lamb, cut
   from leg, cut into ½-inch cubes
2 tablespoons fresh lemon juice
1 tablespoon each corn oil and
   Italian olive oil, combined
3 large cloves garlic, minced
1 leek, white part only, well washed
   and cut into ¼-inch slices
1 medium sweet green pepper, cut
   into ¼-inch slivers
1 small onion, minced
¼ cup dry vermouth
1 fresh tomato, skinned, cored, and
   coarsely chopped
1 cup canned tomatoes (no salt
   added)
½ to ¾ cup tomato juice (no salt
   added)
¾ teaspoon each cuminseed and
   caraway seeds, crushed
½ teaspoon curry powder (no salt or
   pepper added)
8 dashes ground red (cayenne)
   pepper

1. Wash okra under cold running water. Place in bowl. Sprinkle with vinegar, turning to coat. Let stand for 30 minutes. Rinse under cold running water. Drain.

2. Place lamb in small bowl. Sprinkle with lemon juice, turning to coat. Let stand for 30 minutes. Drain on paper toweling. Pat dry.

3. Soak clay pot in tepid water for 20 minutes.

4. Heat 1 tablespoon combined oils in iron skillet until hot. Add meat and brown lightly on all sides. Transfer to plate.

5. Heat balance of oil in skillet. Sauté garlic, leek, green pepper, and onion until lightly browned. Return meat to skillet. Stir.

6. Add vermouth. Stir and cook for 1 minute.

7. Add tomato, ½ cup tomato juice, and spices. Bring to simmering point. Pour into clay pot. Cover tightly. Place clay pot in center section of cold oven. Set oven at 400°F. Bake for 1 hour 20 minutes.

8. Remove from oven. Uncover and stir. Mixture will be thick, but should not stick to pot. Add a little more tomato juice, if desired.

9. Pour into serving bowl and serve.

Yield: Serves 4

Serving suggestions: Serve over a bed of cooked brown rice, or with diced, cooked Idaho potatoes.

Note: I prefer fresh okra, but when it's not available, frozen okra can thaw and blend into a reasonable facsimile. Partially thaw, then follow step 1.

CAL	F	P:S	SOD	CAR	CHO	PRO
388.5	16	1.2:1	17	10	132	41.5

Succulent Stuffed Cabbage Rolls

1 *loose head (2½ pounds) green cabbage*
½ *pound each ground lean veal and beef*
1 *tablespoon toasted wheat germ (no sugar added)*
½ *cup slightly undercooked rice*
½ *teaspoon each dried sage and thyme leaves, crushed*
8 *dashes ground red (cayenne) pepper*
1 *tablespoon corn oil*
3 *cloves garlic, minced*
½ *inch slice fresh ginger, peeled and minced*
1 *small leek, white part only, well washed and minced*
2 *tablespoons dry vermouth*
½ *cup Rich Chicken Stock (page 94)*
2 *tablespoons fresh lemon juice*
¼ *cup apple juice (no sugar added)*
1 *cup canned tomatoes (no salt added), chopped*
2 *teaspoons curry powder (no salt or pepper added)*
¼ *cup raisins (optional)*
Bouquet garni (1 sprig fresh parsley, 1 bay leaf, tied together with white thread)

1. Soak clay pot in tepid water for 20 minutes.

2. Wash cabbage. Discard tough outer leaves. Remove core. Gently loosen 12 large leaves. Drop into large pot of rapidly boiling water. Bring to boil again and cook until leaves are pliable (about 5 minutes). Remove from water and drain. Set aside.

3. Combine and blend meats, wheat germ, rice, herbs, and ground red pepper in bowl.

4. Heat oil in nonstick skillet until hot. Sauté garlic, ginger, and leek until wilted. Add vermouth. Cook for 1 min-ute. Pour into bowl with meat. Blend well. (Fingers do the best job here.)

5. Layout all 12 cabbage leaves on board. Place a mound of meat mixture on each leaf, leaving enough of each leaf uncovered so it can be rolled up and sides tucked in.

6. In small saucepan, combine balance of ingredients except for bouquet garni. Heat until hot. our half of mixture into clay pot, spreading to cover bottom. Place cabbage rolls in one layer, seam side down, on top of mixture. Pour other half of mixture over cabbage rolls. Add bouquet garni. Cover tightly.

7. Place clay pot in center section of cold oven. Set oven at 400°F. Bake for 1 hour 45 minutes. Remove from oven. Spoon cooking juices over cabbage rolls. Re-cover and let stand for 5 minutes. Remove bouquet garni.

8. Arrange on warmed individual serving plates and serve.

Yield: Serves 6 as appetizer, 4 as main course

CAL	F	P:S	SOD	CAR	CHO	PRO
Appetizer (without raisins):						
190	8	1.4:1	57.5	14.5	39	14.5
Appetizer (with raisins):						
210	8	1.4:1	59.5	20.5	39	14.5
Main course (without raisins):						
285.5	12	1.4:1	86	21.5	59	22
Main course (with raisins):						
315.5	12	1.4:1	89	29.5	59	22

Roast Pork Chops with Fruit

12 dried pitted prunes
1 cup apple juice (no sugar added)
4 center-cut pork chops (about 1½ pounds), well trimmed
½ teaspoon each dried thyme and rosemary leaves, crushed
2 teaspoons corn oil
1 medium onion, minced
2 large cloves garlic, minced
¼ pound fresh mushrooms, washed, dried, trimmed, and sliced
½ teaspoon each ground ginger and cinnamon
3 whole cloves
4 dashes ground red (cayenne) pepper
1 tablespoon fresh lemon juice
2 tablespoons medium-dry sherry

1. Soak clay pot in tepid water for 20 minutes.
2. Combine prunes and ½ cup apple juice in heavy-bottomed saucepan. Bring to simmering point. Cover partially and simmer for 5 minutes. Stir. Let prunes cool in pot. Drain prunes, reserving any cooking juices. Cut each prune into quarters and put in bowl. Pour cooking juices into bowl. Set aside.
3. Wipe chops with paper toweling. Rub on both sides with dried herbs. Place in clay pot.
4. Heat oil in nonstick skillet until hot. Sauté onion, garlic, and mushrooms until wilted but not browned.
5. Add spices, balance of apple juice, lemon juice, and sherry. Bring to simmering point. Pour over chops. Cover pot tightly. Place in center section of cold oven. Set oven at 400°F. Bake for 1 hour.
6. Remove pot from oven. Add prunes, stirring into cooking juices. Turn chops. Re-cover. Return to oven and bake for 20 minutes.

7. Serve chops on warmed individual plates surrounded by thick vegetable-fruit mixture.

Yield: Serves 4

CAL	F	P:S	SOD	CAR	CHO	PRO
335.5	18	1.1:1	72	27.5	70.5	25.5

Sources of Some Favored Ingredients

1. Low-sodium baking powder, low-sodium prepared Dijon mustard, low-sodium tomato juice, low-sodium tomato purée, low-sodium tomato paste, low-sodium canned tuna and salmon, packaged stone-ground flours, natural honeys, jellies made with honey, natural dried fruits, date powder, whole kasha, dried beans and legumes, nonfat dry milk, and smoked yeast are available in health food stores such as GNC (General Nutrition Corporation).
2. Bottled spices, herbs, juniper berries, and arrowroot flour can be found in supermarkets under the trade name Spice Islands. Manufacturer is

Specialty Brands, Inc., San Francisco, CA 94111.

3. Loose spices, herbs, juniper berries, couscous, dark rye flour, and other specialty flours can be purchased by mail from H. Roth & Son, 1577 First Avenue, New York, NY 10028.

4. Dietetic tuna, tomato juice, and canned whole tomatoes are generally available on the diet shelves of supermarkets.

5. Evaporated skim milk (manufactured by Carnation) is generally available in supermarkets.

6. Sap Sago cheese (imported by Emmental Cheese Corp., 175 Clearbrook Road, Elmsford, NY 10523) is available in cheese specialty stores or gourmet shops.

7. Plain matzohs (manufactured by Manischewitz) are generally available in supermarkets.

Index